Landscapes of Poverty

Landscapes of Poverty

JEREMY SEABROOK

Basil Blackwell

First published 1985

Basil Blackwell Ltd
108 Cowley Road, Oxford OX4 1JF, UK

British Library Cataloguing in Publication Data
Seabrook, Jeremy
    Landscapes of Poverty.
    1. Poverty
    1. Title
    339.4'6   HC79.P6
    ISBN 0-631-14508-7

Typeset by Dentset, St. Clements, Oxford.

Printed in Great Britain by Billings Ltd, Worcester

Contents

Acknowledgements

This book evolved out of reading and discussion and meeting the poor over a number of years, and in that sense I cannot really lay claim to it as my own. I am grateful to Susan Richards, with whom the idea was first developed for a television documentary that was never made. I am indebted to my shared work with Trevor Blackwell, to Tom Burke, Ivan Ruff and Barry Davis. I owe much to Vince and Janet Rocks in Scunthorpe, to my friends in Walsall Labour Party, to Elen Noor and the Southwark Radio Project, and to members of successive evening classes at the Working Men's College in North London. Above all I am grateful to those people who have shared their experience of being poor with such generosity of spirit, in some cases over many years.

I should like to thank Elizabeth Stamp of Oxfam, and also all the Oxfam representatives I met in their humane and enlightened projects in India, especially Geoffrey Salkeld in Nagpur, the Rev. Karim David at the Nagpur Industrial Services Institute, Mrs Sugandha Shende at the Hostel for Girls from the Depressed Classes, Sister Joaquina in Ghatkopar, Bombay, and Dr Parikh at Streehitakarini in Parel, Bombay. I am grateful to Mr Kanitkar, who taught me just enough Marathi for me not to have to address the people of India in a foreign tongue. I should like to express my gratitude to Paul Barker at *New Society*, and to thank him for permitting me to republish pages 89–95, a version of which first appeared there, and to Richard Gott at the *Guardian* for allowing me to develop some of the themes of the book in that paper.

Among the books I found particularly stimulating while writing were Peter Worsley, *The Three Worlds* (Weidenfeld & Nicolson, London, 1984); Michael Redclift, *Development and the Environmental Crisis – Red or Green Alternatives?* (Methuen, London, 1984); Rudolf Bahro, *Socialism and Survival* (Heretic Books, 1982); Guy Debord, *The Society of the Spectacle* (Black and Red, Detroit, 1977); William Leiss, *The Limits to Satisfaction* (University of Toronto Press, Toronto, 1976); Beatrix Campbell, *Wigan Pier Revisited* (Virago, London, 1984); Susan George,

How the Other Half Dies (Penguin, Harmondsworth, 1977); Frances Moore Lappé and Joseph Collins, *Food First* (Sphere, London, 1982); Gillian Tindall, *City of Gold, The Biography of Bombay* (Temple Smith, London, 1982); Brian Inglis, *Poverty and the Industrial Revolution* (Hodder & Stoughton, 1971); Dennis Hardy, *Alternative Communities in Nineteenth Century England* (Longman, London, 1974); Geoffrey Moorhouse, *Calcutta* (Penguin, Harmondsworth, 1974); and Michael Ignatieff, *The Needs of Strangers* (Chatto & Windus, London, 1984).

Jeremy Seabrook

Preface

The questions raised in this book are only part of an ancient and recurring argument about the persistence of poverty and the nature of human need, at least as old as the challenge of the prophet Isaiah: 'Wherefore do ye spend money on that which is not bread, and your labour on that which satisfieth not?' (55:i). The question was debated vigorously in the late Middle Ages, as traditional teachings of the Church, which sought to restrain economic appetites, came up against the waxing energies of early capitalism. Tawney, in *Religion and the Rise of Capitalism*, traces the eclipse of doctrines such as that expressed in the fourteenth century by Henry of Langenstein: 'He who has enough to satisfy his wants and nevertheless ceaselessly labours to acquire riches, either in order to obtain a higher social position, or that subsequently he may have enough to live without labour, or that his sons may become men of wealth and importance – all such are incited by a damnable avarice, sensuality or pride', and the epochal change, whereby the exploitation of public necessities for private gain was transformed from being a heinous sin in the Middle Ages into the summit of virtue by the eighteenth century. The argument is resumed in the modern world in the still unresolved issue of whether humanity has been enslaved by its needs as natural scarcity gives way to social scarcity (Rousseau), or is being emancipated by the development of its productive possibilities (Adam Smith).[1]

At the time of the early industrial era it seemed that the power of capital to release human inventiveness and its ability to create wealth had settled the argument. It was only when the instinctive and inchoate resistances of labour to its role in this process had been formulated in the apocalyptic and sulphurous vision of Marx that the challenge to capitalism was made concrete; and even then Marx did not contest the underlying productivist assumptions of industrial society. He was certainly not seeking to moderate

---

[1] See Michael Ignatieff, *The Needs of Strangers* (Chatto & Windus, London, 1984).

human appetites, but rather to transcend the ugly inequalities of capitalism. His insistence, however, on the primacy and the liberating potential of labour meant that he was, at least in part, calling upon a much older tradition, one that led Tawney to refer to him as 'the last of the schoolmen' of the Middle Ages.

The efforts of socialism, not to inhibit but to redirect human needs, have faltered in the mid-twentieth century, not only in the rigidities and inflexibilities of those societies in which 'actually existing socialism' prevails (that materialized dream of secular redemption made nightmare), but also in the regenerated and global dynamism of capital, which has dazzled the world with its limitless wealth. But just when it seemed that the argument had once more been definitively settled – just as it must have appeared to those of the early industrial era – it has struck against new constraints. When it seems that the West has offered a model of development and a source of emulation, not only to the poor of the earth but also to those increasingly beleaguered people in countries that call themselves socialist, it is menaced by limitations and obstructions previously undreamed of. The reign of universal capital is threatened by the limits to resources, the degradation of the global environment, the further impoverishment of the poorest countries, uncontainable urbanization, as well as by the damaged spirit and nameless wounds inflicted on growing numbers of people in the overdeveloped world. This is what has made the 'Greens' and the environmentalists return, not so much to the formulations of the early socialists (except insofar as these asked for nothing more than sufficiency for all) but to more ancient arguments, in order to make their case for moderating the predations of the rich upon the Earth's treasures, for the sort of frugality and restraint that would have been recognized by St. Bernard of Clairvaux no less than by twentieth century Gandhians. We are rediscovering old and slumbering truths that had been allowed to lapse in recent times, and these are now being spoken again with an even more compelling urgency, in order not only that the poor shall have the space to live but also that the human race itself may survive. The argument that seemed reduced to silence in the presence of human control over nature, once more rouses stirring echoes in those who see the mastery over what has passed for humanity's own nature as an even more imperative task.

1

Introduction

The model of development that has evolved in the West is now widely acknowledged to be inappropriate for the culture and experience of much of the Third World. What is less widely conceded is that it may be inappropriate for the tendentiously named First World too: what is violent, exploitative and destructive in the poor countries cannot be miraculously cleansed in the metropolitan areas, cannot there be made fit, as it were, for human consumption.

To contest the way in which we have developed is to invite derision. Although it is sometimes granted that the profusion of products, symbols, services and commodities which the rich capitalist countries believe to be the signs of advanced civilization may have consequences that are baleful and damaging for the poor of the earth, the criticism that these things might also be oppressive to those whose lives are dominated by them has never been taken seriously. Just as at the time of the first industrial era the possibility of development in Britain readily quelled any anxieties about the nature of that development, so, from our contemporary perspective, we can no longer conceive of any alternative to that which has actually occurred, and can contemplate with composure its spread over the whole globe. We are then compelled to close our eyes to all the awkward and intractable by-products of a version of progress that has taken on the force of a deterministic inevitability.

That what Rudolf Bahro calls 'actually existing socialism'[1] has equally pursued a cult of productivism, a shared dedication to growth, has been a measure of the collusive symbiosis of capitalists and socialists in the twentieth century. The yoking of these apparently conflicting ideologies has until quite recently effectively marginalized the real alternative. This has to do with the search for sufficiency, a formulation perhaps best summed up in the Book of Proverbs: 'Give me neither riches nor poverty,

---

[1] Rudolf Bahro, *The Alternative in Eastern Europe* (New Left Books, London, 1978).

but enough for my sustenance.'[2] The model which we have lived, and which we have been at pains to torment the whole world into accepting, is one that bypasses such modest and easily achievable goals.

Such an aim was the hope of the early labour movement: freedom from want, hunger, insecurity. This limited claim upon the treasures of the Earth would have been perfectly compatible with the alleviation of hunger and poverty in the Third World, no less than in the industrial West. What the labour movement foresaw was a continuing frugality, a careful husbanding of things, an only moderate appetite for possession. This might well have served as the basis for a very different kind of development from that which we have seen. Indeed, people's ancient respect for material resources – for all that it was forced upon them by poverty – was not a response of such little worth that it could afford to be squandered. And it is repeated today in the attitude of the poor in the Third World. Those people in the slums and shanties are, in important ways, living our past all over again. They are taking up the one-time cry of our labour movement, which remains such a blasphemy against the imperatives of capitalism (and has therefore been smothered in the West) – 'enough for our sustenance'.

What we have to learn from our own past experience has nothing to do with nostalgia, for it remains the daily lived ordeal of the workers in the slums of Manila, the *chawls* of Bombay, the despairing inhabitants of the *favelas* and *barrios* of South America. For them, other possibilities of development have not quite been suppressed, even though we in the West can scarcely imagine any future other than one in which the rich must go on getting richer before the poverty of the majority of humankind can be mitigated. This is why we are not anxious to look clearly at the way in which other ideas of development were crushed by an obsession with growth that has nothing to do with sufficiency, but everything to do with an autonomous economy that is not articulated to human need.

What an irony it is that the 'new' formulations of the green and ecology movements are so similar to those evolved by the early socialists; and that they should match the sober claims of those poor people who see their children perish in a world of abundance today: the possibility of a humanity 'not wasted by penury or luxury' in William Morris's words,[3] but living securely within the bounds of enough. Such was the vision of the early labour movement; and it still represents the limit of the hopes of half a billion people living on the edge of survival in the South. To disavow our own past is to add insult to the injury we inflict upon the present-day poor.

[2] Quoted in R.H. Tawney, *Religion and the Rise of Capitalism*, 1926 (Penguin, Harmondsworth, 1964).
[3] William Morris, *News from Nowhere* (Lawrence & Wishart, London, 1977).

The Left has been reluctant to examine too closely the transformation of humanity which has taken place in the West in our lifetime because that transformation has been paid for with the eclipse of those more modest socialist ambitions, and the metamorphosis of socialism into an emulous and competitive shadow of what it came into being to supplant. For we, the people of the West, have become, not so much the sullen and reluctant labour that unwillingly propels the machinery of capitalist production, as the willing agents of its driven and tormented trajectory: we have ourselves become its need for growth and expansion. We have permitted our needs to become identified with its necessity. It is as though we had been turned into the very machines to which we were tethered in the early industrial era. The process of attaching Left-wing parties to capitalist growth has been the external symbol of this profound inner transformation. By this means, the creation of real alternatives was evicted to a position outside that occupied by an ossifying and ageing Left.

The other side of this catastrophe, of course, is that the socialist aim of sufficiency remains; overtaken, submerged perhaps, but still there in the dreams of the poor of the Earth; and, who knows, perhaps still palpitating, seething gently beneath the market profligacy of the rich world with all its superfluities that nevertheless leave so many human needs achingly unanswered.

What we can say is that we have seen the spoiling of one kind of potential for change: the possibility of more sustainable claims upon the Earth's fragile abundance, an opportunity to make the most of human resources to supplement scarce material things, whereby we would not appropriate more than our fair share of them. We have been deceived into believing that deliverance from capitalist poverty could lie only through its own distorted version of plenty, a belief that has become the more entrenched as we have been turned into the very engines that drive its need for growth and expansion. It is this vision of 'development' that we have willed upon the whole world; and because we surrendered so long ago to its logic, we are slower to see the inadmissible disgrace and scandal at its heart.

In *Towards 2000*, Raymond Williams dissects the word 'development'.

This is based on an idea of the unfolding, the unrolling, indeed the evolution of an inherent process. The eighteenth century idea of a unilinear process of civilisation, through all the stages from savagery to barbarism to societies of the type in which the process itself was defined, was strengthened by nineteenth-century evolutionary ideas: 'nations proceed in a course of Development, their later manifestations being potentially present in the earliest elements'. This could still mean different kinds of development, as for example into different species in the biological model, but steadily, in the twentieth century, a unilinear sense was assumed, and was even seen as 'natural' . . . Thus all societies other than the old industrial societies were 'naturally' seen as either 'undeveloped' or 'developing', and their futures were theoretically assumed to be governed by this pre-existent model . . . Thus 'development' became an inherently ideological term.[4]

This book examines two significant moments in this model: the process of urbanization (with or without industrialization) characteristic of early nineteenth-century England and of much of the contemporary Third World, and at the later moment, the phase of de-industrialization, or the evolution of a post-industrial or service or leisure-oriented economy which, so far, only the 'advanced' Western countries have passed through, and then only incompletely. The book observes the way in which poverty passes intact through both these phases, to re-emerge in a modernized form in even the richest societies the world has ever known. If at the earlier moment of industrialization the persistence of poverty could be explained by a productive capacity only rudimentarily established, such an excuse is no longer possible. It becomes clear, therefore, that the survival of poverty is essential for ideological and not material reasons. Indeed, the maintenance of a felt experience of insufficiency is essential to any capitalist version of development. For this to be achieved, human beings must be radically reshaped; and it is the manner of this restructuring of human beings and their needs in rich Western society that is the core of this book. In many ways, this transformation of people in our era echoes the turbulent and driven process of the first industrial period, which moulded a dying peasantry into a disciplined manufacturing population – that change which is occurring all over the world today. Only this time, the change in the West has at least one major difference: it has been an internal transformation, a dismantling of the psychic structures of the old working class, and their rebuilding in the interests of a new phase of capitalist evolution, a modified international division of labour. This is why the change has been possible without the external violence that characterized the first industrial revolution. Quite the reverse, in fact: the violence has been contained. The pain of this drastic reshaping of the human substance has been internal; and at the same time the outer landscapes have been cleansed and refurbished. It should come as no surprise if the evils that stem from this change should be psychic and emotional, mental and moral disorders, so much more readily attributable to weak or unsound individuals rather than to epic social and economic upheavals. This is territory that remains largely uncharted; and it is the harder to reach for not being susceptible to description in terms of the material squalor and ugliness of the first Industrial Revolution, or of the chaotic process of urbanization in the South today.

[4] Raymond Williams, *Towards 2000* (Chatto & Windus, London, 1983).

Peter Worsley indicates how crucial the moment of urbanization is in contemporary experience.

'Beginning with the Great Transformation (the capitalist modernization of agriculture and the rise of machinofacture) the city has triumphed over the countryside, and the industrialised countries over the agrarian ones. In the world's first major capitalist country, Britain, there were already more people living in towns and cities than in the countryside as early as 1861 . . . That flight from the land is being repeated, now, in the Third World. And within our lifetime the majority of us will be living in towns and cities, not in the countryside. The future is an urban future'.[5]

It is therefore the more urgent that we look critically at the likely subsequent fate of those new urban poor, and reflect on what needs to be done if they are not simply to pass from one form of poverty into another.

The locking together of forms of overdevelopment in the North with underdevelopment in the South has been widely documented by, among others, Susan George and Lappé and Collins.[6] The poor cannot be freed from the cruel visitations of their poverty unless the rich are at the same time emancipated from the diseases – physical, moral and spiritual – of their wealth. This book is an attempt to understand how rich and poor are caught up in a symbiotic dependency; and it asks how disengagement from the machinery that perpetuates that cruel equilibrium is possible. It is a project requiring a language of liberation that has so far eluded us in the West, because of the pervasive and overwhelming association of our riches with all that is good and desirable, and because of the fateful and insistent transmission of their images across the whole world. What does emerge is that despite all the promises of capitalist wealth, poverty, in one guise or another, remains its constant attendant and its most carefully protected product. The question to which we return is whether deliverance from poverty is possible within a system which sets at the heart of its purpose the maintenance of a felt and immitigable insufficiency. The argument is an old one, but it is given new urgency in a world threatened by both ecological disaster and nuclear catastrophe. In the West, the Peace, Womens' and Green movements have begun to address these issues. Our most urgent task lies not only in the organic coming together of these, but their fusion with the liberation movements of the South in a shared emancipation from what R. Panikkar calls 'the pan-economic ideology: just as some people accept that we need some demilitarized zones, we should begin to demonetize values. Let me give an

---

[5] Peter Worsley, *The Three Worlds* (Weidenfeld & Nicolson, London, 1984).

[6] Susan George, *How the Other Half Dies* (Penguin, Harmondsworth, 1977); Frances Lappé and Joseph Collins, *Food First* (Sphere, London, 1982).

example of a demonetized culture in which I lived for a few months recently with great joy: Nagaland. Among the nagas, food (rice) is not monetizable, not marketable; you cannot buy it or sell it in any way; it is simply distributed to each household by a very sophisticated system. As a result there is no anxiety since there is rice for everybody. Similarly houses are not marketable or monetizable; there is no real estate. To deal in real estate would be a criminally punishable activity. Houses are not negotiable as human bodies are not – the house being a prolongation of the human body . . . You don't need to pay for breathing, but in Nagaland also not for eating and dwelling. You can live without such burden and anxiety'.[7] All over the world there are growing numbers of people resolved not to permit the vision of sufficiency for all go down before the vain and always disappointed promises of limitless wealth.

[7] R. Panikkar, in *Negations* (Trivandrum, Kerala, spring 1984).

2

What we have Lived Through

It is not easy for us to imagine now the turbulence and anxiety in the lives of people at the turn of the nineteenth century. Then, a raw and inexperienced agricultural population, dispossessed by enclosures and agricultural improvements, moved from the impoverished countryside into the factory towns – 'the barracks of industry', as the Hammonds called them.[1] There, unfamiliar with the rules of political economy, they were coerced, wrenched into the disciplined shape required by the rhythm of mills and manufactories. In this process there was a radical reworking of the human material: in the 1790s there were twice as many people employed in agriculture as in manufacture; by 1840 this proportion had been reversed.

And yet, all this disturbance should not be strange to us. For we have lived, in our epoch, through a shadow of that drastic change; in some ways, almost an undoing of it. This time, it has been the proportion of people in the 'new' manufacturing industries of the nineteenth century that has changed in relation to the numbers employed in service industries.

The echoes and correspondences between these two major convulsions are not often emphasized, perhaps because the restructuring of the working class has not involved the same physical plucking up of people from their living places. There has not been the same flow of half-starved and uprooted migrants from Ireland, or from the overburdened villages after the enclosures of the late eighteenth century into the new towns (although the migrants from the Caribbean and Asia have undergone an experience that was more general at the time of the industrial revolution). But that difference – the absence of such disruptive mobility – has been crucial in the current remoulding of a working class that had become as archaic as a peasantry confronted by the exigencies of industrialization. This time, it has been only the psychic structures that have been broken

[1] J.L. and Barbara Hammond, *The Town Labourer* (Longman, Green, London, 1925).

and reassembled. It is the internal landscapes that have borne the scars, in that mutation of a working class from what was thought of as its 'classic' industrial form, into the new shape required by a modified and global division of labour. This time, it has all been so much more tidy than when the pauper apprentices were conveyed northwards from the London workhouses to serve in the factories, and the despairing agricultural labourers walked from their squalid vilages for the last time, and the handloom weavers, unable to retain even the last vestiges of control over their work, and full of resentment and bitterness, sent their children to work in the mills.

Other factors have also been at work to blur the similarities. The developments we have seen have been accompanied by far more obvious improvements in living standards than those erratic and ill-distributed gains of the early nineteenth century; and give less room for dispute as to whether most people experienced them as material advance or as immiseration, in the way that occurred at the time of the industrial revolution. It has therefore been all the easier to efface or elide the parallels, the continuities with that earlier upheaval, even though it has all been in the interests of the same exacting and impersonal forces.

But it does not mean that the experience this time has been wholly beneficent. For what we have seen in the past two generations or so has been nothing less than the dismantling of the identity of the old working class and the reorganization of its psychic structures in comformity with the demands of capital, shifting in its means, but constant in its purpose. It may come to be seen that what we have lived through has been in its own way as far-reaching, as implacable as that earlier transformation that created a new kind of human being out of a wasting and uncomprehending peasantry – 'just as in the last century the peasants and the manufactory workers changed their entire way of life, and themselves became quite different people when they were drawn into large-scale Industry', as Marx and Engels stated in the *Communist Manifesto*.[2]

For the manipulation of the human substance has been just as profound. It is sometimes acknowledged, as a popular cliché, that we are going through a second (or even third) industrial revolution. But the common wisdom interprets this blandly, in terms of 'modernization', or 'social change', something neutral and inoffensive. And there has been no dearth of commentators and wise men (nearly always men) to declare that this is as desirable as it is necessary, and that even if there are painful consequences for certain groups of workers and certain kinds of communities, it cannot fail to benefit 'the nation as a whole' in the long term. But then, even at the moment of that earlier unquiet transformation,

[2] Karl Marx and Friedrich Engels, *Communist Manifesto* (Progress Publishers, Moscow, 1977).

there were many eager to point out the inestimable benefits to the people in their removal to the towns, where they would work in the wholesome and salubrious atmosphere of an airy manufactory. Thus, Sir Frederick Eden in 1797 extolled the virtues of enclosure, not only for the sake of greater efficiency in agriculture but because this would release the poor from scratching a living, 'picking up a few dry sticks, or grubbing up, on some bleak moor, a little furze or heath'; they would be enabled to turn to more regular labour, be freed from their petty concern for their 'starved pig or a few wandering goslings', and free to earn a more regular income through manufacture.[3] The same arguments have been deployed in our time to demonstrate to the workers the wisdom of a system that has been evicting large numbers of them from settled employment in manufacturing, and urging upon them the advantages of future service industry. Not only are such changes always represented as being to everyone's advantage, they are also declared to be inevitable. That all our experience of change has been in the interests of the same processes that tore people up by the roots almost two centuries ago is readily seen in the recurring official justifications. The threat of impoverishment and loss if we fail to become competitive in the markets of the world echoes down the years; and the reflection of Ricardo from the 1820s has a curiously contemporary resonance, when he wondered 'whether it was worth a capitalist's while to continue in a country where profits were so small, and every pecuniary motive compelled him to quit rather than remain'.

That the reshaping of humanity for the benefit of the factory system was not an easy undertaking was widely conceded. It was a violent and tormented enterprise in a driven and dislocated time. Richard Arkwright recognized how difficult it was to train human beings 'to renounce their desultory habits of work, and identify themselves with the unvarying regularity of the complex automaton'.[4] The punitive rhetoric of those for whom the labour of the people had to be moulded into a commodity found its highest expression in the words of those who framed the Poor Law Amendment of 1834, when they complained that the old poor law 'By saving the labouring poor from the natural consequences of their improvidence, was putting a premium on indolence . . . In some parts of the country they had reached the conclusion that there was no point in working, as they would be supported out of the rates.'[5] This too has been familiar in our time, and has been heard in the lament of those who claim that the welfare state has tempted people to remain on the dole rather than seek work, and has encouraged them in idleness and debilitating dependency.

[3] Sir Fredrick Eden, *The State of the Poor* (1797).
[4] Quoted in Karl Marx, *Capital* (Vol.I, Lawrence & Wishart, London, 1977).
[5] Poor Law Amendment Act, 1834.

Even though the arguments remain constant, we are nevertheless asked to believe that the present refashioning of the working class is wholly benign. And it can be presented the more plausibly this time, because the human transformation has coincided with a period of spectacular material advance. This has obscured to those it has so deeply affected the depth and tenacity of those old recurrences, those unvarying severities, that strangely elusive repeat of an earlier history, so wounding and so violent that we were perhaps only too ready to forget it. The defenders of the working class have perhaps failed to be alert to the scope and profundity of changes that have all been in the interests of resisting change. But who is to say that the emotional violence, the twistings of the feelings, the pounding of the sensibility, the ravages of the heart and spirit have been any less than those earlier pressures that drove people from the familiar places? Of course, the squalor, the hunger, the brutality of the poverty have not been the same. We have not paid in the same coin as that demanded by that other epochal disruption; we have paid another form of tribute. As a consequence of seisms that are internal, this cannot always be seen. It lies in the realm of feeling, and does not leave the same blots and scars in the outer world; for it involves a breaking of relationships, a destruction of associations, with their accompanying absences and loneliness, mental disturbance and emotional breakdown, violence against ourselves and each other; dependence on drugs or alcohol, addictions to commodities both permitted and prohibited from junk food to heroin, a search for escape from the wounded sense of purpose, the effaced function of superseded skills and functions. This is where we have to look for the consequences of the dismantled identity, and the unceremonious reassembling of the sensibility of the old working class. Of course, all this occurred also at the time of that earlier transformation. An important difference this time is that we have, as yet, been less capable of resistance to the violence done to us. We have been induced to accept the by-products of convulsive change as individual disorders and derangements; we are less sure that they have been socially produced. What the old working class learned – however slowly and partially – from their experience was that however hard they worked, they could still never secure themselves and their families against the threat of poverty. They had daily evidence that the pain inflicted upon them came from an alien and external force; and one of the primary effects of the capitalist welfare state has been to smother the evidence that socially produced afflictions are not all the consequence of personal or individual failings.

The reason for this more ready acceptance of individual responsibility for socially determined ills is not far to seek: it was the condition demanded in return for a capitalist promise of riches, a capitalist version of answering need. Because relief from primary poverty and insecurity were what the working class needed above all else, the terms on which that relief was granted were not contested. Thus our celebrated cherishing of individuals has a darker side – the imposition upon them of the burden of responsibility for socially created afflictions; and this is too much to bear for the many individuals who break beneath it. In the same way, that earlier upheaval broke the spirit as well as the body of countless people. There were, after all, thirty lunatic asylums in England and Wales in the 1790s; by the 1840s there were over three hundred. Even after allowance is made for increase in population and changes in public attitudes to madness, this growth is startling.

Although the demolition and reconstruction of the human personality has all taken place within, as the dust begins to settle and we can see this major transformation for what it is, we can observe how curiously it has been reflected in the tearing down and rebuilding of the external landscapes, the towns and cities in which the 'classic' working class lived and laboured. Indeed, that internal convulsion has been crucially linked to the external cleansing and work of reparation.

It is not difficult to see why this complete reform has been necessary in our time. The vastly augmented capacity of the capitalist economies to produce has meant that what many have known for almost two hundred years – that we no longer live in a society of scarcity – can no longer be concealed, even from the very poorest. The productive power of capital always implied the possibility of an end to poverty; indeed, it was precisely this that made Marx see as progressive the rise of the bourgeoisie. But what was less easily foreseeable was the extent to which a sense of insufficiency, an experience of continuing privation could be maintained, even in the midst of an abundance unparalleled in human history, and equally unparalleled in the range of its distribution. Just how this extraordinary achievement has been accomplished deserves more attention that it has received. Even this is no new argument. Tawney wrote:

Mankind, it seems, hates nothing so much as its own prosperity. Menaced with an accession of riches which would lighten its toil, it makes haste to redouble its labours, and to pour away the perilous stuff, which might deprive of plausibility the complaint that it is poor. Applied to the arts of peace, the new resources commanded by Europe during the first half of the sixteenth century might have done something to exorcise the spectres of pestilence and famine, and to raise the material fabric of civilization to undreamed-of heights. Its rulers, secular and ecclesiastical alike, thought otherwise. When pestilence and famine were ceasing to be necessities imposed by nature they re-established them by political art.[6]

[6] R.H. Tawney, *Religion and the Rise of Capitalism* (Penguin, Harmondsworth, 1977).

The same could be said for the twentieth century, but this time on a global scale. The means whereby this has been accomplished in our time has involved the appropriation of human need, and its irretrievable dispersal through a vast proliferation of capitalist commodities which deform and mutilate it; a process which directly reflects the capitalist appropriation and misshaping of human labour. In other words, the vast division of labour into so many fragmented tasks has its analogue in the splintering of alienated needs.

As a consequence, scarcity has had to be redefined, the idea of poverty reformulated. For within capitalism, that which it seemed to promise, and which reconciled many to its logic – sufficiency – is inadmissible. Enough is anathema to a system devoted to its accumulation, and in which the answering of human need is only a tangential and subordinate purpose. Poverty and illusions of scarcity are ideologically indispensable to capitalism; for without them all the desperate energy and striving in the search for growth and expansion and accumulation would be undermined; and indeed, there might be a serious danger that its inner dynamic would simply exhaust itself. Thus the effort and ingenuity that have gone into ensuring the survival of poverty are one of the wonders of the modern world; of a piece, in their way, with splittng the atom or walking on the moon.

The maintenance of the subjective experience of being poor in the presence of its manifest redundancy has been at the heart of the transformation of the people; and it is to this end that the inner landscapes, the minds and feelings of women and men and children have been systematically reworked. In the interests of this vast, ignoble design, the defences against an earlier capitalist poverty have been swept away, cleared, as the Highlands of Scotland were once cleared for the sake of more profitable sheep, as the countryside was cleared of people for more profitable agriculture, as the poor have always been cleared from the land they occupy, as it becomes more valuable and is turned over to railways, property or cash crops. What invasions of the old resistances of the working class have been necessary in order that new and alien needs and wants might be implanted, just as cotton or coffee or sisal were planted in the lands people once cultivated for subsistence? What strange conversions have been required to change the very hearts of women and men into the manufactories of desire for all that promiscuous spillage of capitalist manufacture and marketing, what intensification of suppressed need has been worked up, just as the steam was once built up with sufficient force to drive the engines of early capitalist production?

The migrations of a driven and restless population can occur again. This time, however, they have been accomplished in secrecy and silence, in the dark internal places, safe from the scrutiny of Engels or Marx or Mayhew or Booth, where no Children's Employment Commissioners or Factory

Inspectors can penetrate and depict those glowering and unforgettable landscapes. If the same things recur, they do so in an inaccessible place, where they cannot be so easily recognized for what they are; and we respond with bemused incomprehension when children are disturbed and angry and violent, take drugs, run away, destroy themselves with solvents or drink; when women are afraid to walk out in the dark; when the old fear the young; when the poor prey on the poor; when needs and abundant commodities seem to be eternally mismatched and our yearnings unassuaged by them; when ancient wrongs seem to live on, perversely, inexplicably, surviving all the changes and improvements that were to have eradicated them for ever.

So many of the plagues of the heyday of *laissez-faire* capitalism recur; not simply as a result of the ravages of a free labour market upon the workers, but also as a result of the warpings of consumer markets upon those who seek to express their leashed and dependent freedoms through them. For we have internalized those alien mechanisms of the early industrial period, by which our labour was regulated, and we still live to their remorseless rhythms; and if our part in the labour process has been mitigated through struggle, it is only in order that our part in the competitive fight for the fruits of the labour of others might be intensified. Guy Debord, in *The Society of the Spectacle*, observes 'The present "liberation from labour" and the increase in leisure is in no way a liberation within labour, nor a liberation from the world shaped by this labour. None of the activity lost in labour can be regained in the submission to its result – non-work, inactivity; this inactivity is in no way liberated from productive activity; it depends on productive activity, and is an uneasy and admiring submission to the necessities and results of production.'[7] Subordination to the flow of never-finished work, when children commonly worked a thirteen- or fourteen-hour day, where 'recreation is out of the question; there is scarcely any time for meals, the very period of sleep is often abridged, nay, the children are sometimes waked even in the night', as the Leeds doctor H. Turner Thackrah said in his support for the Ten-Hour Bill, has become a different, but parallel subjugation. This time it is not to a deregulation of labour that children are subjected but to a deregulation of desire, in which they become apprentices to never-ending and insatiable longings for the fruits of all that productive capacity. Just as the pauper apprentices once provided an inexhaustible supply of hands to the mills, our children become, in this new phase of capitalist expansion, indentured to their own appetites. And the wants which they learn to express in this way are no more their own than the labour they formerly performed was for their own satisfaction,

[7] Guy Debord, *The Society of the Spectacle* (Black and Red, Detroit, 1977).

but have been generated by the apparently infinite powers of production of the great impersonal engines of capitalist manufacture.

Our needs have been yoked to production and profit, confiscated by an alien power, in such a way that we do not distinguish between where human needs cease and the promptings of that power begin. The limit is blurred between our human impulses and the vast machinery in which these have been caught up – like those images in Engels, of people being trapped in the wheels and belts and pulleys of factory machines, and spun round until every bone in their body was broken. Humanity itself has become the raw material for strange new products. We feed the invisible but ubiquitous machine, and what is produced out of inexpressible longings, our isolation and wonder at the dissolution of our earlier part in the processes of production, out of our anguish and confusion, is a vast reservoir of desire, a cistern of amorphous and indefinable hopes and wants, which have to be assorted with the pyramids of merchandise, the heaps of commodities that pile up and are distributed through the great vending machine in which we live.

Many human needs are doomed never to be satisfied in this way, because they belong to an order of experience that simply bears no relation to what can be bought and sold. As Michael Ignatieff observes:

Needs which lack a language adequate to their expression do not simply pass out of speech: they may cease to be felt. The generations that have grown up without ever hearing the language of religion may not feel the slightest glimmer of a religious need. If our needs are historical, they can have a beginning and an end, and the end arrives when the words for their expression begin to ring hollow in our ears.[8]

Simply because goods or services or experiences are marketed, and indeed achieve great sales, does not necessarily mean that they *answer* a need. Human needs are so complex and difficult that what we buy in order to satisfy them may be only the roughest approximation to an answer; or they may be a substitute for things that cannot be bought yet cannot be discovered anywhere else in our culture; or indeed, may be consolations for absences and yearnings that are either not available to us in our society or, what is worse, have been suppressed by it. It may well be that the driven and pervasive insistence on buying and selling is itself a means of crowding out all the precious things that cannot be had for money, or, even more disturbing, is a sympton of the way in which needs are misshaped and distorted until they do correspond, at least vaguely, to what can be sold as commodity or service. In this way, just as the workers of an earlier phase of industrial society were theoretically free to choose to whom they would sell their labour, so our 'free' choices of what to buy are

---

[8] Michael Igniateff, *The Needs of Strangers* (Chatto & Windus, London, 1984).

not quite as they appear; but are often gropings, formless and captive longings, sharply disciplined, rigidly channelled responses that leave many basic (more complex) needs untouched and unappeased. Indeed, because they cannot be satisfied in this way these only grow more insistent and restless. It is this that has made sufficiency an impossible achievement. Frustrated and suppressed needs keep alive the striving and the energy that drive the machine – the machine we have become in our vain attempt to absorb, to ingest and lay waste that unstoppable outpouring. And this is how it can happen that humanity continues to be wrecked and wasted in one way or another, whether by scarcity or abundance, because neither phase of capitalist development bears any direct relation to our needs. In this way, direct continuity is maintained between those early victims of industrial society, who were 'not citizens of this or that town, but hands of this or that master',[9] and their descendants, equally disturbed, who have become simple aggregates of over-stimulated needs, a fascia of appetites which belong not to ourselves but to the unchained productive power which manipulates them.

It is easy for us to mistake the rhythm of capitalist making and selling for the rhythms of our own humanity. We have internalized it until we take the driven machinery for the gentler pulse of our own body; we don't distinguish its relentless exactions from the throb of our life-blood, its churning and grinding from the dilations and contractions of our spirit, its pitiless simulation of life from the rise and fall of our heart.

It is not simply as metaphor that continuity with an earlier moment of industrialism is assured, but as lived experience. It is not easy to reach into the places that belong to the spirit and the imagination and feelings. Even as the disabling workload of industrial production is lessened, the space created is immediately filled with the disabling fantasies that belong to capitalism as surely as the old burden of labour did. It is the internal location of that kneading and reworking of the human substance that makes contemporary definitions of poverty so elusive. Peter Townsend, writing of *Poverty in the United Kingdom*, says: 'Conceptions of poverty as absolute" were found to be inappropriate and misleading. People's needs, even for food, are conditioned by the society to which individuals belong.'[10] This makes good sense, as do Runciman's insights into relative deprivation.[11] Townsend states that 'needs arise by virtue of the kind of society to which individuals belong'; but underlying all the attempts to reach a definition of poverty is an assumption that needs occur as a by-product of different and widely varying cultures. What poverty means,

[9] Hammond and Hammond, *The Town Labourer*.
[10] Peter Townsend, *Poverty in the United Kingdom* (Penguin, Harmondsworth, 1979).
[11] Runciman, *Relative Deprivation and Social Justice* (Routledge & Kegan Paul, London, 1966).

in a society in which the creation and manipulation of need itself is a primary purpose, is the great conundrum, before which definitions falter and remedies appear impossible. This is what happened with us; and thus it is that needs become measureless and unanswerable, and the task of fulfilling them as hopeless as that of Sisyphus or the daughters of Danaus. This is what has defied judgements of what constitutes poverty in the West. It has made the well-to-do feel insecure, the affluent experience constant insufficiency, and even the very rich aware of their impoverishment. What we are dealing with is the expropriation of need, and its refraction, vast, moving, irretrievably lost in the panoply of capitalist selling, the 'spectacle that is capital to such a degree of accumulation that it becomes image'.[12] When we talk, as Townsend does, of poverty as the exlusion of people from the norms, standards and customary activities of their society, that is beyond dispute; but when these norms and standards are themselves all centred on fugitive notions of increase – more, better, higher, bigger, all of them comparative terms detached from their positive degree – then any definition of poverty becomes as mobile and untenable as any gesture towards sufficiency. This preoccupation has been described by William Leiss as 'a culture of wanting', in which commodities and marketed services 'cease to be straightforward objects, but are progressively more unstable, temporary collections of a mixture of objective and imputed characteristics – that is highly complex material-symbolic entities', and easily escape practical attempts to define need.[13]

When we turn to some of the classic texts on the industrial revolution, our sense of continuity, and the repeat – albeit in a different form – of historic processes, are only enhanced. A book like the Hammonds' *The Town Labourer*, with its familiar story of the transformation of the peasantry into the 'new' working class, strikes not as something remote and finished with, but as the beginnings of a process that has an urgent and contemporary resonance. Their account of the violent formation of a new kind of being – the industrial worker – foreshadows a parallel mutation of our time. Their picture is bleak enough, and at first sight could scarcely be more different from that of present-day Western societies: 'No economist of the day, in estimating the gains and losses of factory employment, ever allowed for the strain and violence that a man suffered in his feelings when he passed from a life in which he could smoke or eat or dig or sleep as he pleased, to one in which somebody turned the key on him, and for 14 hours he had not even the right to whistle. It was like entering the airless and laughterless life of a prison. Unless one keeps this moral sacrifice in mind, we shall not understand why the handloom

[12] Debord, *Society of the Spectacle.*
[13] William Leiss, *Limits to Satisfaction* (University of Toronto Press, Toronto, 1976).

weavers refused to go into the power-loom factories, where they would have earned much higher wages . . . Moreover, although to the authors of the books on the advantages of machinery, invention seemed to have lightened the drudgery of men and women, it had introduced a wearing tension: the nervous strain of watching machinery and working with it aged people faster than the heaviest physical exertions; the machinery never tired.'[14] What remains in our experience is not the machinery, but the compelling and accelerated rhythms of production, and the tense and competitive adaptation of people to the world of capitalist commodities; the effort and stress that go into *keeping pace*, maintaining a tempo of human life in accord with an alien music; not keeping up with the Joneses, as the popular phrase suggests, but keeping up with the unflagging productivism of the whole capitalist machine. And the airless prison of the Hammonds' period is reproduced, this time within each individual, alone with his or her needs that gnaw the soul.

What James Philip Kay said in 1832 is curiously evocative of the restless fevers of contemporary life: 'Whilst the engine runs, the people must work – men, women and children are yoked together with iron and steam. The animal machine – breakable in the best case, subject to a thousand sources of suffering – is chained fast to the iron machine, which knows no suffering and no weariness.'[15] It is no accident that so much of the disease of this age derives from stress and tension, nervous debility and exhaustion.

There are even more telling echoes in Marx. The division of labour into isolated repetitive actions has its direct counterpart in the fragmenting of need. The confiscation of skills and their incorporation into machinery has its equivalent in the dispersal of need in the vast depersonalized machinery of selling, and the dance of commodities, in which it is as difficult for us to recognize our human impulses as it was for the detail labourer to have any sense of his worth and creativity in the alien processes that manipulated him. The subordination of humanity to capital for the sake of production is directly reflected in the leashed freedoms promised by market-distributed rewards. When capital comes to offer a remedy for its own inflictions – some relief from its version of poverty – the mechanism whereby this benign end is to be achieved is not what it appears to be; and the markets through which human needs purport to be answered are no more innocent than those 'free' markets whereby labour is ensnared and enslaved. And just as the workers were led into an unbreakable symbiosis with the machinery of which they were an extension, so market-machinery grinds human need to dust in its workings. The growth of markets to fit the world-wide productive capacity

[14] Hammond, *Town Labourer.*
[15] James Philip Kay, *Moral and Physical Conditions of Operatives Engaged in Cotton Manufacture in Manchester.*

of capital involves a warping of humanity no less than the systematic disciplining of people until they had been deformed to fit the machinery of production in nineteenth-century Britain; this has been the work of our epoch.

Just as the labour of the workperson was isolated and riveted to a single action within an incomprehensible labour process, so the individual, seeking to satisfy his or her needs, finds they have become obscurely indefinable, inaccessible in multitudes of objects, symbols, substances and services that it would require all the money in the world to unlock. What we need, no less than what we can do, has been captured in complex impersonal processes, and frozen there, immobilized; and the restless attempt to buy back that living substance, which flickers like a will o' the wisp, beckoningly, enticingly, over the spectacle of merchandise, is always doomed; and we are victims of that 'permanent opium war which aims to make people identify goods with commodities and satisifaction with survival that increases according to its own laws'.[16] The possession by any individual of the whole Aladdin's cave would not even begin to satisfy the desires, because the dead merchandise occurs in a realm that bears no relation to those desires, and indeed, is sealed from them by the money through which it is conducted. Our attempts to buy what has been taken from us with money has its equivalent in the expenditure of labour, by which we could never secure ourselves enough for the subsistence of ourselves and those who depended on us. Like the machinery of the early nineteenth-century factory, the markets create 'an industrial perpetuum mobile, that would go on producing for ever, did it not meet with certain natural obstructions: the weak bodies and strong wills of its human attendants'[17] (or perhaps the markets flourish precisely because of the strong bodies and weak wills).

In the early part of the nineteenth century a memory of a less fragmented labour process was extraordinarily tenacious – the dream of land and the subsistence that was to be won from it, perhaps, or the memory, which many members of my family in the boot and shoe industry retained, of having control over their work-time, before they went grudgingly into the factories in the second half of the nineteenth century. Marx appends a note to page 456 of *Capital*, quoting the *Works* of Dugal Stewart, Edinburgh, 1855:

In some parts of the Highlands of Scotland, not many years ago, every peasant, according to the Statistical Account, made his own shoes of leather tanned by himself. Many a shepherd and cottar too, with his wife and children, appeared at

[16] Debord, *Society of Spectacle*.
[17] Marx, *Capital*.

Church in clothes which had been touched by no hands but their own, since they were shorn from the sheep and sown in the flaxfield. In the preparation of these, it is added, scarcely a single article had been purchased, except in the weaving. The dyes, too, were chiefly extracted by the women from trees, shrubs and herbs.[18]

Similar stories persist in the testimony of those who come into the rich Western societies as migrants from other cultures. But perhaps what is even more significant is the memory that remains of a more integral and organic answering of need which continues to trouble the experience of so many of the old urban working class – the persistent (and devalued) litany of those who still repine for a less fragmented and more human version of caring for each other, that reiterated story of mutual support, of leaving the door open day and night, helping and succouring, sharing insufficient material things, the bowl of broth for the sick, the human presence around the dying. This nostalgia for another way of answering need is the analogue of the nostalgia of those who recalled a less disciplined way of working; for it marks the passing of something equally irrecoverable.

This is the terrain that has been invaded during the current restructuring of human beings. Since the present phase has been, as always, in the interests of thé rich and powerful, the rhetoric that has accompanied it has echoed that which originated at the time of the first industrial revolution. We are urged, as our ancestors were, to go gracefully and unresistingly with the grain of those changes which we cannot, in any case, more than briefly delay. Naturally, there are disarming differences in the way we are encouraged not to resist. Indeed, those who protested most vigorously against any shortening of the fourteen-hour day for operatives in the cotton industry (Nothing is more favourable to morals than habits of early subordination, industry and regularity) have their heirs in those who have sought to persuade working people to set aside hard-won skills, not to stand in the way of technological change, and who hold out the glittering prospect of a future of leisure and comfort if only they will not throw obstacles in the path of the evolution of capitalism. Those groups of workers who do resist are like those who resisted 'modern industry, which threatens by taking away the instruments of labour, to snatch from their hands the means of subsistence'.[19] And whether they are steelmen, shipbuilders, miners or printers, they are called 'latter-day Luddites', 'wreckers' or 'Canutes'; and they are mocked to scorn if they express doubts about the benefits to be showered upon us if only we will co-operate to the full with processes which are, we are assured, inevitable anyway.

Those who were passionately convinced 150 years ago that any

[18] Ibid.
[19] Ibid.

abridgement of the hours of child labour would 'raise the price of goods to the consumers, which will affect the home trade considerably and will produce the most serious effects upon the prosperity of the district, by tending to foster the manufacturers of foreign nations, our trade with whom depends on the cheap and advantageous terms on which we now supply them with goods, and whose manufactures would be enabled by an advance of price successfully to compete with the British merchant' are heard once more; using the identical argument in urging us 'to price ourselves back into jobs', to compete with workers controlled by poverty, underemployment or military dictatorships in the Third World, by accepting lower wages.

The great advantage which the present reconstruction of the working class enjoys is that we have long become accustomed to the arguments, and the resistance which occurred in the first stage of industrialism has been far less intense. There has not been the same recalcitrance as when workers broke the stocking frames or fired ricks. It all appears, superficially at least, as though this contemporary reshaping has been far milder, altogether less painful.

But the relative ease with which it has all been accomplished is deceptive, for the violence has this time been more easily contained. It would be an error to believe that the conversion of human beings into the engine that drives the system can be achieved without damage and pain. It means that our spirit and heart become the sites of a different kind of production, where absences and voids and achings are created for which capitalist manufacture presents itself as a healing answer. It is not easy to find the language for these psychic reversals that have turned the internal landscapes into the locations of another kind of industry, which is a kind of inversion of an earlier form of exploitation. It is sometimes easier to express in metaphor and image than to rely on the incomplete formulations of economics, psychology or sociology. Guy Debord uses the appropriate metaphor when he says, 'When economic necessity is replaced by the necessity for boundless economic development, the satisfaction of primary human needs is replaced by an uninterrupted FABRICATION of pseudo-needs, which are reduced to the single need of maintaining the reign of the autonomous economy.'[20] The images of industrialism have all turned inwards. We have to ask ourselves what excavations in the region of the sensibility have been necessary to prepare the ground for this change; what minings and quarryings have occurred there; what veins and seams have been tapped for the purposes of profit, what faults and fissures prised open? How shall we describe the strange new products that have been hammered and forged and tempered in the dusty heat of foundries of

[20] Debord, *Society of Spectacle.*

the imagination; where are the hot dark mills in which the fabrics of fantasy are woven, that endless tissue of dreams spun by capital on the looms of human desire? 'Dissatisfaction itself became a commodity as soon as economic abundance could extend production to the processing of such raw materials.'[21] Perhaps the greatest artefact from these secret factories is poverty, a limitless and abstract fabrication, created in such a way that no amount of wealth and no heaping up of merchandise will ever answer it. We are ourselves the workshops and the refineries, the places where human needs are melted down, the forge where raw substances can be blended and shaped so that they will appear to fit the marketed response to them. The fires are stoked so that they cannot be extinguished. Here takes place a distilling of need, the casting and moulding of want, the shaping of desire; a threshing and winnowing of old longings; a refining of ancient appetites, a polishing of requirements; as well as an unending process of sorting, separating and matching – a labour without limit. Plenty becomes the raw material out of which a new poverty is fashioned: instead of withholding from the people the necessities of life, poverty becomes a transmutation of desires into such forms as to render them incapable of fulfilment. Rich and poor alike in the advanced societies are subject to the same experience; with this difference – that the poor are denied the money even to reach for the consolations that are permitted the rich, the pursuit of those approximations, the repeat of disappointment and the renewal of that mismatch between their agitated desires and the marketed deformities that sometimes give an illusion of responding to them.

It is here that we need to look in order to understand the completeness of that rebuilding of the psyche of the people in the rich world. It has been as total as that reconstitution at the beginning of the nineteenth century.

During the era of transformation that is now drawing to a close the people, worried by the decay of 'traditional' labour which shaped their lives, have been reassured that their future, and the future of their children, will lie in 'service industries'. This vision has been temptingly held out as a further inducement to co-operate with those benign processes characterized by such a palpable improvement in material standards. And indeed, this too looks wholly desirable to those people who, for generations, could only dream of seeing their children lifted out of the dirty and dangerous occupations associated with heavy industry and manufacture. The response of the mother of a young miner was characteristic. When she saw him going off to work in the pit on his first day, she said, 'I wept when he'd gone. I wanted something better for him; and if his father hadn't died, we would have struggled so that he shouldn't have to go off and work in the dark like that. I felt an utter failure that

[21] Ibid.

day.' Most people have been ready to meet more than half way the prospect of service industries. How proud they have been, those parents who *have* seen their children go, in clean clothes, not following the rhythmic regularity of the factory hooter, but to offices and shops and places of further education where dirt would not soon become etched into their hands and faces, where they would not be constantly at risk from industrial accidents, and they themselves would never again be subject to the terror of seeing one they love being borne home on a stretcher, or the labour-power squeezed out with the blood of a hand mangled in some unguarded machine.

It is service, then, that has been presented to the working class, in happy conjunction with the decline of manufacture, as a liberation from the burden of labour which has cast such a long shadow over their lives. It has all seemed so reasonable; even though these new services are under the control of the same imperious master who pressed us into manufacture, and before that kept us in the unknowing bondage to the soil: the wealth of others. But because the offer of 'service' seemed to be allied to a respite from an older, more familiar poverty, we have accepted it, without examining the contradiction contained in the idea of service as liberation; for the word service still means 'having the status of a servant'.

And indeed, this is what the mutation now completing itself is about – the remoulding of the human in the contours of a new servitude. There is nothing new in this, as the memories of farm servants, domestic servants or even the nineteenth-century 'wage slaves' testify. Only this time, a certain increase in material well-being has masked the fact that this is merely a recurrence of a familiar process. Wealth has been offered as a substitute for emancipation.

Those who exemplify this contemporary form of subjection are already so numerous that we take their presence for granted, scarcely even notice that they exist. Even those who claim to be the true defenders of labour have appeared indifferent, or perhaps made complacent by past victories, and have failed to take account of the actual experience of the working class as it has been reshaped.

The new servitors of capital are as invisible and self-effacing as the manipulators of that which they serve. It isn't simply that we don't see the Filippino chambermaids in their squalid accommodation under the roofs of the big hotels; it isn't merely the submissive manner of those migrants working in kitchens, cleaning lobbies, stations, halls and airports, lost in an expanse of bare marble and smoked glass and the spreading fronds of tropical plants; nor the silence of the vigilant janitors and night-watchmen in the darkened reception areas of great corporations through the small hours, with no company but a tinny transistor and the clatter of mop against pail from the invisible army of contract-cleaning women dispersed throughout the twenty-storey buiding; rather, it is that we have become blunted to their presence. We are used to the sleep-walking dependency of the young, raised on too much junk food, spiritual as well as material, on make-work projects, landscaping the inner city or engaged on the endless labour of clearing plates and cigarette ends from plastic tables in the fast-food chains, or sitting at the check-out, with closed, bored faces, not even looking at the people whose hands they brush; and those recent immigrants, with their eagerness to please, who have not yet learnt the rules of the game and assumed the stony impassivity of their elders, cleaning, carrying, opening doors for others. We are barely aware of those who serve money more nakedly, enfolded in offices that are smooth cliffs of granite and glass, with chipboard partitions pinned with holiday postcards, gunmetal cabinets and vending machines and a man-made climate that dries the nose and makes the throat permanently sore; those locked into word processors and visual display units with the shimmering green figures that leave such a persistent after-image on the retina and blur the black print of the evening paper; the shadowless glare of white strip-lighting, the fingerprints in the dust on the slats of the blind, the Busy Lizzie in the cottage-cheese pot, the lunch of dry Ryvita and Golden Delicious apples; and those older people, mostly men, with a more total devotion to finance, with their fur hats and real leather cases full of computer print-outs, crime novels and yachting magazines, jowls shaken by the commuter train as they stand in silence on the platform, with their shadowed chins and dry hands that rustle like paper money, on their way home in the dark to the garden they love but scarcely see half the year; all the subaltern humanity in banks and offices, the young women protected by glass, immaculate as orchids on display, fretting over the nail broken by the keyboard, and keeping a wary eye open in case one of the customers is concealing a shotgun under his raincoat. There is a whole population in the service of merchandise – not just selling, but in distribution and retailing; all those who wait for the next whim of the markets that will claim their service in new ways impossible to anticipate, infinitely flexible, inexhaustibly patient; as well as those celebrities who can be persuaded to promote some star commodity, differentiating it with the lustre of their fame from everything else that crowds the market; those who serve time, place and other abstractions, dancing attendance on money: the security guards patrolling the empty warehouses at night, flashing their torches on the stacks of merchandise at the slightest sound, and jumping at the echo of the baying Alsatian on its chain; the youngster in the petrol forecourt, blinking and yawning in the early hours in the glass kiosk, with its bags of sweets on hooks and its cans of oil, the striplighting crackling in the silence, and the rainbow-splashes of oil winking on the concrete; those whose service to humanity in the health service is dependent upon the

wealth of others, pensioners of the superfluity by whose grace the social
services exist at all; the black women on the early bus, the cleaners, whose
business is with blood and shit and vomit, waiting in the windy indigo
dawn for transport that is always late.

These services are what have replaced the making of things. They have
displaced from the hands of a great number of working people the tools
and the materials and the skills with which they might have fashioned
goods for need rather than for the caprice of the markets. And this is what
we are bidden to welcome as emancipation.

The meaning of a reconstituted working class becomes a little clearer.
The de-skilling and the decay of produtive industry result in labour that is
expendable, easily replaceable; all that is wanted is a succession of faint
competences, the adaptability of a protean vassalage that can be counted
upon to accommodate itself to whatever will make money for others; in
other words, the development of a form of labour that cannot be so easily
turned against those who abuse it. What is required all over again is a long
procession of mute subordination, a population of wraiths, dwarfed and
diminished by the power of the money they serve. With the loss of so
many of the tools and skills of basic manufacture, the possibility of
disengagement from the terms laid down by capital becomes less. While
the funciton of making essential goods remained, there was always the
(perhaps faint) chance of turning that function to an alternative end; while
the more overt service of money, the rise of distributive, service, leisure
and entertainment industries, permits no such imaginative vision of
alternatives: they represent, not the basis for self-sufficiency, but a mere
fragment of a world-wide division of labour. They disarm and disable the
working class of a single country. What we are confronted with are new
and unfamiliar patterns of subordination; and this is what we have been
slow to face.

The reason for this reluctance is clear. The release from the dirt and
squalor of much of traditional industry coincided with one of the periods
of greatest material improvement that the working class has ever seen.
And because that remission from an older poverty and insecurity was what
working people had struggled for above everything, the diminution of
power that accompanied it was not immediately obvious. Their position
was the same as that of people in the 'developing' countries – the
possibility of any kind of development at all was better than none, without
worrying about its nature and direction. But the modest – and not
necessarily lasting – increase of our freedom to exist within capitalism, by
means of a steadily rising income, became a substitute for our freedom to
change that system completely. In this way, we have permitted the idea of
freedom to become identified with a process which, in important ways,
actually erodes it: that human beings may be able to consume more, and at

the same time have their capacity for formulating social, political and moral alternatives abridged, is a novel combination; so unfamiliar, in fact, that for a long time the bargain that appeared to guarantee that purchasing power would go on increasing for ever, seemed benign. It is with this contradiction that we are now faced: the increasing identification of the needs of the working class with the needs of capitalism in a shared dedication to growth has been a snare. That version of emancipation leads into new forms of dependency.

And we can see something of the profile of the new jobs that have been promised when the current restructuring is completed. It is precisely what that deceptively homely term – jobs – suggests: jobs, rather than work, something which will be, for the majority of people, casualized, inexpert and insecure, responding to the monetary whim of the market, that will suck in the labour of workers and spew it out when that fad is past, leaving no residue, little skill, scarcely even a trace in the memory. It is sometimes referred to as 'flexibility' or 'adaptability'. What it means is that there will be no rest for the working class, no roots, no anchoring in transmitted skills or a particular locality: that kind of stability suggests inelasticity and resistance. This does not mean that the working class will be undisciplined. It will be discipline not, for the majority, of back-breaking labour, but a discipline of silence and renunciation, an almost monastic devotion to the service of wealth. The reconstitution of service in its present guise is a more austere and abstract dedication to wealth than Victorian service ever was. That the working class is being exhorted to welcome this as a deliverance from the horrors of manufacture is made worse by the fact that it was always capitalist manufacture, and never manufacture for need; the revulsion against real horrors is exploited to smother the extinction of things of real worth.

The contemporary forms of service are diminishing enough even to those who enter them with scepticism and reserve; but there are many who are paid to counterfeit a sort of enjoyment of their menial and often humiliating tasks, so that they do not disturb the sleepwalking fantasies of those who pay for them – the bought smile and the purchased cheerfulness, simulated sometimes painfully through worn faces and tired eyes; those women, for instance, whose sexuality has been driven to market like cattle, those whose image has been sold for money, which they are compelled to inhabit, as constricting as a prison cell. We often do not see them, because we take for granted that they are there, or because their hours of work do not coincide with our own. They catch the early bus, standing and straining to shake off the lethargy of inadequate sleep, all those of whom it is said, sometimes defiantly, sometimes defensively, 'Well, somebody has to do the shit-jobs.' We don't see their resistances either, the accommodations made by individuals with the terms of their service: the puritanical fastidiousness of the prostitute and her contempt for those who use her; the woman tending the lavatory in the department store, treated as though she didn't exist, and who says that at the end of each day she has 'to go and look in the mirror to see if I'm still there'; the bitter black woman who says that because white people think all blacks look the same, she will become three different people; and she does three jobs under different names, travelling across London at all hours when the streets are empty and the last tube has gone; the embattled employees in the public service who regard those they serve as their mortal enemies.

And those who serve the diffuse and invisible power of money become like it, as thin as the air that has swallowed their masters. In this way, resentment, anger at their condition can less easily be turned against a system that has sought to identify itself as coterminous with the conditions of human existence itself. People more easily turn against each other, or inwards, against themselves; and especially against those workers who remain in manufacture, when these express their eroded collective power against that which failed to enslave them. But those silent, effaced millions are learning to acknowledge their subordination, like members of a strange new caste. They are the ones who recognize the folly of resistance, and are eager to propitiate the vast, inhuman power, anxious to identify their own interests with it, in the hope that it will not crush them, will not evict them from that servitude which at least offers them a foothold in its riches, provides them with some rudimentary sense of function, and does not cast them out altogether in the whirling blackness of unemployment and despair.

What we are seeing has been as sweeping a change as that which occurred when the fields sent their population into the manufacture. We have lived through the demolition of the sensibility that was formed (and which, as E.P. Thompson has reminded us, formed itself[22]), and its recomposition in the interests of a servitude which appears more innocent, because it has not demanded the disordered physical displacement of an earlier period. Only it has nothing to do with emancipation. And this is the price that has been paid, that stealthy accompaniment of all the material improvements that have been won only on the terms of capital; those confusing, contradictory changes, that balance of gain and loss that made us feel richer, yet less free in that it became unimaginable that we should disengage ourselves from the rhythms and imperatives of a system that has penetrated the very depths of being, a system whose necessity is hopelessly, inextricably entangled with our needs.

---

[22] E.P. Thompson, *The Making of the English Working Class* (Penguin, Harmondsworth, 1968).

3

Landscaping Capitalism

The breaking and remaking of the whole character of the working class in response to a new international division of labour would never have been possible without that transformation of what came to be thought of as the 'classic' landscapes of capitalism. This is why, during the second half of the twentieth century, the familiar images of industrialization have been so carefully reworked. The factory chimneys with their parabola of smoke bending to the wind, the dust and heat of the foundries, the rows of houses subsiding on their ledge of a mountain of coal, the metal skeletons of the shipyards – all those things that seemed to have eaten into the soul of the working class, just as the acid and soot ate into the brick of the places where they lived – are in the way of being effaced. A sustained effort has been made, it seems, to wipe out the traces of the industrial revolution, to modify the decor of its ravaged cities. The scars of that epic ugliness have been healed. This has all been represented, no longer as inescapable attributes of capitalism but as a necessary, but mercifully vanished, interlude; a prologue to a more lasting plenty. But it is possible to see in this metamorphosis a more sinister aspect: a reconstruction of history, a cleansing, a gilding even, of the great catastrophe and its secular baleful effects on those pressed into its service, the working class.

In all the industrial districts, they have been burying the remains. It has the grandeur of the careful concealment of some epic crime. The Welsh valleys, where the air was always heavy with grit and the black dust swirled down the hillside, collecting in drifts, blackening the washing and accumulating in the lungs of the people, have been planted with conifers and covered with turf, turned into man-made forests and pastures. The rusting machinery has been dismantled, the pit-head replaced by a children's playground, with its bright red swings and roundabout, or the pastel-coloured slabs of a shopping piazza. In the manufacturing towns, the dying industrial function has been sublimated in decorative mural and mosaic, to brighten the wall of a shopping mall or to relieve the menacing gloom of an underpass; towers of glass rise, with soaring innocence, reflecting only a sky of scalloped clouds where formerly the iron-puddlers and chain- and nail-makers sweated, half-naked, in hot airless workshops. Docks have been preserved as marinas, and white-sailed yachts rest, serene as sea-birds on sheltered waters, where the green and barnacled wood of the shipyard has been reclaimed by the sea. The crafts and occupations which gave the manufacturing towns their reason for existence have been embalmed in local museums, all carefully reproduced to the last meticulous detail; sometimes even working to turn out samples of an archaic product – pottery, woollens, lace. In Northampton Museum there are even stuffed rats playing among the scraps of leather distributed on the floor of the Victorian cobbler's shop, behind the protective sheet of glass. The oldest workers have confided the secrets of their dying skills to the tape-recorders of labour historians, ostensibly for the sake of continuity with those who will come after, but really in the same valedictory way as those who spoke of decayed country practices and beliefs to the ethnographers and folklorists of the nineteenth century.

That brief moment of apparent coherence, when it seemed that most objects in daily household use could be securely identified with the precise locality of their manufacture, lasted no more than two or three generations. As a child just after the Second World War, I can remember thinking of the material things in the houses I knew in terms of the town or city where they were made: the cutlery from Sheffield, the lino on the floor from Lancashire, the linen from Belfast, the soap from Port Sunlight, the woollens from the West Riding, the lavatory pan from Burslem or Hanley, as indeed was the best china also, with its smudged gold stamp at the base of the cup; while the boots we wore could have been nothing but pieces of locally tanned leather. It created a false sense of security, because even then that whole fragile structure was on the verge of collapse and change.

The working-class areas of the industrial cities, those crowded places of mills and factories and industrial dwellings, where Lowryesque figures without features or feelings were simply shapes and smudges against smoke and brick, have been recast. Those grassy humps and smoothed-over ruins, planted with saplings, have the vague shape of tumuli, the remains of buried civilizations. All the old buildings are converted – chapels into bingo halls, warehouses into discos, factories have become depositories for things made elsewhere – imported wines or car spares, toys and video games from the Far East. And in those central city areas that have not yet been rebuilt there remain great breaches and absences: abandoned town halls with their *trompe-l'œil* pillars and gargoyles effaced by soot, factories invaded by weeds and wild flowers, and concrete car parks blanketing the vanished streets.

The evidence of that calamitous upheaval of the industrial age is being erased, not only from the sites of its occurrence but, even more significantly, from the memories of those who were its victims and of their descendants. The slums, courts, tenements and workplaces have been obliterated, the red-brick streets plucked up. And with this, the spectre of a threatening and intractable proletariat is being exorcised at last.

It is sometimes represented as progress, altruism, remorse; or the desire to redress vanished and irredeemable wrongs. But it has all been a removing of stains, a mending and restoring, a covering up and concealing; a reshaping of those places of hardship, despair and struggle. It has been a change of scenery; a shift made easier by a natural human desire to forget old injuries – even at the risk of preparing greater ones. The abruptness and manner of their erasure are disturbing. The dissolution of these places, and of the sensibility of those people which was formed by them and for them, looks like a deep discontinuity, and indeed is experienced as such, even though it has occurred precisely in the interests of maintaining everything in place.

Capital has tried to tell another story. Not content with dissimulating its own violent and bloody birth, it has sought to revise the story of those it created in such strife and pain, the working class. The refurbishing of the outer landscapes is the counterpart of that deeper variation in which capitalism has sought to present itself: from bringer of insufficiency, degradation and toil, it has turned itself into provider of plenty, harmony and opportunity. It has taken on the guise of something so wise and beneficent that it would be not only perverse and idle to seek alternatives, but destructive and unnatural too. Capitalism has striven to assimilate itself once more to the natural order, so that it informs the very air we breathe; and is seen, no longer as one of many possible ways of organizing human affairs, but as something cosmic and unalterable, in such a way that to struggle against its inexorable laws is not only futile but unthinkable.

It is not hard to see what is behind this swift alteration of what looked like fixed landscapes. The dazzling mutation has occurred at the same time as that prodigality with which its manufactures and services and promises have rolled across the Western world like the promiscuous spillage of a vast cornucopia. Capitalism has provided its own answer to the consequences of its own earlier darkest visitations. It has taken on the task of alleviating the poverty and absences which it created. In other words, it has become a closed system. And it is this illusion of wholeness that has required the service of so many hucksters, promoters and merchandisers, for it has been their function to complete the magic of transformation by exhibiting the meaningless circularity of its movement, not as treadmill but as carousel.

And yet those old landscapes are surely not so easily disassembled. The lineaments of an older poverty cannot be so readily effaced. They have become part of our culture, those factories with their racing machines, and the tormented lives that served them. And in any case, even if those things have been occluded by the scouring of the mind and the washing away of memory, they have been fixed in the pages of Engels or Dickens or Booth or Mayhew: the cliffs of stone, the greasy offal-strewn cobbles, the crowded tenements, the sickly children swarming in the alleys, the population of scavengers and rag-pickers, the cripples and beggars and pickpockets and dollymops. Surely a revision of that past is not so easy.

And indeed, the old landscapes are far from having been eliminated, however they may have been veiled, smothered, enfolded in the collapsible decor. Their survival, in one form or another, is essential to the dynamic of capitalism: for the landscapes of poverty, with their cruel disciplines, are what drive the people on in their search for escape, or at least refuge, from their destructive, dehumanizing power. But if those familiar scenes are no longer to be discerned in the material environment – and our senses tell us that they are not – this is only that they might be the more effectively preserved elsewhere.

We sometimes use the word 'Dickensian' to describe the survival of things felt to belong to the period of early Victorian England: Dickensian living conditons are sometimes discovered, examples of misery and squalor still to be detected beneath the surface. Within the last couple of years I have come across a number of examples: an old woman living in a house full of cats, which went on growing in number and were never allowed out, so that she was living in appalling filth, while the roof leaked and the fireplace was so choked with cinders that the coals had burned holes in the floorboards; a young man of nineteen, sexually abused by his father throughout his childhood, and turned out by his stepmother when he was fourteen. For four years he lived in the mouth of the workings of an abandoned mineshaft, begging and scavenging, spending his time between launderette and betting-shop to keep warm. When he was discovered, he had lost the ability to use a knife and fork, was covered in sores and unable to communicate with anyone. There was a family with a baby of six months, living in a wheel-less car in a lay-by on the edge of a Midland town, with a few scraps of cardboard blocking the draughts from the broken window, sleeping in the seats, cooking and defecating in the adjacent fields. There was the family who lived without power for three years in a run-down terraced house – their four-year-old had never seen electric light. A group of children who had been cheating old-age pensioners in Barnsley in October 1983 were referred to by the press as a 'Fagin gang'; while the Church of England Children's Society's concern with teenage runaways in 1984 meant that it was 'celebrating' its centenary by doing what Barnado had been doing in the mid-nineteenth century –

rescuing children whose home was the streets of the capital. But the way in which such things are presented to us – as curiosities, survivals from an earlier time – only reinforces the idea that we have securely left all that behind. Such examples only illuminate the road we have travelled since then, flatter us with an agreeable sense of our progress and enlightenment. It all serves to conceal what has happened to those disfigured and graceless scenes that were not so long ago far more general.

Before tracing what has happened to those classic images of poverty in the late twentieth century, it is worth recalling some of the nineteenth-century originals. For a century and a half investigators, observers, reformers and novelists had portrayed what looked like an unchanging, enduring picture. It seemed this must be an ineradicable product of capitalism, whatever other wonders it had achieved. Peter Gaskell, in *The Manufacturing Population of England* wrote in 1833 'Any man who has stood at twelve o'clock in the single narrow doorway which serves as a place of exit for the hands employed in the great cotton mills must acknowledge that an uglier set of men and women, of boys and girls, it would be impossible to congregate in a small compass.'[1] De Tocqueville in 1935 evoked the growing city of Manchester.

Who could describe the interiors of these quarters set apart, home of vice and poverty, which surround the huge palaces of industry and clasp them in their hideous folds? . . . Narrow twisting roads . . . are lined with one-storey houses whose ill-fitting planks and broken windows show them up, even from a distance, as the last refuge a man might find between poverty and death . . . The fetid, muddy waters, stained with a thousand colours by the factories they pass, wander slowly round this refuge of poverty. They are nowhere kept in place by the quays: houses are built haphazard on their banks. It is the Styx of this new Hades. Look up and all around this place and you will see the huge palaces of industry. You will hear the noise of furnaces, the whistle of steam. These vast structures keep air and light out of the human habitations which they dominate; they envelop them in perpetual fog; here is the slave, there the master; there is the wealth of some, the poverty of most.[2]

The descriptions are always those of the distant observer: they evoke only the outer appearance of people's lives, their blighted living places. They do not penetrate the domestic interiors, and even less the state of mind of the people.

---

[1] Peter Gaskell, *The Manufacturing Population of England* (1833).
[2] Alexis de Tocqueville, *Journeys to England and Ireland* 1835 (Faber, London, 1958).

Engels' picture of unrelieved desolation in his *Condition of the Working Class* in 1834 reserves his most lurid language for the portrait of Manchester:

At the bottom flows, or rather, stagnates, the Irk, a narrow coal-black foul-smelling stream, full of debris and refuse which it deposits on the shallower right bank. In dry weather, a long string of the most disgusting blackish-green slime pools are left standing on the bank, from the depths of which bubbles of miasmic gas constantly give forth a stench undendurable even on the bridge forty or fifty feet above the stream . . . Above the bridge are the tanneries, bonemills and gasworks, from which all drains and refuse find their way into the Irk, which receives further the contents of all the neighbouring sewers and privies . . . Here the background embraces the pauper burial-ground, the station of the Liverpool and Leeds railways, and, in the rear of this, the Workhouse, the 'Poor Law Bastille' of Manchester, which, like a citadel, looks threatening down from behind its high walls and parapets on the hill-top upon the working people's quarter below.[3]

Most of those who tried to evoke the conditions of the early industrial population fall into the stylized manner of Engels: the words are emotionally charged, but general, imprecise – 'ruin', 'filth', 'debris'. The recurring expressions are admissions of defeat by the appalled observer – 'indescribable', 'unbearable', 'unspeakable'. And indeed, in looking at the material equivalents of these places in the slums of Asia, Africa or South America, the same awkwardness is seen, a temptation to retreat into generalities of nausea and revulsion. It means that the landscapes are always slightly blurred, misted over by the shocked sensibility of the observer.

Mayhew in the mid-century gets closer to the people he is writing about. His evocation of the Saturday night markets in New Cut and the Brill have the vividness and the feel of markets in the shanties of the contemporary Third World city:

The scene in these parts has more the character of a fair than a market. There are hundreds of stalls, and every stall has its one or two lights; either it is illuminated by the intense white light of the new self-generating gas-lamp, or else it is brightened up by the red smoky flare of the old-fashioned grease-lamp . . . Here is a stall glittering with new tin saucepans; there another, bright with its blue and yellow crockery, sparkling with white glass. Now you come to a row of old shoes arranged along the pavement; now to a stand of gaudy tea-trays; then to a shop with red handkerchiefs and blue-checked shirts, fluttering backwards and forwards. At the door of a tea-shop with its hundred white globes of light, stands a

[3] Friedrich Engels, *Condition of the Working Class in England*, 1845 (Allen & Unwin, London, 1968).

man delivering bills, thanking the public for past favours, and 'defying competition'.

As Mayhew writes of the prosperous years of the 1850s and 1860s his words have a curiously modern ring: 'Of late years everything connected with the industrious classes has undergone as complete a transformation as any magic can effect upon the stage. Not only is the condition of the people changed, but they themselves are as effectually metamorphosed.' Here is the answer to those who see capital as something static and constant in its effects, rather than as the mobile and shifting force that is always about its work of change.

And Mayhew does penetrate the living places of the poorest; and he leaves memorable images of what he found there – even when in full denunciation of the idle and dissolute.

The first room we entered contained a Lascar, who had come over in some vessel, and his woman. There was a sickly smell in the chamber, that I discovered came from the opium he had been smoking. The Lascar was lying on a palliasse, placed upon the floor (there was no bedstead), apparently stupefied from the effects of the opium he had been taking. By his bedside sat his woman, who was half idiotically endeavouring to derive some stupefaction from the ashes he had left in his pipe. Her face was grimy and unwashed, and her hands so black and filthy that mustard and cress might have been sown successfully upon them. As she was huddled up with her back against the wall she appeared an animated bundle of rags.[4]

Even to the most sympathetic observers, the people are so remote from their own sense of what is human, they become part of the landscape: people and places seems to form part of a continuous nightmare. Indeed, in order to authenticate their own impressions, they often had recourse to newspapers, or even government reports and official documents; as though their personal exploration alone was unlikely to be believed.

Those glowering scenes, with their sulphurous atmosphere, their mangled and barely human figures, are scarcely at all amplified even by the novelists of the mid-century. Mrs Gaskell's description of the industrial town of Milton in *North and South* is sketchy in the extreme, not much more than a smudge of smoke on the winter sky. In *Scenes from Clerical Life* George Eliot's Nuneaton is simply 'a dingy town, surrounded by flat fields, lopped elms and sprawling manufacturing villages'. Disraeli's Wodgate in *Sybil* is stylized and without detail: 'Here, during the days of business, the sound of the hammer and the file never ceased, amid gutters of abomination, and piles of foulness, and stagnant pools of

[4] Henry Mayhew, *London Labour and the London Poor, 1851–62* (Constable, London, 1968).

filth; reservoirs of leprosy and plague, whose exhalations were sufficient to taint the atmosphere of the whole kingdom, and to fill the country with fever and pestilence.' Dickens' version of Preston in *Hard Times* was the result of one brief visit:

It was a town of red brick, or of brick that would have been red if the smoke and ashes had allowed it: but as matters stood, it was a town of unnatural red and black like the painted face of a savage. It was a town of machinery and tall chimneys, out of which interminable serpents of smoke trailed themselves for ever and ever, and never got uncoiled. It had a black canal in it, and a river that ran purple with evil-smelling dye, and vast piles of buildings full of windows where there was a rattling and a trembling all day long, and where the piston of the steam-engine worked monotonously up and down like the head of an elephant in a state of melancholy madness.

Apart from some rather stretched imagery, little is added to the accounts of de Tocqueville or Engels.

But however repetitive and wanting in detail these pictures are, they were no brief aberration, fixed in the writings of a single generation. Those who reported later in the nineteenth century were struck by similar aspects of the industrial setting. This generation approached the people more closely; and they began to refer to journeys 'into a region which lies at our own doors – into a dark continent that is within easy walking distance of the General Post Office'.[5] This was the time of Booth's Darkest England, which

like Darkest Africa, reeks with malaria. The foul and fetid breath of the slums is almost as poisonous as that of the African swamp. Fever is almost as chronic there as one the Equator. Every year thousands of children are killed off by what are called defects of our sanitary system. They are in reality starved and poisoned, and all that can be said is that, in many cases, it is better for them that they were taken away from the trouble to come.[6]

The metaphor of an unexplored continent beneath our noses was not new. Mayhew had already dwelt on the irony of his excursion into unknown territories, and he contrasted his own domestic undertaking with that of the colonizers and adventurers whose voyages took them to the remotest places on Earth. It was – and remains – a powerful idea; one that resonates in our time. For, with every corner of the globe known, and every frontier conquered, we too have to follow a new and scantily investigated region, in our pursuit of those preserved landscapes of poverty.

Jack London's *People of the Abyss* contains little that Engels would not

[5] George Sims, *How the Poor Live* (1883).
[6] William Booth, *In Darkest England, and the Way Out* (1890).

have recognized half a century before. Once again, it is the brooding ugliness of the places that remains, defying all efforts at cancellation.

No more dreary spectacle can be found on this earth that the whole of the 'awful East'. The colour of life is grey and drab. Everything is helpless, hopeless, unrelieved and dirty . . . Strange vagrant odours come drifting along the greasy wind, and the rain when it falls is more like grease than water from heaven . . . Here lives a population as dull and unimaginative as its long grey miles of dingy brick . . . Here in the East End, the obscenities and brute vulgarities are rampant. There is no privacy. The bad corrupts the good, and all fester together. Innocent childhood is sweet and beautiful; but in East London, innocence is a fleeting thing, and you must catch them before they crawl out of the cradle, or you will find the very babes as unholily wise as you.[7]

The working people do take on distinguishing characteristics – the docker, the carter, the carpenter; but they are still part of a frieze of bowed an broken humanity. And as the mysterious interiors of the poor are opened up, they seem to be a continuation of the world outside, an extension of the dirty and impoverished city streets.

Even within living memory Orwell, writing of Wigan and Sheffield in the 1930s, could still describe the living places of working people in terms that do not vary markedly from the horrors evoked by those writing a century before. 'As you walk through the industrial towns you lose yourself in labyrinths of little brick houses blackened by smoke, festering in planless chaos around miry alleys and little cindered yards where there are stinking dustbins and lines of grimy washing and half-ruinous WCs.' He recalls 'a dreadful room in Wigan where all the furniture seemed to be made of packing cases and barrel staves and was coming to pieces at that; and an old woman with a blackened neck and her hair coming down denouncing her landlord in a Lancashire-Irish accent; and her mother, aged well over ninety, sitting in the background on the barrel that served her as commode and regarding us blankly with a yellow cretinous face.'[8]

It is sometimes hard to believe that those scenes have really vanished. Should we perhaps not be wary of deception, a trick of the eye, some kind of masquerade? In the light of such long tenacious experience, is the recent alteration to do simply with appearances? Are the young people who sit in the marble shopping plaza, with their bloom and health, really the descendants of yesterday's stunted and prematurely aged poor? If so, then the change has taken place with such speed that we should look in the realm, not so much of economic miracles, as in that of myth and magic, if we are adequately to describe such a reversal.

[7] Jack London, *People of the Abyss* (Journeyman Press, London, 1977).
[8] George Orwell, *The Road to Wigan Pier* (Gollancz, London, 1937).

The persistence of reminders of past misery had this advantage: they kept alive a manifest need for continuing growth and increase, the wealth that would ultimately abolish it. Indeed, from the beginning of the industrial period it was insisted that the great merit of the new system was that its power to produce would one day overcome the insecurity of poverty. Even so, long before Marx, there were those who reiterated the ancient argument that 'true wealth must be distinguished from riches', among them the Earl of Lauderdale in 1806; with the suggestion that capitalist accumulation meant the unambiguous preoccupation with the latter. John Poulett Scrope, brother of the Whig Minister, wrote in 1833:

It is utterly false that every increase of wealth is a proportionate increase of the aggregate means of enjoyment. Nay, some kinds of wealth may be vastly augmented with little or no increase of the means of enjoyment, and a very small increase of some sorts of wealth is often more beneficial to mankind than a large increase of others. Suppose, for illustration, a race of absolute sovereigns to have a taste for jewels, and to employ several thousands of their subjects or slaves, generation after generation, in toiling to procure them. These treasures will be wealth of enormous *value*, but add barely anything to the aggregate means of enjoyment. Suppose another race of sovereigns to have employed equal numbers of workmen during the same time in making roads, docks and canals throughout their dominions, or on erecting hospitals and public buildings for education or amusement. These acquisitions to the wealth of the country, having cost the same labour, may be of equal *exchangeable value* as the diamonds of the other sovereigns; but are they to be reckoned only equally *useful*, equal accessions to the aggregate means of human gratification?[9]

Of political economy, Thomas Love Peacock had said in 1831: 'The upshot of your so-called science is this: that you increase the wealth of a nation by increasing in it the quantity of things which are produced by labour: no matter what they are, no matter how produced, no matter how distributed.'[10] In the year of depression 1842, when Thomas Carlyle was writing *Past and Present*, and there were, in the official report, '221,687 Indoor and 1,207,089 Outdoor Paupers', he insisted that

England is full of wealth, of multifarious produce, supply for human want of every kind; yet England is dying of inanition. With unabated bounty the land of England blooms and grows: waving with yellow harvests; thick-studded with workshops, industrial implements, with fifteen millions of workers, understood to be the strongest, the cunningest and the willingest our Earth ever had. Of these successful, skilful workers some two millions, it is now counted, sit in Workhouses, Poor-law prisons; or have 'out-relief' flung over the walls to them –

⁹ John Poulett Scrope, *Principles of Political Economy* (1833).
¹⁰ T.L. Peacock, *Crotchett Castle* (Everyman edn, London 1962).

the workhouse Bastilles being filled to bursting . . . workhouses, pleasantly so-named because work cannot be done in them. . . . This successful industry of England, with its plethoric wealth, has as yet made nobody rich; it is an enchanted wealth, belongs yet to nobody. We might ask Which of us has it enriched? We can spend thousands where once we spent hundreds; but we can purchase nothing good with them.[11]

The poor, sequestered and isolated in their rude industrial suburbs, were well sheltered from any such unsettling arguments. The slow and intermittent gains won through struggle still left many in a state of chronic insufficiency; and they remained, for the most part, unaware that their suffering had, as time went by, less and less an existential cause (sheer lack of resources) and an increasingly ideological one (the dynamic relationship between accumulation on the one hand, and the misery that fuels it on the other), a process whereby, in Goldsmith's phrase, 'wealth accumulates and men decay.'

By the mid-twentieth century, such illusions of scarcity as a cause of poverty could no longer be maintained in the rich societies. It could no longer be kept from the poor that the need for their poverty was the need of capitalism to goad its people into a continued competitive striving. And this realization, with the threat it implied of an increasingly self-conscious and more organized working class, has been the impulse for the startling and swift work of transformation. The world was suddenly full of its own hymns and rhapsodies to its limitless capacity to provide. The bulldozers and cranes were busy, gouging the city centres, the great hammers swung at factory and tenement walls until they buckled and fell, the old sites of squalor and pain were pulverized. And all this coincided with the reworking of the psychic terrain. If the ugliness without was brusquely swept away, it was only that it might be the better preserved within.

These new settings of a transformed material world do, however, have an eerie familiarity. It is not difficult to trace their origin and antecedents. For they are nothing less than the materialization of older figments and fantasies. It is an old story that the consolations which capitalism suggested to us for the material desolation of the early industrial era should also have been formulated in terms that were physical and palpable. If the ideological fight always sought to conquer the abstrct terrain of the heart and imagination of the people, to be effective it always required images, landscapes in fact. The visions of release which were offered to that captive population were of a popular version of paradise: promises of streets of jasper and gold, the heavenly city; the everlasting feast was the pledge to the hungry, the mansions of the blessed to the

---

[11] Thomas Carlyle, *Past and Present* (Everyman edn, London 1960)

homeless, the raiment of white to those in rags. Promises of an afterlife sustained people through miseries scarcely to be borne. 'A tent or a cottage, why should I care? They're building a palace for me over there.'[12]

And indeed, the appearance of those enclosures of selling that have been superimposed on the old industrial areas, those shrines and cloisters dedicated to commodities have been a making material – with their ghostly atmosphere, their ice-blue lighting and moving stairways, their offerings of flawlessness, their invitations to fulfilment – of those earlier landscapes which were of the imagination, born of privation and despair. Capitalism has always offered its own compensations for the injuries it inflicted, the distant progenitors of the images of perfection and models of emulation that are projected through the contemporary capitalist publicity machine are idealized images of Christ's perfection. (It has, of course, nothing to do with the religious impulse itself, but everything to do with the way in which pre-existing cultural forms could be applied to the alien purpose of disciplining a turbulent and refractory labour force.) E.P. Thompson refers in particular to Methodism as 'the desolate inner landscape of Utilitarianism in an era of transition to the work-discipline of industrial capitalism'. Of the emotional transports it provided, Thompson writes, 'We may see here in its lurid figurative expression the psychic ordeal in which the character-structure of the rebellious pre-industrial labourer or artisan was violently recast into that of the submissive industrial worker.' He sees 'the box-like blackening chapels . . . in the industrial districts like great traps for the human psyche'.[13]

The Hammonds speak in more measured terms than Thompson, and with somewhat more understanding, of the emotional exaltation and release afforded to the materially starved industrial worker. The periodic revivals

fed the imagination of the new population on the exciting history of a fierce and warlike race, living under conditions very unlike those of Manchester or Leeds, leaving a literature rich in metaphor and image, which awakened amid the bare and colourless life of the new civilisation, dreams and reveries and visions full of awe and splendour . . . For the miner or weaver, the Chapel with its summons to the emotions, its music and singing, took the place that theatres, picture galleries, operas, occupied in the lives of others.[14]

The myths of rescue from bondage, the stories of deliverance, of wilderness, journeyings and exile gave a borrowed lustre to brief and humble lives; gave them the conviction that it was not all without meaning

[12] Moody & Sankey, *Hymnal*.

[13] E. P. Thompson, *The Making of the English Working Class* (Penguin, Harmondsworth, 1968).

[14] J.L. and Barbara Hammond, *The Town Labourer* (Longman, Green, London, 1925).

and purpose; and, what is more significant, furnished an imagery that was to enrich an important strand of resistance in working-class culture.

But the compensatory quality of those celestial landscapes was their most persistent feature. Even those who were sceptical of religious observances and had no particular faith believed in the literalness of heaven. Many who distrusted ministers of religion and the social disciplines with which they associated them still believed that when they died, they would be greeted by those they had loved in life. I can remember the mournful and reflective conversations whenever my own family gathered about 'where they would put us all' – as though paradise were an unearthly prolongation of the housing problem, how they would spend their time, how they would occupy themselves throughout eternity, which they saw as an indefinite extension of the closest thing they knew, a sort of Bank Holiday Monday without end.

But if the blackened chapels trapped the souls of the people in the industrial era, the present-day equivalents are far more seductive, and indeed far more effective; even though their object is of a piece with earlier, less palpable visions and exaltations. And just as the abuse of religion has nothing to do with deep human impulses, so the abuse of materialism has nothing to do with profound needs for sufficiency and security.

The majority of the poor nevertheless remained unmoved by promises of a compensatory afterlife. For most, gin, laudanum, the sleep of exhaustion were their only release; and their dreams were more likely to be of a good feed and a warm fire; or possibly of a return to a countryside as it had never been. The early accounts of industrialism, before, as Hobsbawm expresses it, the workers 'learnt the rules of the game',[15] fail to indicate that the poor could find within themselves the resources to resist the conditions of those brutal landscapes: the squalor without easily breached the defences of bewildered and uninstructed factory workers, many of them still half-rural. The poorest were in many ways simply a mirror to the cruelties without. Robert Owen recognized this in his *New View of Society*: 'Theft and the receipt of stolen goods was their trade, idleness and drunkenness their habit, falsehood and deception their garb, dissensions, civil and religious, their daily practice.'[16] Later, Mayhew recognized the ways in which the values of political economy were faithfully reflected in its victims; only, perhaps not surprisingly, he blames them for it, as though it originated with those who suffered most from its workings. Thus, of the costers, 'Among the costers the term education is merely understood as having a complete knowledge of "buying in the cheapest

[15] Eric Hobsbawm, *Labouring Man* (Weidenfeld & Nicolson, London, 1964).
[16] Robert Owen, *A New View of Society*, (1813) (Everyman edn, London 1972).

market and selling in the dearest" . . . Lads possessed of a mental acuteness almost wonderful, will educate themselves in vice if we neglect to train them to virtue . . . ' Mayhew speaks of the 'undeveloped minds of the poor'.[17] In spite of the resistances of labour, the growth of Chartism, there remains little sense of any distinction between the inner and outer worlds of the poorest. Marx himself, citing the Children's Employment Commission of 1866, said 'It is unhappily, to a painful degree, apparent throughout the whole of the evidence, that against no persons do the children require protection as against their parents.'[18]

The state of mind of the poor is glimpsed throughout the century: lives dominated by ignorance and isolation. Cole and Postgate quote the Glasgow superintendent of police who said of a tenement district in the city in the 1840s, 'I should be able to find a thousand children who have no name whatever, or only nicknames like dogs.'[19] Engels quoted from the report of the Commission of Enquiry into the Employment of Children and Young Persons in Mines and Collieries in 1842: 'To the question who Christ was, a youth of 16 said "He was a king of London long ago"; a girl of eleven years who had attended both day and Sunday school "had never heard of another world, of heaven, of another life". Several boys had never heard of London, or Willenhall, though the latter was but an hour's walk from their homes.'[20]

The resistances of a growing and increasingly conscious working class had to be created not only against this abjection and ignorance but also against the pervasive imagery of capitalist ideology. If these defences were to catch the understanding of people, they too had to be formulated in vivid material terms. The great labour alternative was also conceived in terms of landscapes; and these were deeply coloured by those other-worldly ones which had fed chapel imagery. The labour movement fought on the same terrain, and fixed its secularized version of those imagined celestial landscapes. Their promise too was of a pilgrimage, long wanderings in the desert, a long search – but this time for the earthly paradise, the land of peace and plenty. The images themselves were forged in antagonism to the violence and degradation of the real material world; and they took on the shape – for what other was there? – of the indefinitely deferred setting for the capitalist reward, which it became their ambition to make material. Their new Jerusalem was an emancipation that should have as its goal life, and not death. At times this fused with nostalgia for a pre-industrial world, as in the Chartist land scheme. But as the socialist vision developed and was elaborated, it became an expropriation of those

[17] Mayhew, *London Labour*.
[18] Karl Marx, *Capital* (vol. I, Lawrence & Wishart, London, 1977).
[19] G. Cole and R. Postgate, *The Common People* (Methuen, London, 1971).
[20] Engels, *The Working Classes*.

heavenly kingdoms, a struggle for the territory that had been colonized by capitalism and conjured out of sight in a life to come.

Industrialization itself ensured that earlier Utopian ideas had changed. An idealized past of man-in-nature versus man-in-society gave way to a contrast between future emancipation and the squalor and disorder of the present. Industrialism itself, with its possibility of untold riches, became the source of hope for a different kind of transformation from that wrought by capitalism. Robert Owen's *New View of Society* was conceived as landscape at New Lanark:

It is intended that in the most pleasant situation near the present village, neat and convenient dwellings should be erected, with gardens attached; that they should be surrounded and sheltered by plantations, through which public walks should be formed; and the whole arranged to give the occupiers the most substantial comforts.[21]

The emancipatory power of landscape – or environment as it later came to be called – has always been a powerful, somewhat mystical impulse in socialist thought. In 1834 the Owenite journal, the *New Moral World*, declared: 'The hour of deliverance from sin and misery is at hand. Behold the coming of that new life, when the world shall be so changed that every man shall sit under his own vine and his own fig-tree, and there shall be none to make him afraid.' Owen's New Harmony in Indiana was an actually existing landscape: 'the high lands of Harmony, from two to four miles from the river and its island, of which the inhabitants will have a beautiful and extensive view . . . ' His Harmony Hall in Hampshire was criticized as being too ornate; 'a monument of ill-timed magnificence' it was called. With its promenades and landscapes, and the plan to light up the towers 'by powerful apparatus, the new kiniophostic light, which would brilliantly illuminate the whole square' it betrays its inspiration in the splendour and unreality of the mansions of the blessed.[22]

O'Connor's land plan, and the five Chartist settlements which were founded in the 1840s, were conceived in terms of a return, a homecoming to the land; an escape from industrial society that proved more material, if not much more practicable, than the fantasies of celestial deliverance. The land at Charterville was going to be converted 'from a wilderness into a paradise'. At the opening of Snig's End in Gloucestershire in June 1842, O'Connor wrote in the *Northern Star* of

The pleasurable aspect of 80 families, heretofore slaves, and living in underground cellars, taking possession of their own castles and their own labour fields. Delight

---

[21] Owen, *A New View of Society.*
[22] *New Model World*, June 1940.

is no term to describe their feelings – it was one of pride, of independence and thanksgiving. All – strangers and all – confessed that the eye had never beheld such a sight, nor has it . . . The day was wet, for it poured showers of gold, and I was pleased to be wet to the skin, because it went to the roots of the seed, which will yield my children their harvest.[23]

The idea of reclaiming land from alien occupation and reordering the landscape underlies the formulation of many nineteenth-century alternatives. But the very oppression and poverty of the existing industrial landscapes made the possibility of such visions remote and painful. Thus the socialist impulse was always rivalled by messianic cults which promised irrational and immediate transformations in place of the more arduous toil required for real change. The borderline between the inturned fantasies of despairing people – faith in a consummation that could only occur with death, and the often thankless labour of plucking hopes of change out of an intractable existing misery – was always a thin and shifting one. Certainly the earthly paradises that were underpinned by religious faith, the urgency of the Second Coming or the last days, were always more durable than those that rested on more secular faith. D.H. Lawrence catches something of the energy that remained so hard to win over to more secular beliefs. In *Apocalypse* he evokes 'Strange marvellous black nights of the North Midlands, with the gas light hissing in the chapel, and the roaring of the strong-voiced colliers. Popular religion: a religion of self-glorification and power, for ever! and of darkness . . . the self-glorification of the humble.'

Well into the twentieth century Edward Carpenter, expressing his idea of the free commune, wrote in terms of a transformed material world:

I see a great land poised as in a dream – waiting for the word by which it may live again . . . I see a great land waiting for its own people to come and take possession of it.

Between a great people and the earth springs a passionate attachment, lifelong – and the earth loves indeed her children, broad-breasted, broad-bowed, and talks with them night and day, storm and sunshine, summer and winter alike . . . Owners and occupiers then fall into their places; the trees wave proud and free upon the headlands; the little brooks run with a wonderful new music under the brambles and the grass . . .

Freedom emerges, the love of the land – the broad waters, the air, the undulating fields, the flow of cities and the people therein, their faces and the looks of them no less than the rush of the tides and the slow hardy growth of the oak and the tender herbage of spring and stiff clay and storms and transparent air.[24]

---

[23] Dennis Hardy, *Alternative Communities in Nineteenth Century England* (Longman, London, 1974).

[24] Edward Carpenter, *Towards Democracy* (Allen & Unwin, London, 1917).

As the nineteenth century advanced, agrarianism and other-worldliness were displaced by more urban-based alternatives: the Brotherhood Workshop in Leeds was called 'an oasis in the desert of commercialism'. The claim of Marx that the new society would emerge out of the old, on the same site, as it were, meant that there was less need for those socialists who came under his influence to take refuge in fantasy. It no longer seemed that the alternative would occur somewhere else, in a vague future, another place, in Thomas Spence's 'country in Fairyland situated between Utopia and Oceania'.[25] But there still remained the problem of describing just what it would look like. The expression of the changed socialist landscape always retained an ethereal, dreamlike quality, a visionary shimmer influenced by that Utopian tradition despised by Marx, but calculated to appeal to people whose language had been deeply penetrated by millennarian imagery and biblical language. Even William Morris's portrait of the new socialist country in *News from Nowhere* – perhaps the most fully elaborated of all – is nevertheless placed within a dream, in which it has more in common with *Pilgrim's Progress* than with Marx.

I was going to say 'But is this the Thames?' but held my peace in wonder, and turned my bewildered eyes eastward to look at the bridge again, and thence to the shores of the London river; and surely there was enough to astonish me. For though there was a bridge across the stream and houses on its banks, how all was changed from last night! The soap-works with their smoke-vomiting chimneys were gone; the engineer's works gone; the lead-works gone; and no sound of riveting and hammering came down the west wind from Thorneycroft's. Then the bridge! I had perhaps dreamed of such a bridge, but never seen such a one out of an illuminated manuscript; for not even the Ponte Vecchio at Florence came anywhere near it.

Morris saw a London become pastoral and leafy, in which the dreamer awakes to a Hammersmith Broadway consisting of 'a range of buildings and courts, low but very handsomely built and ornamented', while Kensington has become largely forest, and Piccadilly an arcade 'of what I should have called shops, if it had not been that, as far as I could see, the people were ignorant of the arts of buying and selling'. In this world, necessary labour has been rendered rich and satisfying, while the manufacture of superfluities for profit has been abandoned; the creative abilities of the people have been set free, and the power of money has decayed; so that the dustman 'wears more gold than a medieval baron, and writes novels in his spare time', and the road-menders 'look much more like a boating party would have looked in the days I remembered'. He

[25] T. Spence, *Description of Spensonia* (London, 1795).

talks of England as 'a garden where nothing is wasted and nothing is spoilt', and refers to 'a place called Manchester which has now disappeared'.[26]

What we have lived through has been the repossession by capital of those alternative landscapes which socialism had made its own. Capitalism has pillaged those places that threatened it with ruin; and has assumed a travesty of their outer aspect the more effectively to lay waste their essence. It has been the material construct of that counterfeit that has lain at the heart of the great scene-change of the mid-twentieth century. To this end, capital has recalled and given life to its earlier non-material promises, themselves originally abstracted from an older religious tradition. Hence this metamorphosis, the appearance of capitalism as force, so benign and new in a world it had torn and mutilated, that it can scarcely be recognized for what it is. It has been reborn in the rich Western societies, revitalized, a great pagan deity whose shrines now stand at the heart of all the working-class places, lately so poor and disfigured by its earlier incarnation.

But of course such victories are never final. It is no accident that in response to all this the most suggestive and creative challenge has come from those in the ecology and environmentalist movements. And it is the women's movement which has dared to speak of healing the ravaged and trampled internal realm of relationships and feeling. The German Greens have urged the need for disengagement from these destructive fantasies of capitalism. Rudolf Bahro expresses it thus:

We must see ourselves somewhat after the fashion of the exodus from Egypt inspired by Moses, or the first Pentecost after Christ's ascension . . . There is an overall crisis of our civilisation, which is backfiring on human nature. Scarcely has the earlier kind of material want been more or less banished from the metropolises, before people are plagued by cancer and crime, heart attacks and mental illness. The destruction of nature by industrial accumulation, the danger of nuclear war, the impoverishment of marginalised masses in the Third World, mental impoverishment in the metropolises – these are the horsemen of the apocalypse at the end of the Second Christian Millennium.[27]

We are far from done with the imagining of alternatives. This is indeed the most urgent task, the reclamation of the newly recolonized territory. We do not yet have the language of liberation from that capitalist increase which is nevertheless not plenty, its riches that only deepen our sense of privation, that universal creation of wealth that goes hand in hand with the manufacture of poverty. The search for sufficiency that was so effortlessly

[26] William Morris, *News from Nowhere* (Lawrence & Wishart, London, 1977).
[27] Rudolf Bahro, *Socialism and Survival* (Heretic Books, London, 1982).

bypassed remains a dream unfulfilled for the rich of the earth as it is for the poor; and it is not to be found in the growth of capitalist economies any more than it is in the barren productivism of Eastern Europe, that frozen shadow of capitalism that has been locked into its sterile circular dance.

The fantasy landscapes of capital have eclipsed and overlaid those earlier socialist possibilities; and they have eroded the defences erected against older forms of exploitation. Those defences – always imperfect, only rudimentary – were nevertheless constructed in struggle and pain, and sustained by visions. Despite the burden of labour, the daily witness of spoliation and loss, the idea of a better life took shape; realizable projects were conceived. These were possible only because of the human warmth kindled against the hardness of brick and stone, the shelter against total dispossession that was shaped out of living flesh, the protection that people offered each other. The breaking of these solidarities has been achieved by capitalism in our time; and the undoing of the work of resistance has its counterpart in the material demolition, the exultant work of destruction on those classic landscapes of capital, as though their ghastly and malign influence could be undone merely by ploughing them back into the earth.

Those sites of capitalism's desolation have not gone away; they have merely retreated. They have been reassembled in the cities of Asia, South America and Africa, where they continue to drive human beings to the same desperate lengths to survive that shocked explorers of the Victorian cities in Britain.

They have, too, a second place of sojourn: and that is the country of the poor in the rich countries – a topography as uncharted as the impenetrable labyrinth of London must once have seemed, a country so securely internal that it is beyond the reach of even the most sophisticated measures of social science. The dissolution of those outer forms of poverty in the rich world has driven them underground, where they take on another shape that will defy not only investigation, but even recognition. Just as Mayhew and Booth contrasted the enthusiasm for exploring distant territories with unknown London, so, while we thrust deeper and deeper into outer space and reach for the planets, so the inner space remains the site of strange sufferings and plagues of which we understand little. There, so many of the elements of classical *laissez-faire* remain; not only as metaphor, as in the Paris of Baudelaire's *Les Fleurs du Mal* or Emily Dickinson's rag-and-bone shop of the heart, but in ways that are directly continuous with and akin to a poverty and ruin that have long been familiar.

4

Recurrences

An estate in an industrial town in north-east England; blocks of flats, four and six storeys, red-brick, grouped around echoing concrete courtyards. They were built in the 1950s but are already ruinous, stained by greasy overflow pipes, disfigured by graffiti, strewn with waste and rubbish – rusty metal, broken glass and waste paper. The estate itself was imposed on a clearance among the dereliction of the once busy nineteenth-century port – the crumbling warehouses and chapels, factories, docks and pubs. These still stand, so the area is now pervaded by the decay not only of the nineteenth-century industrial origins of the city but also of the corroded better world that was to have replaced it all.

This is one of the rare images that make explicit the fate of so many of the reforms, the attempts to relieve older evils. For the most part these have been veiled, but not eliminated; they simply recur in another guise.

Those epic migrations of our great-grandparents through the last century, for instance, from the villages into the overcrowded courts behind the main city thoroughfares, into the dark places hidden by the dazzle of bright gaslight and naphtha flares, have their parallel in the great migrations of the twentieth century. First of all, in the 2½ million people who emigrated from Britain between the turn of the century and the First World War, the willing migration into death of the million men killed in that war; the continuing drain of people from the depressed areas in the inter-war years. Then there has been the migration of people from Asia and the Caribbean and Africa into Western Europe since the Second World War – a process nowhere more powerfully evoked than in John Berger's *A Seventh Man:*

Every day he hears about the metropolis. The name of the city changes. It is all cities, overlaying one another and becoming a city that exists nowhere but which continually transmits promises. These promises are not transmitted by any single means. They are implicit in the accounts of those who have already been to a city. They are transmitted by machinery, by cars, tractors, tin-openers, electric drills, saws. By ready-made clothes. By the planes which fly across the sky. By the nearest main road. In the news. In the music. . .[1]

But there has been an even greater movement of peoples in our time; a long and largely uncommented retreat inwards. These internal wanderings have been in search of escape – away from the insistent pressures to change and adapt. Just as the industrial revolution set in train great shifts of population, broke patterns of living, prised apart human associations, and sent people off into unknown places, so we have been impelled by these same forces; only this time the journeying has been a withdrawal, a descent into self. And when we get there, we find our assignation is with the very pressures we were fleeing – those whose business is with exploiting our unfamiliarity with the terrain, our isolation and confusion; just as factory and mill waited to claim those who had taken up their roots and gone in search of something better. Our migration has been the reverse of those migrations into labour; we find ourselves trapped in a different sort of toil – a lonely work of the imagination, an obsessive concern with a self that is decreasingly defined by social function or purpose.

Just as the migrations from the countryside were given further impetus by enclosure, that taking over of common land and wastes by which country people had supplemented their agricultural wage, so the idea of 'enclosure' has some curious echoes in present-day experience. The appropriation of common resources for improvements in farming has its obvious parallel in the sequestration of the best land in poor countries for 'agribusiness' and cash crops, with the result that even during periods of hunger food may be exported by the absent owners of lands on which people starve. (In the Sahel drought in the early 1970s, 'ships in the Dakar Port bringing in "relief" food departed with stores of peanuts, cotton vegetables and meat for consumers in Europe and North America.'[2])

In rich countries, too, areas of public space have been occupied, common resources impounded – by no means all of them material. There has been a distraint on the shared and communal, a disgracing of the human need for brother- and sisterhood. Expertise and professionalism grow, while faith in ourselves and each other atrophies. In my years as a social worker, the lingering cry was 'I can't cope'. Not knowing – not knowing what to do, where to turn, who to talk to, how to respond – implies a loss of social skills, a decay of public knowledge.

When people in the mid-twentieth century have said that they are afraid to leave their doors open, that they don't even know their neighbours, that

---

[1] John Berger, *A Seventh Man* (Penguin, Harmondsworth, 1975).
[2] Frances Lappé and Joseph Collins, *Food First* (Sphere, London, 1982).

they don't want to get involved; when they refer to the monoliths and tower blocks where they live as Sing-Sing and Alcatraz; when they refer to the agencies of the welfare state as though they existed to coerce and punish, they are speaking of a dwindling control over their own lives, a growing sense of personal impotence – that unspoken counterpart of all our ostentatious concern for the individual. Their voice has its echo in that of John Clare, bemoaning the effects of improvements in his time: 'Ye meadow blooms, ye pasture-flowers farewell!/Ye banished trees, ye made me deeply sigh – Inclosure came, and all your glories fell.' As W.G. Hoskins says, 'So far from disintegrating, the open-field village often grew larger after enclosure, larger, but often more squalid, for there was generally more poverty than there had been before'.[3] The equivalent trespass which we have seen has not yet had its poet, but the evidence is all around us.

Transportation – that enforced change of landscape, which removed to Van Diemen's Land or Australia those rick-burners or felons who survived the journey – has its more widespread analogue today not in the criminal code but in all those services and industries who manufacture fantasy: those transportations of the spirit, calculated to separate and divide people, to disincline them from dangerous combination by keeping them in impotent occupancy of fabricated dreams. See the shrines in the bedrooms of young people, where marketed images cover the walls. For them, the talents of exceptional individuals diminish their own real powers and abilities. The power of these things is enhanced by their unexpressed reference to older cultural forms – the images of Christ and the Virgin and the saints, with all their ambiguous resonances of tenderness, cruelty and emulousness.

If the landlords have vanished now from the slum streets of jerry-built houses, it is only in order that they might reappear in more effective contemporary shape. We wait now in different habitations of despair for other landlords – landlords of knowledge. We depend absolutely on counsellors and experts without whose paid-for information and expertise we are unable to lead our own lives; not simply the social workers, the agony-aunts and the radio phone-in, which invites us to pour out our despair into public anonymity, but all those who tell us how we should spend our money in order to become more desirable, to attach to ourselves those bound to us by blood or duty – children, husbands, wives, lovers; those who will enable us to become less flawed through the miracles and mysteries of the market. There are other landlords too, those who have appropriated the abilities and powers that have been struck from the hands and hearts of women and men. The owners of those resources, whose function it is to

[3] W.G. Hoskins, *The Making of the English Landscape* (Penguin, Harmondsworth, 1970).

teach life-skills, communication, social skills, suggest an ownership
of wisdom, a hoarding of understanding; and the growth of their services
depends absolutely on the failure of transmission of skills and knowledge
elsewhere – through families, friends, community, workplaces. And
we don't hide in the cellar from these landlords and their agents, as
we hid from the rent collector visiting the slums, sending the children
to answer the door with the lie that there was no one at home. We
cannot offer our rent, our tribute, eagerly enough. For without these
people, the professionals, the rentiers of the heart and feelings, we feel
ourselves depleted and inadequate.

By 1977, it had been calculated that the process of production,
distribution and consumption of *knowledge* had already reached twenty-
nine per cent of the yearly national product in the United States. Those
who have enclosed this knowledge will sell it to us, in dribs and drabs, in
such small parcels as they think fit. The word 'landlord' rouses deep
memories in working-class life. If the word 'lord' itself meant 'master of
the bread' (Anglo-Saxon *hlaford*); and landlord came to mean the owner of
the space we occupied and then the house we lived in, it is only to be
expected that the next great invasion would be the seizure of a less material
area. In this way, knowledge and wisdom are transmuted into information
and facts, because in that form they are made marketable commodities, to
be released or withheld according to our ability to pay. This is how the
markets do their work of warping: earlier forms of wisdom and experience
are bent until they take on the shapes that can be bought and sold; and in
the process, they may become tangential or even inimical to the real needs
which they claim to answer.

Uncertainty about how to respond to each other, to our children, to old
age, loss or death, our declining faith in those we love or thought we loved,
allow passage to other sinister figures of working-class folklore – the
bailiffs. They come now for a different sort of eviction, evictions of the
heart, the uprooting of those shallow-planted affections that do not last, so
that the people to whom we are bound become an only impermanent home
for our changeable and unsteady feelings. The moonlight flits from rented
property, those departures in the dead of night to avoid the accumulated
rent that would never be paid – these have their equivalent in all the
noiseless desertions of each other, those mysterious and stealthy defections
of feeling, and the wandering off in search of somewhere more secure;
only we find that our emotions have taken up their new dwelling in a
structure as frail and insecure as the leaky tenement we have just left.
These things find their expression in the secret case-book of the social
worker, whose purpose is to ensure that socially produced unhappiness is
contained by the individuals who suffer; a story of impermanence,
dissatisfaction and discord. I was cheated. He let me down. She took me

in. I saw through him. He pissed off. She left me. He's no good. He broke his promise. He betrayed my trust. They were ungrateful. They don't care. He made demands. I couldn't cope. They took advantage of me. I thought I could count on him. I was conned. Never again. I shall know next time. You can't depend on anyone. Look after yourself. A long litany of bitterness and exploitation; as though we had internalized the values of a society that had misused and damaged us for so long that we have finished by becoming like it in our treatment to each other.

And what of the children abandoned or neglected by these spoilt and temporary sojourns? These are the orphans of our time, the waifs and starvelings, looking for ha'pence of comfort in the sweetshops and the stores, just as their equivalents begged or offered boxes of lucifers on the pavements of Victorian London, or do so today on the sidewalks of Manila and Sao Paolo. It is another kind of orphaning that carries off the absent fathers and departed mothers, and that sends children to a succession of surrogates – brief and random kin, half- and step-brothers and sisters, the make-believe caring of substitutes. Our versions of the infant orphan asylums, the rescue missions and prentice houses are not the individuals to whose care children are given; these are merely agents of the real institutions. The wooden benches, bare distempered walls, cold stone floors, grilles and deal tables, damp straw and lumpy flock, gruel and watery cocoa – this has given way to a different kind of hardness: the stone, brick and metal enter the heart. In the poor areas, what parents say, sorrowing but accepting, 'You've got to grow up hard round here. The kids've got to learn to fight. They'll have to fend for themselves if they want to survive.' The correction and chastisement of the Victorian institutions that schooled children to renunciation and stoicism take on a different form, though the coldness and indifference remain: the lesson is that nobody is going to give you anything for nothing; that you have to take what you want; that you must help yourself to the banquet of life, at which, as Malthus observed, there is no place set for the poor. The meaning is the same, even though the children themselves are transformed from the submissive wraiths at the dusty Gothic windows longing to be free, into the healthy and robust young people wandering around outside the shopping malls. For the real institutions are run by those who market the comforts – the vendors of sweets and palliatives, the consolers, those who hold the key to the golden gates. For these are things that shape the lives of our orphans, just as the red-brick institutions once did, soaring over the industrial suburbs with their menacing red gables and towers. Our institutions are run by those whose function it is to teach, with the insistence of a catechism, not that God is Love, but that money rules. The things that you count on in this life are not so much the people who look after you as what you can get out of them; above all, the healing, restorative power of money.

The dispossession of children whose parents are called away, not to eternal rest but to eternal restlessness, not so much to heaven as to a corner of it in some love-nest on the other side of town, mocks the scenes of parting and loss of the nineteenth century. Reading Mrs Gaskell, I was struck by her description of Mary Barton's feelings on the death of her mother:

Poor Mary, meanwhile, had mechanically helped the neighbour in all the last attentions to the dead; and when she was kissed and spoken to soothingly, tears stole quietly down her cheek; but she reserved the luxury of a full burst of grief till she could be alone. She shut the chamber-door softly, after the neighbour had gone, and then shook the bed by which she knelt in an agony of sorrow.

I was reminded of the young woman in the Midland town, recalling herself as a child of ten, when she realized that her mother had gone for ever.

'My Mum told me to sit with the two little ones while she went out to get something from the shop. She never came back. I sat there, just like she said, and I didn't move. I was afraid if I did, she wouldn't come back. In a way, I knew she wouldn't anyway, because she was all dressed up, and she kissed us before she went out; and you don't do that if you're only going to the chip-shop. It got later and later, and I listened for the footsteps outside; but she never came. The young 'uns fell asleep on the settee, and then the television went off; and then it was the middle of the night. I went to Auntie Joyce next door – it must've been about one in the morning. I said "Me Mam hasn't come back." "Oh she'll be back, duck." "No, she won't." I knew she'd left us. As far as I'm concerned, to me like, she's dead. I could see her tomorrow and not feel a thing. I shall never forgive her, if I live to be a hundred. There wasn't a day went by, all the years I was in care, that I didn't think about her. At first, I used to pray she'd come back; tell us it was all a mistake, she'd had an accident, somebody had made her do it, kidnapped her. But then it turned to hate. I found out later she had a bloke, he'd told her he'd take her but not her kids. And she chose him.'

Or I am reminded of Natalie, a child of three, clutching her packet of Maltesers, tears staining the chocolate on her face as she explains, 'My Daddy's gone away. He doesn't love us any more'; and she strokes the shoulder of her mother who is lying on the bed, crying. 'That's why Mummy is poorly. That's why she's crying.'

What the young learn from *these* parental defections is not that adults are prone to disease and sudden death that abridge relationships before they can fulfil themselves; but rather that adults have their own lives to lead, and cannot be counted on. One consequence of this is that they will turn for reassurance to that which *can* be counted on. As the years went by, Natalie learned to say to every newcomer not 'Will you love me?' but 'What have you got for me?' If their great-grandparents turned to the consolations of the flowery streams and the river where the angel-feet have trod, the promises on offer to their descendants are more tangible; even though they are no more appropriate for the wounded feelings; the mismatch between needs and commodities could not be more glaring. It is not so much that false needs have been created – rather that real needs get waylaid and falsified.

And infant mortality is not to be measured in the pale, waxlike bodies of those who have died in the first year of life, and perhaps placed, like one of my grandmother's dead children, in a top drawer until the funeral; but there is a dying of the imagination, a choking of the sensibility. Children are so easily smothered; their youth and energy overlaid by the noise and show of selling, just as so many infants were overlaid by the bodies of their exhausted parents in overcrowded beds.

The word 'consumption', once used to designate one of the great scourges of the nineteenth century, that wasting away of the human substance from within, is now used to describe, quite accurately, the way we live. What it suggests is that we actually imitate the dread disease, that we have come to resemble that affliction in our ravages upon the resources of the Earth. In consequence, the waste and debris pile up, not only outside. Our inner powers are wasted too, the ashes choke our abilities and clog our will to act. All the garbage and offal strewn about the manufacturing towns have their analogue in the spent residue of sensations, experiences and commodities we have used up; and this is all deposited within, just as the soot from the chimneys eroded the fabric of the towns, just as the acid emissions destroy the forests and kill the life of the rivers. And in the same way, that internal waste is not cleared but lies, obstructing the paths of the imagination, encumbering the feelings, stunting growth and development in much the same way that an earlier poverty did. The kinds of satisfaction that depend upon and belong to the purchased comforts leave a different sort of clinker and ordure, which block and suffocate, creating a demand for even more powerful sensations and compensations. These things as effectively ambush the intelligence and waylay the development of children as the earlier material absences, the distractions of hunger and cold. A report in the autumn of 1984 said that three out of four schoolteachers believed that children starting at primary school were markedly more disruptive, defiant, destructive than they were five years before. Their abilities, too, were believed to have decayed: more children were entering school without toilet training, unable to eat with a knife and fork, and unable to undress and dress themselves.[4]

---

[4] Reported in *The Times* on 7 September 1984.

Just as the sewage flowed through the open drains and middens of the old slum areas, so the effluent of market-culture flows through the imagination, bearing a detritus, the effect of which is only superficially different from those by-products of nineteenth-century urbanization. The exhalations from the canals of Engels' Lancashire rose up in choking vapours; the poisonous fumes of fantasy are given off by what is sometimes called the 'entertainment industry'. I have a composite memory of long afternoons spent in the homes of the poor, in shabby flats and draughty houses, where in the idleness and futility people long for diversion and sensation. A room, furnished with social services or Salvation Army chairs and carpets, bare tables, stained discoloured sofas, flimsy curtains. The only modern items in the room are a video recorder and a television. A group of adults have pooled their resources to provide themselves with some distraction. Four or five children play on the carpet with plastic bricks, comics, Barbie dolls. The video is showing a film. A demented axe-man is on the loose in a small American town, where images of autumn trees and suburban propriety could not be more reassuring. But when the hooded maniac climbs into the girl's bedroom, you see in explicit detail his assault upon her; you hear the sound of the axe on bone, you see the splashes of blood. You can witness the rage of the man-become-monster who is terrorizing the town, and who is a respectable salesman in a shoe-store by day. Each new victim is introduced arbitrarily; and the tension lies in wondering whether the girl in the drugstore who has befriended him will go the same way as all the others. You know who is next. A thrill of anticipation runs through those watching, half a dozen young adults; mostly long-term unemployed. The children notice, yet they do not notice. A brief, troubled glance at something spectacularly horrific, nothing more than a clouding of the eyes, a slight frown; perhaps one of them runs to bury her head in an adult lap, and returns to her dolls with a tube of Smarties.

We are right to be proud of the elimination of the old diseases and epidemics of the slums. But they are echoed in the fevered relationships that use people up so swiftly, the rage and delirium of passions that burn themselves out in a few days. These are the products of another kind of squalor, a different sort of overcrowding from those that engendered the fevers of the early industrial era: a flooding of the senses, a jostling of the heart, an inflaming of the imagination, the effusion of feeling. We sometimes speak of 'outbreaks' of violence, of 'epidemics' of crime, as though acknowledging at some level these obscure continuities and recurrences. In July 1984 Lord Lane, the Lord Chief Justice, said that heroin addiction was worse than cholera or typhoid. In the same month, at a British Medical Association conference, a psychiatrist said; 'Heroin addiction is not an epidemic now, it is a plague.'

This was expressed vividly in some conversations with young people on an estate in South London in the early summer of 1984, fifteen-/to seventeen-year-olds who had become addicted to heroin, and saw in it a means of escape. The metaphors they used – of flying, of ecstasy, of living in another world, of feeling like superman, of possessing supernatural powers – were all metaphors of transcendence. Their addiction was the final destination of their wanderings through a life without function or prupose.

Their dependency on heroin – suddenly, mysteriously available, unknown to their parents – seemed to illuminate the many dimensions of the circuits of capital, not only through time but around the world. Young people, unemployed, bored, powerless in the richest societies in the world, seek escape from their condition. They consume a crop grown in the Third World, exported for cash, which makes great profit for all those through whose hands it passes. (That this money is often used to finance the demands of ideology – resistance to the Soviets in Afghanistan or to the military in Turkey – is an irony lost on those whose lives are laid waste in the slums of Chicago, Marseilles or Merseyside.) As a lucrative crop, it will have displaced more modest traditions of subsistence farming. Those who process, refine and distribute it exhibit all the most admired entrepreneurial skills; transporting it is a very high-risk business which calls forth qualities of great inventiveness and imagination. And the despair of those who have no other means of making a living than by cultivating the poppies joins the despair of those captive, immobilized consumers in the barrack-like estates of South London. Those who have become addicted will do anything to get the money they need. The renewed increase in crime in South London in 1984 has been attributed to the desperate and ruthless efforts of those who have become obsessed with the fulfilment of their addiction. It illuminates the nature of 'demand' in a capitalist economy in ways not often so nakedly displayed.

What heroin shows is not so much the destructive power of a single damaging substance, but rather, in an exaggerated way, the mechanism whereby so many other, legitimate commodities are marketed. It is its very closeness to all the hallowed processes in which our freedoms are supposed to be enshrined that creates the horror. Not only does it reveal its kinship with all the other cash crops which over the years have displaced the poor of the Earth (exploitation of which has always contributed to rising living standards for the working class throughout the colonial period) – tea, tobacco, snuff, chocolate, coffee; but also with those other dependencies which we regard as normal – alcohol, junk food, TV, certain aspects of the entertainment industry.

Heroin is one of the prohibited addictions of an addictive society. It tells us too much about the way we live. Above all, it throws into sharp focus the relationship between needs and commodities. The needs that heroin purports to answer are real enough – that aching sense of futility, absence of function, boredom, despair; but as a commodity it cannot possibly satisfy them. All it can do is create a growing appetite for the sensation it produces. Those for whom exploiting the vulnerability of the young is their daily business are disconcerted by something which they do not control. But the Lord Chief Justice is right in his choice of metaphor. We sometimes refer to the 'climate' which favours the growth of certain social ills; and in this sense the poisoned atmosphere, the miasmal airs of early industrial society have their direct counterpart in these contemporary plagues.

It is, of course, essential not to suggest that things have got worse, or that there ever was a time when resistance to the more ugly visitations of capitalist society was more coherent or deeply rooted. It is not that. It is simply that the tribute paid to capital in human terms remains constant, even though it may take on different forms in different epochs. What we are looking at is the reconstitution of old evils in new shapes. The samenesses are more compelling for being so elusive; no longer, it seems, traceable in a world where they had become familiar. But they remain a presence, more sensed than recognized.

The metamorphoses of capitalism, protean and fluid, mean that it may flow into different contours and yet remain itself; intervene in our lives for the same purpose of impoverishing and taking something from us, and yet remain unscathed. It has been the greatest error of the enemies of capitalism to believe that it has only one way of sucking our substance – through the sweat and blood of labour. They have underestimated its power over other parts of the human frame; not just muscle and sinew but feelings and spirit, and even, in its newest incarnation, the brain and understanding. If we fail to see this, it is perhaps because our eyes are still fixed on a poverty of orange-box furniture, guttering candles and empty hearth, of scavenging for food in the garbage of the rich and seeking fuel on the cinder-heaps; poaching for rabbits and waiting at the factory gates. We have not been alive to those things that have come like a thief in the night, and have been present even in what looked like our victory over older forms of exploitation and loss. It did not occur to us that out of the very abundance of capitalism new and raw materials could be created, out of which another and less tractable poverty might be fashioned.

When we think of all the agencies of punishment and coercion of our industrial past – not only of the work-system, with its hierarchies and disciplines that the men replicated within their families, but also of the punitive regimes of workhouse, gaol, house of correction, reformatory and industrial schools – we think of the obsessive monotony of repeated and meaningless tasks. These have their continued existence in the workhouses of the mind, where neither relief nor rest is possible from worry, anxiety, fear. The treadmill, the crank and the stoneyard prolong their asperities in the compulsions and obsessions of the emotionally, mentally, spiritually disabled; as well as in the recurring nightmare, the wider social restlessness and disquietude. Earlier, imposed disciplines live on in private rituals, incommunicable neuroses, the compulsions of gambling, drink, work, sex, drugs, violence; and are of a piece with the more obvious contemporary disorders – the old man picking up pieces of paper in the street, the woman pursued by noises in her head, those who believe themselves possessed, the people in the psychiatric wards counting, praying, touching, self-proposed rituals without end. These sufferings are only a small space removed from the testimony of older people who started work sixty or seventy years ago, and who say, 'I hear the noise of the looms yet, I hear them in my sleep', or from the witness of unemployed workers who still wake at the same time as they did when they were working, fumble into their clothes, terrified of being late, until they realize that it is finished, and they light a cigarette in the silence of dawn, their heart still pounding, their body still throbbing with the alien rhythms that disturb their rest.

The internal corrosion, that wear and tear of the spirit, calls forth the tranquillizers and drugs and chemicals we need in order to rest; just as the tormented bodies of the factory workers were grateful for the opiates and elixirs. The image of the children observed by the overseer who gave evidence to the Children's Employment Commission remains evocative: 'I have stopped and looked at them for two minutes, going through the motions of piecening, fast asleep, when there was really no work to do, and they were doing nothing.' So many of the diseases of the late twentieth century are said to be related to tension and stress; products of a life in which human beings are still subservient to alien rhythms, are still appendages of a machinery become invisible but still reverberating. Capitalism's own version of healing proves to be a mirror image of its earlier compulsions. We seek relief from the very thing that drives us, just as the palaces of production drove our forebears.

And similar effects are achieved. I remember an old woman in a council flat in Lambeth. She was afraid to go outside her door, for fear of being robbed or attacked. She was as effectively incarcerated as the aged paupers in the Victorian workhouses, even though no one compels her to sit in stiff calico aprons on wooden chairs behind high walls. She said: 'You never feel safe. You're not safe if you go into the streets. You're not safe if you stop at home – they'll break in and beat you up for the sake of a few pounds. You're not even safe when you're dead – they'll dig you up for the sake of the rings on your fingers.'

The homeless of Victorian cities live on in those driven out of their mind –
those shelterless wanderings of people in search of purpose. The great
growth of new sects, of semi-mystical and quasi-religious organizations
parallels those of the nineteenth century – Joanna Southcott and all those
prophets and founders of sects, all the satanists and the Moonies, the
Scientologists, and the Hell's Angels with their blood-feuds, the
astrologers and fortune-tellers, have offered provisional shelter, just as the
asylums, night shelters and casual wards once did; a scavenged and
provisional rest, a sleep of exhaustion, before the people are sent on the
tramp once more in the early morning.

'The story of 19th century labour is one of movement and migration,'
says Eric Hobsbawm in *The Tramping Artisan.*[5] That persistent,
involuntary wandering that drove people on in search of a night's lodging,
a day's work, a better rate of pay, has its echo in the restless movement of
those young people evicted, like their forebears, from any anchorage in
place or purpose. Ironically, many of the young have been severed from
the tradition of labour, which was the source of such disturbance to their
great-grandparents; and they live in a kind of abstract vagabondage. Early
in 1984, concern was expressed about children who run away from home,
following estimates that 50,000 teenagers disappear in the United States
each year. About a tenth of these are subsequently found dead. The same
phenomenon is spreading in Britain. Young people invited to express their
feelings about how such things are possible say they are bored. They want
to be free. They want to find themselves. They must be left alone to
discover who they are. Then the professionals have their say. The man
from the charity, the psychiatrist, the youth worker. More research is
needed. They have just been to the USA or Scandinavia to see how such
problems are dealt with over there. Oh yes, quite common. A very
interesting new project is just getting off the ground in South London . . .

But the people suffer – frightened faces, tense with lack of sleep, fear,
anger – are carefully preserved from any understanding. Why me? they
ask the impassive reporter, the mute camera. Why did she have to leave
home? We gave them the best of everything. Where did we go wrong? The
sense of injury floats, detached. It cannot be lodged anywhere. It just
happens. The violence that has been committed is inaccessible to its
victims. So they yield, and acquiesce in a superior wisom that is none.
More research, yes. Perhaps they'll come up with something. And if all
those clever people whose job it is to know cannot make head or tail of it,
who are we . . .

And those parents reading the papers or watching television say under
their breath, 'There but for the grace of God'; and they remember the
funny smell of glue in the son's bedroom that time when he said he

[5] Eric Hobsbawm, *The Tramping Artisan* (Weidenfeld & Nicolson, London, 1968).

thought he could fly and was going to jump from the bedroom window; they wonder what was behind it, that time the police came looking for someone who was supposed to have attacked an old woman, and they said their son was in school, when all the time . . .

And there it rests. We cannot probe the social causes of these things because they have been declared out of bounds. Off limits. Even so, this particular scare – teenagers, little more than children, running away, living rough, changing their identity, stealing, taking drugs – clearly has causes that must be at least partly social.

The society that produces these aberrations mocks the invididuals it claims to cherish but whose lives it scars. All the ostentatious caring, the solicitude and concern, suggest that these are problems of unstable individuals. Nothing to do with society, and even less with capitalism which has, as it were, disappeared from our lives. It was different when people were destitute, hungry, wretched. But now that it asks nothing more than to be able to heap its bounty upon us, there can no longer be anything wrong with it. Now, there are just individuals, living their lives. Freely. As they want to. Choosing.

Our tenderness for the individual has another, darker purpose; and that is to exculpate all social determinants from their part in his or her suffering. The sovereignty of the individual goes hand in hand with the eclipse of the social; even when it is blindingly clear that the whole raising of children in the West depends upon what can be described only as a sustained and systematic disturbance of them from their earliest years. In their partial release from labour, they must be shaped into markets for the labour of others; for the most part remote, unintelligible others, from whose pain and sweat in the production of what they consume they are invited to live in collusion dissociation. They live in a world of jostling goods and services, the origins of which are wrapped in mystery, and might as well have been wafted into their lives by supernatural powers for all they know of them. But what they do have to learn is how to want, and in a very particular way.

In other words, the very basis of the social formation of our children is a systematic and permitted violation of them; a shaping of their growth that follows the configuration of the markets; markets that, far from being a response to need, become a major determinant upon it; with the result that the exigencies of capitalist growth become inextricably entwined with the growth of the young. Their earliest learning is of the imperatives of buying, the urgency of purchased excitements and stimulants. Their development itself is yoked to an expression of needs, which become:

progressively fragmented into smaller and smaller bits, which are then recombined in response to market cues into patterns that are temporary, fluid and unstable.

The constant revision and recombination of need-fragments renders it increasingly difficult, if not impossible, for individuals to develop a coherent set of objectives for their needs and thus to make judgments about the suitability of particular goods for them.[6]

In spite of all the agencies of caring, the elaborate and hard-won structures of the welfare state, the same old cruelties re-form themselves; and the palliatives and reforms serve as a distorting prism through which the altered form of those baleful, inseparable attendants of capitalism are not recognized for what they are.

Laissez-faire occurs in some strange guises. If the curbing of the rights of employers over the bodies of children in the early nineteenth century was so strenuously resisted, it is only to be expected that our contemporary debauching of children's spirits should come to be regarded not as a monstrous aberrancy but as something acceptable, even normal. There was no shortage of apologists at that time for the system of child labour, and their heirs are not difficult to find in those defenders of the present plunder of the substance of the young, that molestation of their powers and abilities, that leeching on their vulnerability by those who recognize soft markets, as the old cotton employers saw the advantages of easy and flexible labour of pauper infants, malleable and unprotected. As H. Turner Thackrah, the Leeds doctor who campaigned against the long hours of child labour in the struggle for the Ten-Hour Bill, said, 'We underrate evils to which we are accustomed .' The machinery that waited to claim their energies and deft fingers still lies in ambush for them; only now they oil the machinery with money. And money wears away their substance no less than factory engines wore away their muscle and flesh.

I think of Michelle. At fifteen her hair was one day red, the next blonde, then jet-black, then teased into Afro kinks and after that rats' tails, then plaited, and then cropped so it glistened close to the skull. She wore a nose-stud, and then her ears were pierced; in them bright feathers, rhinestones or ceramic or silver. Her lips were scarlet, then purple, then black. Her face was ghost-white and then peach-coloured, then bronze as though it were cast in metal. Pursued by dreams of flight, she left home at sixteen to be with her boyfriend, who was twenty-six. If they took her home, she said, she would kill herself. 'But I've always let you do what you want,' her mother protested. 'This is what I want.' At eighteen she returned to her mother, with two children, after she had been badly beaten by her man. She sat in the bedroom which she had fled three years earlier; the faded photos of yesterday's pop stars still stared down from the walls. She said she felt a hundred years old. She felt weary. She'd tried all that life could offer. Nothing else was left.

[6] William Leiss, *The Limits of Satisfaction* (University of Toronto Press, Toronto, 1976).

She reminded me of those people evoked by Jack London, prematurely aged by work; even though Michelle still has her health and youth. That image of people worn out at forty by work, childbearing and undernourishment was a familiar one in Victorian England, and continues to haunt us in the spectres on the Oxfam envelope and television news. Engels spoke of early ageing of the cotton operatives 'so universal that almost every man of forty would be taken for ten or fifteen years older. A list of 131 spinners contained but seven over 45 years, and yet the whole 131 were rejected by the manufacturers to whom they applied for work as too old, and were without means of support by reason of old age.'[7]

This early using up of people has a different resonance in the late twentieth century. Not, of course, in physical signs – far from it. In a world governed by the dictatorship of illusion, where appearances are of primordial importance, the preservation of the semblance of youth – even in the old – has become an obsession. But the maintenance of polished surfaces only dissimulates the wastage within. Many of Michelle's age feel they have been through everything, have become cynical and jaded without becoming wise. The prodigality of experience leaves no residue; and life itself has become a commodity, out of which enough fun, sex or money can never be got. Talking to young adults on the poor estates over the past few years, I have a sense of life lived at such an accelerated tempo, accompanied by such a violent gutting of experience, that they seem to have used up a lifetime in just a few years.

Red is twenty-one. He has two children, one with his wife, from whom he is divorced, the other with a girlfriend from whom he is separated. He feels he has been to the limits of experience, and has nothing else to live for. He lived stoned out of his head for a year, lived rough, took his bike round Europe, stealing and thieving to survive. He fought with rivals to gain admittance to his Hell's Angels chapter, and punctured a guy's lung in the process. He has fucked a chick seven times in succession in one night. He doesn't want to live to be old. But he does want to die spectacularly, so that his children will have something to remember. He didn't want them to be disillusioned with him, as he had been with his parents. He said a curious thing, this man of twenty-one: 'I think my kids will have a better chance in life without me.' He gambles with his life every time he goes out on his bike. This, he says, is the only thing that excites him – half courting the one experience he hasn't yet known. He is sometimes tempted to drive off Beachy Head, or to keep going in the face of the oncoming lights on the motorway. That way, at least, he says, I'll die happy. When he is at home, in the council flat with its walls covered

[7] Friedrich Engels, *Condition of the Working Class in England* (Allen & Unwin, London, 1968).

with photos of gleaming bikes, he listens to heavy metal music. He likes the pounding of the music, which penetrates and possesses you. Looking at the bitten nails, the mobile eyes, his inability to sit still, it is possible to gain just a glimpse of the affliction within. He and his friends worship dead pop heroes – Eddie Cochran, Gene Vincent, Elvis. And the palliatives which capitalism offers to allay this 'restless and migratory spirit', which was deplored in the workers of the early industrial era, and which it has recreated in another context – all the marketed escapism, evasions and distractions – are, like the lessons of resignation, fortitude and discipline of a previous age, calculated only to compound the violence and aggravate what they claim to cure.

Just as an unhappy child may sometimes internalize the cruelties she or he has endured and may reproduce these in adult relationships that bring only suffering which, however hard to bear, is at least familiar, so, it seems, the same thing may happen to whole classes or groups of people with their socially derived pain. Engels, describing the brutalities of the factory system, turned to the *Manchester Guardian* between June and August 1842, in order to document a series of accidents.

June 12th, a boy died in Manchester of lockjaw, caused by his hand being crushed between wheels; June 16th, a youth in Saddleworth seized by a wheel and carried round by it; died, utterly mangled. June 29th, a young man at Green Acres Moor near Manchester, at work in a machine shop, fell under the grindstone, which broke two of his ribs and lacerated him terribly. July 24th, a girl in Oldham, carried around fifty times by a strap; no bone unbroken. July 27th, a girl in Manchester seized by the blower (the first machine that received the raw cotton) and died of injuries received. August 3rd, a bobbins turner died in Dukenfield, caught in a strap, every rib broken. In the year 1843, the Manchester Infirmary treated 962 cases of wounds and mutilations caused by machinery.[8]

This remains a powerful metaphor for the absorption of humanity into the very machinery of capitalism – like Zola's coalmine, named 'Le Voreux'.[9] But where Engels was recording the mutilations suffered in factories, we can read in the local paper of any large town or city a similar sequence of violence and damage, not only as accidents but more clearly as an outcrop of the disturbance within, of those internalized machines run out of control. Of course these same things, horrible crimes and murders, also blemished the early nineteenth century; but then the violence of work told a far more sustained disregard for human life than the actions of disordered individuals. Now – especially with the recurrence of mass unemployment – work, any work on almost any conditions, is desirable;

[8] Ibid.
[9] Emile Zola, *Germinal*.

and it is the people who are left to mangle and humuliate each other.

In March 1983 I went to work in Walsall in the West Midlands. The local paper on the day I arrived furnished as much horror in one night as the *Manchester Guardian* yielded to Engels over a six-week period. The headline is: 'Horror of a Midnight Rapist – vicious sex attack on widow, 85. The man pounced on the helpless screaming woman as she lay in bed in her home in Tettenhall and subjected her to a series of sexual assaults.' On the same day, it is reported that a youth had nine months of madness, causing actual bodily harm to one of his victims; a former schoolteacher is accused of three offences of having sex with a thirteen-year-old girl; a policeman with eighteen years' impeccable service made a telephone call threatening to kill or scar for life a man he thought was associated with his wife; a Tipton man who stabbed his brother to death is to marry the mother of the dead man's children; a man accused of raping a drug addict after whipping her with a wire coat-hanger told a court she agreed to have sex with him; a twenty-year-old man denied that he and his mother – an ex-special policewoman – ran a cannabis sales service at all-night 'blues' parties.

The indignities that the poor inflict on each other give an only intermittent glimpse of the ruin within. They are in some ways even more terrifying – because impalpable – than the known cruelties imposed from without. The first time I ever heard anyone say 'They ought to bring back the workhouse' was in the East End of London, the last place, one might have thought, to hear such nostalgia articulated. She was a woman, herself on social security, whose daughter had been attacked by an unemployed subnormal man in the block where they lived who had 'got away' with a prison sentence of only two years. But the feeling runs deep. '*Bring back* . . .' is the cry – the rope, the birch; a yearning for familiar disciplines and punishments by people so disoriented and frightened by change that they themselves cry out for a return, a going back, for a reanimation of those landscapes with all the correctives and controls that accompanied them. These longings are easily articulated by the popular press through the hysterias they provoke – the outcry against muggers, rapists, vandals, child-molesters, wreckers, thugs, rouse all the sleeping horrors, and make more thinkable the reimposition of older coercions. In this way the atmosphere is created in which the ghosts can be conjured forth; an older ideology is revived, in spite of the altered landscape, an ideology which, like the bacillus at the end of Camus' novel *The Plague* never disappears completely, 'but can remain for years and years, sleeping in old furniture and linen, can wait patiently in bedrooms and cellars, packing-cases, handkerchiefs and old papers, for the day when, in the cause of the suffering and the instruction of humanity, it will rouse up its rats and send them out to die in a serenely unsuspecting city.'

One of the most vivid indications of change came from an old woman in Sheffield, who said; 'Money used to be the root of all evil; now it's the source of all the good you can imagine.' This transformation corresponds directly to the ways in which the other-worldly promises of capitalism have been displaced by its more material ones, and the way to salvation has been charted on a more manifest topography than the misty uplands of an afterlife.

Writing of the role of Methodism in the making of the industrial working class, E.P. Thompson has closely analysed the nature of the emotional and psychological dramas that individuals experienced in their search for salvation.[10] The passport to the heavenly home depended not upon a once-for-all conversion, one definitive act of repentance, but on a state of election that remained always 'conditional and provisory'. The striving for salvation was always characterized by backslidings, by periods of remorse and self-abasement:

> *Alas and did my Saviour bleed*
> *And did my Saviour die?*
> *And did He hang upon the tree*
> *For such a worm as I?*

The fragility of the state of grace, the fall and the renewal, the exaltation of the moment of triumph and the ensuing despair, all this offered a profound emotional release to people in whose daily lives there was little room for such heightened feeling. The Hammonds express it thus:

The Methodists taught that heaven was really a Fifth Act, in which the supreme artist would give a happy issue to the tribulations of this life, and the greater the sufferings endured with patience in these passing scenes, the greater would be the triumph of faith and courage in the day when the plot of the life of mankind received the final disentanglement.[11]

Thompson points out that the tension was maintained by the absence of any permanent state of grace. It had always to be won afresh after every sinning. 'Thus it became the doctrine that forgiveness of sin lasted only so long as the penitent went and sinned no more.' This meant that nothing was ever definitively gained; always threatened, the state of grace required constant effort and anxiety.

And so it is with the contemporary version of this doctrine, and the more tangible rewards in which it is embodied.

There has always been something slightly insubstantial in that sudden

[10] E. P. Thompson, *The Making of the English Working Class* (Penguin, Harmondsworth, 1968).

[11] J.L. and Barbara Hammond, *The Town Labourer* (Longman, Green, London, 1925).

appearance of the cathedrals of merchandise in the old industrial towns
and cities. They have the shimmering aspect of a mirage. The promises
they hold of tangible reward in the here- and-now are real enough, the
Word made flesh, as it were. But there remains something mythic and
mysterious in the apparition. Milton Keynes, with its million square feet
of shopping space in the middle of nowhere is a kind of myth itself, with
its hanging gardens, its palms and tropical lianas, its expanse of marble – a
substance itself traditionally associated with funerary monuments and the
hope of resurrection. One reaches to the realms of religious poetry to
describe its effects:

> *Cosi la mente mia tutta sospesa*
> *Mirava fissa, immobile ed attenta,*
> *E sempre più nel mirar faceasi accesa . . .* [12]

It is as though the pie had miraculously descended from the sky; and the
medium between the unworthy individual and these wonders is, of course,
money, which has undergone the sort of transsubstantiation the old
women in Sheffield was hinting at. It has become a secular equivalent of
divine grace. Although it is everywhere, infinitely available, we can never
be sure of getting enough; it must be constantly replenished. Money has
been assimilated to the enabling agent of grace, which can alone give
release. The intense spiritual individualism of Methodism is readily
adapted to this more prosaic form. The soul of the individual achieves
absolution from sin at the moment of real repentance – and the imagery
suggests the blinding flash, the sudden stilling of the inner turbulence –
and this has its counterpart in the hope of the stroke of good fortune, the
big win, the sudden windfall, the lucky number, the winning ticket. (It
may well be this profane version of salvation that has radicalized sections
of the clergy in our time. Many are deeply disturbed by this encroachment
on a terrain that seemed to belong securely to the Church.)

Southey said that the Methodists made of religion 'a thing of sensation
and passion, craving perpetually for sympathy and stimulants'. This has
its direct sequel in the succession of marketed crazes and sensations of
consumer capitalism. For example, at Christman 1983 a rage for
possession of what were called Cabbage Patch dolls swept the children of
the United States. (These were rag dolls, each one different, and all
foundlings. Each doll came with adoption papers that the child was
expected to sign, pledging to take care of it.) These objects were soon all
sold; and the television showed distraught parents asking what they
should tell their unfortunate children who would be disappointed. ('What

---

[12] Canto XXXIII of Dante's *Paradiso*: And so my mind, bedazzled and amazed,/Stood
fixed in wonder, montionless, intent,/And still my wonder kindled as I gazed.

can I say to my children?' one angry mother demanded, 'Should I say that Father Christmas ran out?') That these dolls answered a profound emotional need is not in doubt; but whether those needs were significantly answered by that particular commodity is another question. Perhaps the need is triggered by the object, but it may well have been created at a far deeper level than that of the need to sell dolls. What was really being marketed was the children's sense of their own orphaned state. Need is turned against life.

This arousal of deep yearnings and unnameable achings by a sequence of images, symbols and suggestions has its earlier root in the sighs and groans of chapel crowds in the presence of that imagery of cross and suffering. That swelling sound of anguish and frustration has its direct descendant in the intense atmosphere of certain pop concerts, in which the frail but unattainable figure of the performer expresses the anguish of all in a surreal ghostly glare. Words are indistinct, but waves of sound rise up from the congregation; a moan that sometimes rises to a scream of longing. Perhaps it is a protest, too, amorphous and not specific; the sound of an exile that cannot be defined, only felt. The longings flow outwards and merge with the blue haze of cigarette smoke and coloured lights until they become almost a solid thing, a texture of sound and desire. These are the equivalents of E.P. Thompson's

Sabbath orgasms of feeling, which made more possible the single-minded weekday direction of those energies to the consummation of productive labour. Moreover, since salvation was never assured, and temptations lurked on every side, there was a constant inner goading to sober and industrious behaviour – the visible sign of grace – every hour of the day and every day of the year. Not only 'the sack' but the flames of hell might be the consequence of indiscipline at work. God was the most vigilant overlooker of all . . . Work was the Cross from which the transformed industrial worker hung.[13]

In this way, the *excruciating* quality of poverty is maintained too. If the discipline of money looms greater than the shadow of work, its unappealable imperatives become the more compelling. One of the happy (at least for the continued vigour of capitalism) consequences of this is that the rich have become sacralised; objects of veneration and emulation rather than the expropriators and oppressors of the people; models of aspiration and striving. In this way, cruel inequalities are once more acceptable.

Naturally, those who in Victorian England did not disdain to spread messages of salvation in the pestilential poor quarters, those who set up Sabbath schools to assist in the training of the uninstructed mind, those

[13] Thompson, *English Working Class.*

who sought to implant the living germ of goodness and to awaken the
kindliest affections of the human soul – they also have their secular heirs
today. These are, of course, the bringers of a more beguiling message of
salvation, the prophets and seers of marketing, the salesmen and singers of
the more immediate joys of all that money can buy.

Of course, the despair of the outcast attracts a different kind of
missionary too, just as those other missionaries of socialism went into
slums and poor quarters and 'made socialists' under the very noses of
those preaching salvation. Only this time, with the secular gospel having
been appropriated by the prophets of capital, it is the sectarians of the Left
who appear to be talking of an unreal, unearthly life elsewhere, when they
deliver their fervours of fraternity and peace; and it is their peculiarly
insubstantial pie that looks more remote and unattainable than the sky
itself. All the would-be teachers and activists of the Leftist factions, selling
their tracts of salvation outside windy factory gates and on rainswept
shopping squares where the people hanker after false gods – it is now their
turn to cry their version of truth and redemption to the empty air. And
they find themselves crying until they are hoarse of the love of man and
woman, as their counterparts once spoke of the love of God, and they are
told 'Get back to Russia', just as their forerunners were told to get back
into their churches. Their message falls on deaf ears, on stony ground; and
they rejoice over one or two conversions, no less than those who had
brought a single soul to salvation. The old urban missionaries might have
shaken their heads at their powerlessness to transform roguery and
idleness into a readiness to accept God's grace; while the new evangelists
find that the mass conversions into a properly revolutionary frame of mind
elude them; when it is all so obvious, so close at hand, and yet so hard of
attainment.

Into the poor communities, those estates where violence and fear rule in
the acres of stained concrete and mildewed walls come those who live off
the remains left even by the poorest – the gatherers of waste, the totters
and tinkers; not, this time, smelly old men with primitive carts full of
rusty iron and disgusting rags and discarded bottles, crying out in their
croaking, barely human, voices. The new scavengers are those who live off
them, those who come to report on their shames, to tell of their suffering –
mother kept child in cupboard, mother sells daughter for sex, murder and
rape and disgrace. It is the people from television and the newspapers, the
reporters, interpreters, commentators and investigators too, all those who
live off the poverty and despair. We visit the ghettos, and listen to people
who tell us what it is like to be poor, unemployed, destitute, incapacitated
in so many, not always physical, ways. We pick over lives offered up so
eagerly, listen to the expiatory confessions; capture on film, tape, video, in
words, so many things that can make their reappearance only in marketed

form. In this way, the lives of the poor get strangely transmuted. The sympathy of the reporter who promises to keep in touch, the tale of woe that elicits such fellow-feeling, the story of loss that is so overwhelming, the testimony of aloneness and grief – all become commodities. And the moment of these personal encounters, so full of hope and promise, is always deceived. In the end, something is taken away from the poor; something else in addition to all the other distraints – the very substance of their life becomes a part of somebody else's career. (I do not, of course, exclude myself from this process. It is impossible for invididuals to transcend the values of the society of which they are in part a product.) The lives of the poorest are exposed everywhere, ostensibly for our concern. In reality, their ubiquitous presence is more like an older form of warning to us, like the corpses of deviants and malefactors swinging on a gibbet as example to the rest.

The beautified external landscapes have been accompanied, then, by a reconstitution of some of the old brutalities within. A dynamic connection exists between a transformed material world and the realm of human relationships. The latter are increasingly represented as being unreliable, brief, mutually exploitative, arbitrary and aggressive. Unhappily-ever-after has been the main cultural expression of films, plays, stories; and this has replaced the bland ideas of justice and happiness, of everything-coming-out-all-right-in-the-end of an earlier phase of capitalist culture. Human consolations are all right for a culture of poverty, it seems, when there is precious little chance of anything else; but in a culture which is based upon dissatisfaction, more sombre and disturbing messages are called for.

When we think of the great age of capital expansion in the eighteenth and nineteenth centuries, it is a story or markets being opened up all over the world; a vast increase in manufacture and its distribution across the continents, and the expansion of (mainly) British power; the sombre adventure of slavery, cotton and Lancashire, the breakdown of local economies in different parts of the world and their subordination to that of Britain (in India, the decay and extinction of indigenous industries[14]), the substitution of monocultural cash crops for subsistence; an undertaking of audacious enterprise and ruthless piracy. This great conquest, which mistook its might for civilizing mission and its strength for a manifestation of divine providence, has struck deep roots in our consciousness. The stories of these adventurers, too, were of landscapes – the frozen wastes of Canada, the disease-bearing jungles of West Africa, the shimmering heat

[14] See E. Hobsbawm, *Industry and Empire* (Penguin, Harmondsworth, 1982).

of the Deccan Plain, the burning emptiness of the Australian desert.

The story of British decline – in some versions already more than a hundred years old – is sometimes confused with the exhaustion of capitalism itself. Because the industrial epoch began here, the decay of our industrial strength and the dissolution of empire have led us to believe that there are no more frontiers. Our loss of that sense of limitless horizons, of vast spaces to be conquered and colonized, has made it seem as if capitalism itself must be in a state of permanent and intensifying crisis. We have identified our own reduced status with signs of decline in a system which we initiated and which seemed to serve us absolutely.

But of course there was never any reason for capitalism to be in retreat in sympathetic conjunction with the diminution of British power. Our feeling of narrowing space, of closing frontiers, of no new worlds to win, is an only partial view. It is not simply that the global reach of the capitalist enterprise has made it easier and cheaper to invest in manufacturing industry in countries where raw materials and labour are close at hand and cost less; nor yet that once-remote parts of the world now serve as 'offshore production units' for growing luxury crops – strawberries, flowers or cucumbers – for the rich countries, or as extensions of farms and ranches. It is also that new territories have indeed continued to be opened up all the time; whole undiscovered tracts of land have been conquered, annexed, laid under a form of contributions; not only in the form of jungle clearances in Brazil or Guatemala, but even in the metropolitan countries themselves. Indeed, Britain too has become the object of some of those colonizing forces which it helped to unleash on the world in the first place. But because the new territories opened up in more recent times have not always been definable countries, indeed, sometimes not even geographical entities at all, we fail to recognize these recurrences for what they are. Markets have continued to be created, as indeed they must be, for the growth and expansion of capital. The restless and invasive adventuring of the eighteenth and nineteenth centuries has not ceased; the unequal transactions between rich and poor, whereby human beings are dispossessed of something vital and capital continues to accumulate, have not let up for a moment.

One area in which we have suffered some of the most daring incursions in the mid-twentieth century has been penetrated almost by stealth, unnoticed until it had become irreversible – that vast, almost virgin territory of working-class defences; a country of the (it was believed) indefeasible strength of labour, a terrain gained by labour itself in its resistance to earlier capitalist plunder. The encroachment of intensifying market-relationships upon this domain is the parallel of that process which has destroyed subsistence and self-sufficiency elsewhere in the world; and has damaged the defences of the poor. This is not to exaggerate the achievements of working-class resistance. The terrain protected by the labour movement was always fragile and threatened. Its very growth had depended upon the slow spread of some of the fruits of colonialism; and it had maintained the subordination of large numbers of those it sought to defend – women and children in particular. But it contained important elements of resistance, the living germ of an alternative that made only modest claims upon the earth's riches.

The analogy with the buccaneering invasions of British merchants into the poorest parts of the world cannot be too strongly emphasized; only this time, instead of a dominating vast areas of land and naming them after their conqueror – Rhodesia – or in honour of the monarchs under whose reign the excursion of 'discovery' occurred – Louisiana or Virginia – or indeed, giving any name that seemed to fit the produce or the climate, this time the territory has been in terms of human beings who are to be turned into markets and then controlled – teenagers, senior citizens, the upwardly mobile, young marrieds, housewives, the under-fives, ABs; groups of people as blithely unaware of their separate identity as the inhabitants of Mali or the Sudan, until they became inscribed upon the charts of all the vendors and salesmen and hucksters who have come in search of these new and underdeveloped territories.

The taking of this region has given rise to a regenerated language of mastery and capture, of ascendancy and annexation. If Britain is not now the centre, but rather an internal colony of the global capitalist empire, this is surely what it means. And those people who received the most meagre benefits from an earlier phase of colonialism have themselves become the object of this more recent incursion. The merchants and conquistadors have gone forth bravely with their battle-cries of peddling and merchandizing, their superior magic which turns all things into commodities and thence into money, their alchemy that transforms everything into manufactures and services, their ability to make material even human dreams, to give manifest form to the most precious, intangible, human things.

If the protests at these invasions into lives which had always suffered want and insufficiency were muted, it was because the conquerors seemed to bring great wealth that promised release from an ancient poverty. But that release has been into a different form of subordination. One man caught what has happened when he said, 'We used to be proud of how much we could do with very little money; now people are ashamed of how little they can do without a lot.' It seems that we have been laid under an enchantment by what promised freedom from poverty. Money, as cure for the damage money has caused, was the new gospel that the invaders brought; and in this circular and inescapable creed rich and poor are locked together.

The most important locus of these triumphs has been in the places where a poor working class erected its always inadequate defences against the ravages of an older poverty. Although this territory was known long ago, it remained for many years forbidden; unexplored. It was in the USA that the discovery was first made that 'the largest potential market was to be found in the rising incomes of the mass of working citizens in economically developed countries'.[15] And although this development was foreshadowed, incipiently in the late nineteenth century and again in the inter-war period, it was not until after 1945, and particularly after 1951, that the new gold rush started, a Yukon of space was opened up, another continent and a strange new way of life found, waiting to be taken over. All previously hidden, internal landscapes were ripe for development, all the hazy *terrain vague* concealed until then from the eyes of the predators suddenly appeared in a new and radiant light.

Because large numbers of working people had always been excluded from the advantages of industrial production (and, indeed, often from the very necessities of life also), they had been compelled to evolve alternative strategies for surviuval; not only in scavenging, begging or filching of inadequate material resources but also in a collective sense of their shared predicament, a pooling of human resources that would supplement a chronic want of material things; an extensive but fragile structure of mutuality and support. The demolition of these things and the capitalist victory over them have, of course, been expressed in the language of deliverance. The process that was to free people from old patterns of poverty was spoken of in terms of 'economic miracles', the *Wirtschaftswunder*, the magic of the markets – even the words are borrowed from the realm of religion and magic. And the capitalists staked their claims in this land that appeared to belong to no one – just as they had discovered that North America or Africa 'belonged' to no one – and there they tended needs and wants and desires that they had previously expended blood and money in suppressing. They refashioned the landscape, changed the shape, the beliefs and values and observances they had 'discovered' and set free. They planned and planted, ploughed up all that they found there – in the tradition of those traders and missionaries who discovered the East and saw there nothing but a neglected wilderness of scrub and thorn.

The imagery of this irruption into *terra incognita* gives rise to the same fables of older explorers – tales of undreamed-of riches to be found in a secret realm concealed in the folds of an inhospitable mountain range, the fortunes to be made, the treasure to be had for next to nothing, merely for daring to venture into that region. It is the world of Booth's Darkest

---

[15] Ibid.

England, a place like Stanley's Equatorial Forest, of 'monotonous darkness, with its malaria and its gloom, its dwarfish dehumanised inhabitants, the slavery to which they are subjected and their misery'.[16] The opening up of these places has furnished the marketers and salesmen with bold picaresque stories in which they are the heroes, epics of daredevilry and courage; a folklore of native peoples eagerly giving up everything they knew – pitiful enough it seemed to these outsiders – for the sake of a string of beads or a few bright ornaments.

It has all happened before. What we visited on half the world has come back to us. And it has brought something of the same unease that we took to the forest people and the peasant farmers, the aboriginals and the Indians. The disturbance and violence we have known is that which follows the collapse of all cultures that have been overrun or contaminated by one that is stronger. We have not always been able to recognize our kinship with those in distant countries whose traditions and defences have fallen into the same wasting sickness; if we had recognized it, we would know that their struggle and ours is the same.

All our experience has its ironic but elusive echoes, its sense of nothing new, its cyclical recurrences of expropriation and loss. Our absence of imagination and lapse of memory condemn us to relive again and again other, modified versions of the same story. Simply because the marauding has moved out of material territory to extend into realms that cannot always be seen, in the same way that the coastline of an unknown continent may be glimpsed through perpetual mists, this does not mean that it has ceased. Indeed, it could not. They are essential, the extracting and pillage, the undermining of settled ways of life, the threat of ruin to every fragile equilibrium, every gesture towards self-sufficiency, the breaking of patterns of resistance. We are dealing with what Rudolf Bahro calls 'the occupied regions of the consciousness',[17] the last, and most elastic frontier of colonialism.

The epic of capital does not pause. Inventive, mobile, unquiet, it strides with buccanneering rapacity unsubdued, making its violent inroads into the spirit and the imagination; and all our defences go down before the brigands and the counterfeiters, with their trinkets and cozenage. And in the plundered and trampled places it stages its dance of victory, its macabre celebration of the annexation of vast territories so rich, not in mineral or cropland, but in human resources.

Capitalism has always required a pool of unskilled labour: 'a disposable industrial reserve army', in Marx's words.[18] This available and malleable

---

[16] William Booth, *In Darkest England and the Way Out*, 1890 (C. Knight, London, 1970).
[17] Rudolf Bahro, *Socialism and Survival* (Heretic Books, London, 1982).
[18] Karl Marx, *Capital* (vol.I, Lawrence Wishart, London 1977).

population is necessary to fulfil the fluid and changing needs of capital. In the early nineteenth century, waves of labour went from the depressed villages into the industrial towns. Later, migrants from Ireland – those who had survived the effects of famine compounded by the ideological obsessions of those who might have mitigated them – filtered from Lancashire into the Midland cities and thence to London. On a smaller scale, refugees from Tsarist pogroms provided a fresh supply of workers for the sweated trades in London at the end of the century. In our time, arrivals from India, Pakistan, Bangladesh have fed a continuous need, not only for 'unspoilt' labour, but also for the kind of human scarecrow, absolutely indispensable for brandishing at the aspiring and the respectable, as a threatening underclass, into which they might fall if they let up on the striving and struggling to better themselves.

In recent years, that reservoir of unskilled labour has been replenished from within the heart of the working class itself. Many of the working-class young have been detached from an older tradition of labour as the established industries have declined. This has severed them from a sense of continuity, an expectation of what looked like enduring forms of work. The experience of the young has suggested to them that theirs is to be a quite different destiny. They are to be exempt from the poverty and the heavy workload of parents and grandparents. And indeed, they have grown within another culture; one which has itself developed around the products, fashions and music and images that belong to capitalism, and which involves the development of cults and rituals around style, a dedication to fantasies and shadows. It has in some ways been the creation of a new, artificial peasantry. Their values are characterized by acceptance, passivity and obedience to patterns of consumption and cycles of buying, the origins and purposes of which are as completely beyond their reach as were the recurring tasks and rhythms of agrarian society, out of which their forebears came. As a result, when they do arrive in the labour market, they are as effectively disadvantaged as if they had indeed just arrived from an alien culture. But if the young are unfamiliar with the rigours of capitalist labour, they are only too throughly grounded in their knowledge of its power to provide all that the heart could desire, and a great deal more besides. This suggests that they may be readier to conform to the disciplines or whatever forms of work await them than those migrants from less malleable cultures. On the other hand, they have been de-energized and deskilled, and might therefore be expected to be less amenable to the asperities of work. But it does mean that they will not be encumbered with any pre-capitalist or extra-capitalist memories which will prompt them to ask awkward questions. They will be less likely to be radicalized. For they will be migrating between two capitalist cultures.

A whole generation has grown, divided from a sense of continuing experience which became such a source of strength to the labour movement. The certainty of what awaited each new generation allowed the transmission of certain values and resistances, 'the degree to which', as Richard Hoggart observed in the 1950s, 'working people still draw, in speech and in the assumptions to which speech is a guide, on oral and local tradition . . . We must not pronounce it dead, when it still has remarkable life.'[19] The story of broken continuity which has been heard from the working-class community for a quarter of a century has gone further and deeper than the customary impatience of each new generation with its elders. 'You can't tell them anything,' the old have complained, 'they don't want to know. They won't listen. You can't talk to them' – all the metaphors are of interrupted transmission. And the response of the young towards those who have expected to prepare them for the life of hardship and work which they had known is, 'They're jealous of us. They live in the past. They don't understand. They don't like us to have all the things they never did.' And their metaphors have been of a new path, a fresh start – a transformation, in fact. The mutual incomprehension corresponds to the restructuring of the working class for a new phase of capitalism. The young speak as if they had been shaped for a different purpose: they are talking from the heart of another culture. And it is true that they have been subject to influences their parents scarcely knew; but whether their destiny will be so different from that of earlier generations is extremely doubtful.

The result of this is already clear. In the West Midlands in 1983 I spent some time with young people on a housing estate; many of them were newly married, some with children or pregnant; most were out of work. At nineteen or twenty they were having to confront a society which they did not understand. What do you have to do to get a house? What do you mean, a waiting list? How do you get on the waiting list? How long will we have to wait? It's driving me mad. It's breaking up our marriage, living in one room. My Mam is getting on my nerves. I've got a doctor's letter. If something doesn't happen, I'll join the army. I'm on tablets as it is. I want my kids to have a good start in life. We're arguing all the time. I'll run away. There's nothing to do round here. He's knocking me about. Me Mam put him out last night, he slept in a doorway. I can't stand it much more. I'll put them in care. I've tried to get rid of it. He's gone away. I don't know where. He said we'd have a better chance without him. Why doesn't somebody do something?

You are left with an impression of anger and incomprehension; the anxiety, the bitten nails, the smudged tattoos, the jumble-sale clothing,

[19] Richard Hoggart, *The Uses of Literacy* (Chatto & Windus, London, 1957).

the frustration at the broken telephone kiosk, the crying baby, the bus that doesn't come, the meter that runs out, the damp bedding, the bread covered with mildew. They wear clothes that have gone out of fashion – cork-heeled boots of plastic that wrinkle up, parti-coloured suedette jackets, flared trousers and mini-skirts; imitation pelt coats, dingy with wear; and inside the heads fragments of pop songs from the late seventies, memories of past fashions and dead crazes and fads that have passed, yesterday's excitements that are used up, novelties gone stale, things that leave so little of substance behind them. And they have no knowledge of what to do, how to cope, how to respond to the society that had seemed so benignly absent while they were young, giving them their freedom; and more often than not, protected by their parents in work, parents who were anxious they should go short of nothing. There is no one to instruct them – just a network of myth and rumour and half-truth, about who is getting a fabulous income from the DHSS, who has a good fiddle going, who is offering a bit of casual work, who bought the key of an empty flat for £50 and then found it occupied; rumours – increasingly justified – that benefit is to be cut, that people are going to be forced to work.

It was reminiscent of the response of people to the building of the new workhouses in the 1830s, when the stories went round that they were poisoning the paupers or chaining them up or even killing them. And the state of impotence and unknowing of these young people is not so different from that of earlier migrants, gullible people from the country, arriving in work-places and being sent on fools' errands, for a penn'orth of pigeon's milk, a sky-hook or a long weight; or being cheated out of a week's wages as a down payment on something they didn't need; or being employed for what sounded like a lot of money in relation to the place where they came from, only to find it will scarcely keep them in food; like the man from Trinidad who, when he arrived at Southampton docks, said: 'When the ship came in my heart was light; I think all them factories, there's plenty work for everybody. I didn't know them factories were people's houses.'

The young have been radically remoulded by and for capitalism. They have arrived from a culture created within it; so that even their ideas of a better world, their notion of freedom and youth, belong to capitalism itself.

Beneath the cliché of a 'generation gap' a profound breach was opened up, through which the transmission of working-class responses faltered. It occurred because the defenders of labour felt they had won permanent gains from capital, and the working class was urged to believe in the magic of capitalism – that we could all get richer painlessly. And because capitalism offered such real and tangible increase to people whose lives had been corroded by poverty, it looked as though all the changes associated with the post-war compromise must be benign. As a result, the young were surrendered to all the cultural influences of capitalism; a transfer that evokes a folklore of poor parents in the nineteenth century, yielding up their sons and daughters to those who could give them a better start in life; and recalls too the scandals of children in India being sold for adoption to wealthy childless couples in the West. At the time, it was hard to imagine that the children were being stolen away by forces that were far from benign. It recalls too, Jack London's description of the children of the East End, of how their energy and grace were to be subdued and defiled by the work that awaited them:

There is one beautiful sight in the East End, and only one . . . and it is the children dancing in the street when the organ-grinder goes his round. It is fascinating to watch them, the new born, the next generation, swaying and stepping, with pretty little mimicries and graceful inventions all their own, with muscles that move swiftly and easily, and bodies that leap airily, waving rhythms never taught in dancing-school . . . But there is a Pied Piper of London Town who steals them all away. They disappear. One never sees them again, or anything that suggests them. You may look for them in vain amongst the generation of grown-ups. Here you will find stunted forms, ugly faces and blunt and stolid minds.[20]

Today's Pied Piper comes in more appealing guise. But a generation has grown installed in another world, one that is merely another artefact of capitalism; but one so full of excitements and stimuli that it easily erases the memory of other ways of being in the world, other values. The consequences of this rupture can be seen, not only in the ease with which mass unemployment and poverty have been so readily imposed, but also in the lack of defences of young people, who are as disarmed and dispossessed in the presence of the labour market as if they had just arrived from outer space. The simile is not inappropriate: for outer space has become a last frontier, a metaphor of escape, whereas the place from which the young are returning is actually their inner space, which the years of parental protection and easy money offered. They are now on a long trek back from the journey into fantasy, the voyage home from cloud seven or over the rainbow, the garden of earthly delights, or from wherever it was that capitalist culture led them in the years of prosperity – that goblin market, where their childhood was expropriated and sold back to them. It is in this sense that the internal migration is the longest and perhaps most anguished of all. For the young have to *come back*; and they do so, defenceless and without resource.

The fact that the culture which has formed tham is a bizarre excrescence that has grown out of the universal selling of things, a strange aberrancy that sees human growth as a sort of by-product of merchandising, makes it

[20] Jack London, *People of the Abyss* (Journeyman Press, London, 1977).

no less intractable. The seizure of the energies and feelings of young people, their direct confiscation for profit, has put them at the mercy of images, ghosts and phantasms, through all the marketed stars and heroes; and in such a way that autonomy, independence and development become unthinkable apart from these things. Just as their limbs and hands were inextricably mixed up with the machinery they operated at a time of more primitive capital accumulation, so now their affections and spirit are entangled with the marketing of shadows; and their identity has taken root there. This is the country the young have inhabited; a never-never land, a land of heart's desire, a dream; but a place too, where energies and powers and abilities lie unused and wasting. Any return is likely to be resented.

When all the young people, those who have been disemployed, those who have grown without skills or function, come to be reintegrated into society as workers, will they discover an older tradition of labour? Will they become wise to their disinheritance, and set about building up the breached defences? Or will they accept the disciplines for the sake of the fruits by which they have been tethered by a deepening dependency over the years? Will they become so desperate that they will be amenable to any work, no matter how trivial and wanting in satisfaction? At present, only one thing is certain: the young are as disabled in dealing with the indignities that are reserved for them as the starving migrants from Ireland in the mid-nineteenth century, or those country people, swinging their legs in the long grass at the back of the carrier's cart and holding on to their bundle, on their way to a city tenement in their search for a better life.

The labour market that does lie in wait for them is transformed, so the instruction their parents might have offered them looks archaic anyway, even though much of the work they do, casualized and unprotected, gives that market something of a far older, nineteenth-century aspect. Many young people, when they first find a job (not work, not even really labour, much less a feeling of having a function) are grateful; even though it is not long before they become aware of the contradictions: the work is diminishing, their contribution is disregarded, the wage itsn't enough to live on, they are taken for granted. Sonya, a seventeen-year-old on the supermarket checkout, wearing a pink check overall with her name on a blue card pinned to her lapel, says that she doesn't know if that is for her benefit or the customers'. Certainly nobody ever calls her by her name. Her arms move at great speed as she sweeps the purchases out of the wire basket (and her wrist is covered with scratches from the rough wire), across the rubberized counter; and the electronic bleep sounds as she registers each item; she has to make a complete turn on her swivel-chair to weigh unwrapped fruit and vegetables, the aubergine, the half-kilo of tomatoes, the Red Delicious apples. It's not the work that is hard so much as the tension and the speed. The queue never gets any less; you can feel the impatience of people, you daren't pause, you don't even look up. At the end of each turn on the checkout she cannot just go and sit down, she has to carry on moving; it's as though the energy is still there.

'You can't let up. When I first started, I heard the sound of the tills in my ears all night. My Mum said I was doing it in my sleep. Now, I can just switch off. Nobody looks at you; they look at the price as it registers on the screen. Nobody talks to you; they're just bodies passing through. You're just part of the machine.' Sonya takes home £49 a week.

Tommy works fifty-five hours a week in an amusement arcade in a Midland town. A small, stocky young man of eighteen, with freckles and chestnut hair and a wide smile, he says it's better than doing nothing. The arcade has a yellow plastic front and a surround of miniature bulbs that go on and off, reflected in the wet pavement outside. The floor is of concrete, cracked and muddy. There are space invader machines as well as more traditional machines and games, where a ball bounces off a bulb which lights up and registers the score on a screen. Tommy wears a sort of butcher's apron with a pocket in front in which he keeps the keys to the machines. His job is to change money, to empty the games, and make sure nobody does any damage. He is paid £46 a week. 'The guy who owns it comes round twice a day to collect the money, so that there's never too much here. There was a robbery here once, two blokes with a gun, they got about six hundred quid. I do nick a bit when I'm emptying the machines, but I have to give it to my mate to go and change it, because if I'm standing here with a pocket full of tenpence pieces it's going to look obvious. I don't pay tax or insurance or anything, so it's money in hand. He tells me it's the equivalent of about £75 a week. I start at half past ten, finish at half nine. Half day off Thursday. I don't know who the owner is. He's called Dave. I just happened to be down here one day, and he was putting a notice up saying Help Wanted, so I said would I do. I'm eighteen. I live at home with my Mum, but I'm getting married in the new year. I enjoy life, but I don't like the work.'

There is a glass booth at one end of the arcade, with a high leather chair, an electric point, a kettle, a dirty jar of Sainsbury's coffee, a sugar-bag and a carton of long-life milk. Tommy goes to the baker's two doors away twice a day; eats a pasty and a doughnut. His Mum cooks for him when he gets home. 'I like dancing, but I'm mostly too tired.'

Greg is nineteen. He works in a video shop that is attached to a more general store – tobacco, sweets, papers, drinks and basic groceries. He was unemployed for two years when he left school, and has worked for twelve months looking after the video section of the shop.

'He's a Paki who owns it; he's all right, but he makes you keep a record of everything you sell, every newspaper and box of matches. I get £60 a week. It's the only shop on the estate, so a lot of the people have to use it. You can't fiddle. But I've got my own business on the side.'

Greg takes home half a dozen videos every Saturday night; and he hires them out to people at £1 a time. That way, they don't have to join the club, £5 membership. What actually happens is that his neighbours hire the films on Saturday night and bring them back on Sunday evening. One night, when I was visiting one of the neighbours, she told me that those who hire the films for £1 each swap them, so that three or four people will get four films for the price of one. On that particular Saturday she had hired *Herbie Goes Bananas* for the children; they had subsequently seen *Rocky II*, *Night Prowler* and *E.T.* It had been a day of marathon viewing, and the children were enervated and listless; but the triumph of having seen four movies for a pound easily overcame the sense of subjecting children of five, seven and ten to a whole day of television. Everyone was satisfied: Greg earned an extra £8; his employer continued to make a living; the people in the neighbourhood felt they had enjoyed something for nothing.

Gina worked in a café while she was still at school; it was owned by a friend of the family. When she left school he offered her a full-time job. As he didn't have any ready money, he asked her if she would mind working for a little while with no pay. It was that he had invested in some new tables and redecoration. He would pay her in due course. In the meantime she could draw the dole, and if anybody said anything, she could say she was just helping out a friend. Gina's father came from Italy in the 1950s, from Calabria. He worked in the brick-fields. She is a dark-haired, intelligent young woman who had wanted to be a children's nurse.

'I worked through the summer. Then at the end of the time he said, "I don't need you on Monday." "When shall I come in, then?" "Don't bother, that's finished." I asked him, "What about my money?" He'd promised me £35 a week plus tips. As it was, I made about a fiver a week from tips, that's all I had, right from May until September. He said, "You've had all you're getting." He said I could piss off. If I didn't leave him alone, he'd go to Social and tell them I'd been working all the summer, and I'd have to pay back the money I'd been drawing. I couldn't do anything. My Dad went up there, and they had a fight over it. But I never got the money. And they'd been friends since they came to this country thirty years ago. My boyfriend broke his window. But I still didn't get what he owed me.'

Sharon got a job in central London when she was seventeen. She lived far out, north of Barnet; a lively and stylish girl, she got a job in a boutique off Oxford Street, and felt that was all she really asked of life. To be in a place at the centre of the world, within reach of discos, on show; it meant she could use her talents at making clothes, could dress up. She had always loved the glamour and the feeling of those open-fronted shops, where music was always playing and the assistants were more like advertisements for the clothes, 'like models, really', than what she had always thought of as shop-workers. She was offered £48 a week, gross. This meant that she was paying almost £20 a week in fares, and she had to buy something to eat in the middle of the day; she had to leave home at 7.30 in the morning, and she was seldom home before 7.30 at night. It worked out that for a twelve-hour day away from home she had an income of less than £20

Barry has always been fat. He was teased and bullied at school. Once a gang of kids sexually assaulted and abused him. He was frightened and stayed away from school. As he was in his last year, it became hopeless to force him to attend. He used to wander the streets, spend his time in betting shops and launderettes or in the shopping centre. One day, as he was going past the railway arches, he met the owner of a rag-business who offered him a job. He spent much of his last two terms at school there, and has worked there since he left. The job is simple: he had to learn the differences between the various materials and sort them into their respective piles – wool, cotton, synthetics. The lorryloads come with the remnants from jumble sales, and they are then sorted into enormous bales. Some of the woollens are exported to South Africa and Bangladesh; Acrilan to Italy. Barry works between seven and ten hours a day, according to the amount of stuff. He stands at a formica-topped table under the light from a single bulb; a tinny transistor at this side, a mountain of rags to be sorted. He is happy here, in the companionship of occasional and casual workers – only Barry and one older man are regular employees, and even they pay no tax. Barry takes home £25 a week. The dust rises up from each garment; the whitewash is peeling from the brick; it is cold; there are festoons of dusty cobwebs around the walls. But nobody teases him, he feels he is doing something that he enjoys. His only dread is of being disturbed, of having to find alternative work.

Barry is more obviously akin to the children in Mayhew; there are many working in unofficial, casual ways, but for the most part they are shielded from scrutiny. Perhaps the most obvious example of the epic circularity of capitalism was the plight of the homeworkers in an inner city area. Mostly, these were young women with small children, living in council accommodation, and doing homework to eke out social security. Knitting, machining, making Christmas crackers, soft toys, buttonholes, sewing sequins, soldering. Christine had hired an industrial machine from the company that brought her leather to sew; by working ten hours a day, seven days a week, she could earn £45. She is twenty-one, and has been working for two years, since her husband left her with two babies. She says her eyesight has suffered, and her back is always painful. She is constantly tense, for fear that someone will hear the machine going. She has padded the room with pieces of foam rubber and Jiffy bags so that the neighbours don't suspect. The materials are delivered late at night so as not to arouse suspicion. She doesn't know who she works for; she simply had to phone Nina, from a card that was in the local newsagent's window. Her friend Janice knits; she will get £5 for a mohair sweater that will then sell for £50. She can do three or four in a week, but it means working late into the night, missing meals. She has done machining too, but she had to lock the children in the bedroom, because they got in the way and resented not having her attention. She felt imprisoned, and guilty that she couldn't look after her children as she would have liked to. She is a single parent; the children are now six and four. She is twenty-two.

5

Figures in the Landscape

Out of the clearances and improvements of the industrial cities a new poverty has been manufactured; a different sort of suffering has been conjured out of the better life we were promised. Those who rejoiced in the obliteration of the old squalor have lived to see another kind of dispossession emerge from the transformations.

The city is Leeds, but it could be anywhere. A chilly windy day in December. This is Hunslet, the site of Richard Hoggart's book about his childhood.[1] He had no illusions about the physical ugliness of the old working-class setting:

To a visitor, they are understandably depressing, these massed proletarian areas; street after street of shoddily uniform houses intersected by a dark pattern of ginnels and snickets (alley-ways) and courts; mean, squalid, and in a permanent half-fog; a study in shades of dirty-grey, without greenness or the blueness of sky; degrees darker than the north or west of the town, than the 'better end'. The brickwork and woodwork are cheap; the wood goes on too long between paintings — landlords are not as anxious to keep up the value of the property as are owner-occupiers. The nearest park or green open space is some distance away, but the terraces are gap-toothed with sour and brick-bespattered bits of waste-ground, and there is a piece of free ground half a mile away, called t'moor. Evocative name: it is a clinkered six-acre stretch surrounded by works and grimy pubs, with a large red-brick urinal at its edge..

Those streets were swept away in what William Morris presciently referred to in the 1880s as 'the great clearing of houses of 1955';[2] only what replaced them was something far removed from the socialist dream he had evoked. Even so, the superficial resemblances to and distorted affinities with what Morris foresaw haunt us with a persistent sense of a vision plundered.

[1] Richard Hoggart, *The Uses of Literacy* (Chatto & Windus, London, 1957).
[2] William Morris, *News from Nowhere*, 1891 (Lawrence & Wishart, London, 1977).

The replacements for the back-to-back houses were blocks of prefabricated flats and maisonettes, four storeys high, at right angles to each other, forming symmetrical courtyards with bright squares of grass at the centre. They are made of concrete, slabs of grey, studded with pebbles. The side of each square is perhaps eight yards long. There are pavements around the base of each; and inside each block is a corridor, with front doors on either side, like a long narrow street. The flats themselves are light and spacious, some of them with spectacular views over the changing city skyline.

The site is a gently rising slope, exposed, so the wind whistles around the concrete and whips the clothes on the plastic clothes-lines so that they billow and sing. It blows through the metal frames in the children's playground, and echoes in the lift-shafts; takes up the waste paper and dead leaves, and deposits them in temporary drifts in the corners of the courtyards.

Only a third of these flats are still occupied, because although only fifteen years old they are unfit and awaiting demolition. They are damp and structurally unsound. Pieces of concrete have fallen from the corners and lie smashed on the ground, panels of thick granite and pebbles. The tinned-up doors, pavements and walls are covered with graffiti; there is a choking smell of urine; dogs, wild and famished, without owners; broken plywood, jagged glass, stains of orange-brown rust where a pipe has overflowed, a growth of soft moss where the paths remain in permanent shadow. Plastic containers, silver-foil trays of meals from the take-away, chicken bones and decaying chips, cartons of washing-up liquid; egg-boxes and kitchen refuse tumbling from a split plastic bag; discarded pieces of furniture – a sofa that has been slashed with a knife is parked on a windy corner, a mocking suggestion of sociability; there is the shell of a television, and a stripped car-frame. The messages scrawled on the surfaces say Janice had her period here – penny a lick; beat inflation – eat cunt; Keep Britain tidy – kill a wog.

In the livid light of winter afternoon there are few people to be seen. Some of the flats have been wrecked; others have gaping black apertures, smoky glass and singed walls where they have been fired – either by occupants desperate to get out, or by persecutors who want them removed. The buildings are hard and angular, without ornament or amenity, the barest form of dwelling-place; stripped, it seems, to the most naked functional limit. And perhaps the physical appearance of these places reflects something of what has happened to the people here. Here, you feel, humanity has been flayed, excoriated, reduced tot he very core, so that the most intense and deepest feelings are exposed. In these places people have been broken, in order that they might be reconstructed in the image of capitalist selling; but something has gone cruelly wrong. For most of those who live here are too poor even to begin that process of healing. The stripping of people to irreducible characteristics – young, old, male, female, black, white, gay, employee, unemployed – has been accomplished in order that we should seek to recreate a sense of identity through all the market-suggested appropriate characteristics. We are offered the possibility of buying back our plundered substance, in ways that are permitted through the mass markets, the conformist images. Perhaps this is why the resistances to that dispossessing power are based upon alternative modes of reconstruction of those basic features – women, blacks, gays; a refusal to accept the manufactured restorative proposed to us by the powers that have dispossessed us in the first place.

The few passers-by in these places are in a hurry – to get out of the wind, to avoid the threat round every corner, the mugger in the lift, the rapist on the stair, the attacker in the shadow.

And yet, these places were built to offer the poor a better life. How is it that the relief from that older, more familiar horror of those airless back-to-backs could have led to this deeper sense of subordination and impotence? The external landscape is not, of course, where people live. The public spaces have been colonized by anxiety and fear. Most people retreat into the domestic interior. Most of the flats here are not without basic warmth, food, even entertainment. But they are still beleaguered. Their doors are bolted, even barricaded, against the human predators. And there is a kind of perverse comfort to be gained in reciting the litany of dishonoured humanity: the child-molesters and rapists, the gypsies and the queers, the glue-sniffers and alkies; the squatters. And the stories are the same everywhere: the woman raped in broad daylight on her way to collect the children after school; the boy knifed after a party and left bleeding in the snow; the family feud over the daughter who stole her mother's boyfriends; the stepfather molesting a 6-year-old, while the mother acquiesced because she was afraid of losing him; the injury to the old woman for the sake of her pension book, and who needed thirty-six stitches in her head; the fear of saying what you know to the police in case of revenge.

The more you enter into the experience of the poor, the clearer it becomes that poverty in the rich world is not the mitigated and protected experience it is assumed to be by those who are not themselves poor. The rag in the window-frame doesn't exclude the draughts; the hot fumy air from the paraffin stove makes the children cough. Meals are sketchy and inadequate – the stained teapot and the sliced loaf, the packets of chips, the boiled potatoes and the tin of Heinz spaghetti rings; the few pence worth of sweets and packets of biscuits, the dented tins bought cheap without labels. The window was broken by somebody who did the meter; and has been repaired with a piece of carboard. The money that was stolen is being deducted by the DHSS every week, because you can't prove you didn't do it yourself. The fallen fences between the gardens are overrun with rank grass and feral cats; pieces of rusty metal and old furniture and sodden wood. The windows are streaked with dirt from the winter-long rains. The plastic flowers are covered with dust, the carpet has lost its colour, the plastic lino in the kitchen is greasy and dark with muddy shoeprints, the gas-stove choked with pots that have boiled over. The red plastic dustbin stained with egg and the sink discoloured by tea-leaves; the walls defaced by children and the sticky marks of hands; the cigarette burn that melted the material of the sofa cushion.

Life consists of long walks to the shops to save bus fares, and buying outdated cakes and rusty tins, so that some days you don't know what you'll eat until you open it and discover that you've got a tin of stewing steak or a tin of rhubarb for your meal. The sameness of the days; the rent stopped at source from the DHSS, the money from the unpaid gas bill or the electricity debt also stopped, so that a woman with four children has £24 to spend for food and clothing, as well as current spending on gas and electricity.

Husbands and wives part so that each will get separate money – that way they may receive a little extra. There is always the temptation of the moneylenders, to whom you discover, when it's too late, that you're paying eighty per cent interest; and in the off-licence on the edge of the estate, with its window boarded up, there is always the chance for a bottle of cider or cheap wine for an evening's escape. Then there are the denunciations of neighbours to Social Security, and the surprise visit, and the attempt to prove you're cohabiting; the humiliation of being told you can have a different man every night if you like, but not the same one. There is the scavenged furniture – the man who fished a radiogram out of the canal and made it work; the woman who dragged a mattress from the rubbish-tip because the promised visit from the Social never came.

Poverty, like everything else, has been modernized, rationalized. Or rather, the people have been rationalized so that poverty can be maintained, would be a more accurate formulation.

In the rich societies of the West the poor cast an unflattering light upon the wealth that produces their poverty. The poor live in the constant presence of that crude mechanism which drives us all, but from which the rich successfully buy exemption: the intensifying penetration of market relationships into every aspect of our lives. This means that freedom begins at the point where money is available; and the quality of that freedom depends upon the quantity of disposable money. The creation of wealth, with its spiritual overtones, is accompanied by an equally opaque process, which is the spiriting away of the human substance, and its reappearance, held fast and frozen in the form of commodities and symbols and services that can be reclaimed only if it profits others.

The effect of consumer capitalism over the past half century has been not to corrupt people through materialism but to invite us to depend less and less upon each other and ourselves, and more and more upon what can be bought: that such an opportunity appeared benign to people haunted by drudgery should not surprise us. But once we have relaxed into that process, it becomes harder and harder to disengage from it; a dependency is set up for which the only answer is more of the same. All the exhortations to let go, enjoy ourselves, all the images of deliverance and freedom are only the surface manifestations of a deepening subordination. While incomes keep on rising there is no reason to question it; there is no awareness of how the human is plundered and has to be retrieved through money. But when it ceases, then we are more able to take stock of what has occurred. And the poor gain no immunity from this process. All the sorry clichés in which they speak – pressure and inability to cope, being overwhelmed, breaking down, cracking up, going under, falling apart, being stranded, marooned, imprisoned; cooped up, caged, losing heart; feeling hopeless, having to run to stand still, existing rather than living, bored and empty, leading a half-life in the shadows – this is the experience we scarcely have words for, so their attempts to express their pain dissolve in what sound like banalities. Their lives are played out in constant exile from all the freedoms that begin with the spending of money; and which have to stand us in the stead of all other liberties – not the least of which is the possibility of choosing another way of being in the world. It is from this recognition that the poor have no escape. For them, of course, even the leashed and restricted nature of market-distributed freedoms is not seen as such; but looked at from the prison that confines them, that freedom appears absolute.

It is only in the light of this that we can understand something of their experience; we can see why they refer to the blocks of flats and tenements as prisons; or why the chalk-marks on the walls plead, as Beatrix Campbell observed, 'Get us out of this hell.'[3] It also begins to make sense of some of the strange phenomena that used to baffle us when we read about them in the newspaper, – especially in the places where they first appeared, in the United States – those individuals who go out and gun down half a dozen strangers at a luncheonette counter because they didn't feel good, the girl who murdered her teachers because she hated Monday mornings; the figures hanging from the top of a skyscraper and threatening to kill themselves, while the television cameras gather in the street below; acts of 'gratuitous' violence that are the misshapen form of a social protest that has been stifled. The response is that these things are incomprehensible,

[3] Beatrix Campbell, *Wigan Pier Revisited* (Virago, London, 1984).

can never be explained. The role of the society in the production of these damaged individuals is the taboo that prohibits understanding. The pretence that is being protected is that there are no longer any social determinants, only free individuals; a hypocrisy well caught by the old unionist who said 'We used to live under capitalism; now they tell us we live in society.' Such extreme acts are only the furthest responses to a torture beyond endurance: the mangled needs, the enforced privations, the taunting without end. Needs which are thwarted by the heaping up of false answers that leave them untouched bring forth their own monstrous and deformed revenge.

When the poor attack each other, fire the ghettos, mutilate others and damage themselves with drugs or alcohol, it has this advantage to the rich, that the connection between them and the poor has been so effectively shrouded that they cannot be accused of complicity in the damage that is done to the poor. The poor can be safely left to demonstrate to the world their instability and violence; and to show that they are poor because they deserve nothing more; while the wealthy proceed, serene and inviolable in the enjoyment of their just deserts, going about their business and only dimly aware of the red glow in the night sky, barely perturbed by the sirens of the ambulances that fetch out their freight of torn and wounded humanity from the impenetrable ghettos. The rich have been delivered from the consequences of their own actions; and it is perhaps only to be expected that this absolution leads to a certain jubilation, an assertiveness which they had, for a brief levelling interlude after 1945, foreborne to parade. After all, the poor ask nothing more than to be able to imitate them; no longer to expropriate, let alone abolish, them.

This is the means by which capitalism proposes that it will cease to be a subject of dispute. It is our natural element. And politics becomes merely a source of mild and equable argument between conservatives and liberals. Those who ask radical questions become anathematized as extremists or wreckers.

But the advantages the rich have gained have actually been won at a price far greater than the money, which represents only their surface value. By an act of faith – a sort of secular version of Pascal's wager about God – we have yielded our freedom to choose other social and economic possibilities for the promise that this one will go on for ever providing us with the money that will permit it to redeem its own promise of perpetual increase. It is a singular gamble; for it makes us all votaries, petitioners, dependants. It gives an incontestable urgency to the persuasion that we must adapt, make way for all the necessary changes required or the regeneration of capitalism; indeed, accept our subservience to its world-wide dictates, and gracefully embrace those service industries into whcih we are now to be pressed. If you are rich, it is perhaps not easy to understand this surrender: a ready and increasing supply of money and the freedoms this provides are a powerful generator of illusions: indeed, the industries devoted to fantasy in the West testify to this; and the decaying area of human autonomy that remains outside market dependency is barely perceived.

The word 'poverty' of course covers a variety of states and conditions. Even the Poor Law Commission of 1834 – not the most sensitive official monument to concern for the poor – sought to distinguish between 'poverty' and 'indigence'; while Gandhi's *aparigraha* (non-possession) is a very different experience from the dispossession of the shanty-town; monastic renunciations have little in common with the sufferings of landless labourers, or even with the pressures and insecurities of the North American ghetto. Our poverty has ben redefined in such a way that all attempts to determine how much would be needed to lift people out of want appear inconclusive and unattainable, or else hopelessly, menacingly costly; and this is because poverty has been set not against need, but against an unlimited capacity to produce and sell. In this way, it has become an insoluble problem; or rather, its solution lies not in remedial action to compensate the poor but with the rich, in whose image the poor have been remade.

6

Aspects of the New Poor

In the living places of the rich – a majority in North America, Japan and Western Europe – the debris and overspill of sated markets heap up. It is not only all the things covered with dust from under-use, the passing fads and caprices; it is also the colonizing of time by gadgets and appliances that purport to enrich it; the food blender and the wok, the waffle irons and the sandwich toaster, the barbecue kit and the garden furniture and patio slabs. But these are only the most glaring symbols. There are also the unread paperbacks, bought because they are widely discussed, the collection of music for all moods, most of which never seem to occur in the haste and exhaustion of living. All the vast perishability of breathless and busy lives soon passes away and leaves so little memory, but so much in the apartment. Experiences succeed each other, soothing or stimulating, exicting or stirring, but always *laving*, wearing away; until they become a torrent that flows through the narrow gorge of the individual sensibility; and over-brimming and occupied life of people trying to rise and to be equal to the immense impersonality of the markets; these, because they are indefatigable and infinite, always defeat us in the end, dwarf and diminish us. All those who expend themselves trying to keep abreast, striving to be in the swim, in the know, anticipating what is in the wind, the next phase, the latest thing . . . The lives of the rich are overwhelmed by sensations and experiences and services.

The houses of the poor present a caricature of the superior products with which the rich are burdened. There are always enough inferior or second-hand things that make the interiors of the poor similarly cluttered; only it is a different order of objects that encumber them. One of the most obvious qualities of today's poverty is its *permeability*, saturated as it is by the images and the simulations of opulence – the onyx and marble and gold- and silver-plate, the fake leopard-skin covers, false ocelot, the plastic Louis Quatorze table, the imitation leather, the sham velvet, the mock jewels and simulated silver – everything contributes to destroy any sense of an existential antagonism between the rich and the poor; which, in turn, mitigates any sense of class divisions. The rich become models to the poor; to imitate and to aspire becomes the only true path. In this way, the rich are no longer the enemies of the poor. They are merely more fortunate; and are as dedicated to the idea of growth and increase as the poor are. In much the same way, the economic surpluses that are heaped up in such lavish quantities by the rich in backward countries are employed to support luxury and excess, which ensures that the aspirations of the poor are captured and manipulated even as they are conceived.

This is why for the majority of the poor in the West it has become meaningless to filter their dispossession through political argument. They merely live their poverty, and seek, as best they may, to redress it. And that means as individuals. In this way, they are perhaps more directly responsive to the system than all the politicians who talk of improving it, reforming it or, rather rarely now, of changing it. If the poor appear to be politically disaffectd, this may be because surviving is a full-time occupation. And one of the reasons why there has been no significant outcry in recent years, why 'intolerable' levels of unemployment have seemed, after all, quite bearable, is that the poor have been compelled to find personal solutions to socially imposed problems.

A culture of surviving has evolved, a form of private – even secret – enterprise, whereby many poor people come to regard state benefit as a sort of basic income, by no means adequate to live on, and which it becomes their object to augment. Those who exist on state benefit alone – and these are the majority – do indeed suffer. But these tend to be not only the respectable poor but also the most cowed, the most helpless: the disabled, the old, the under-endowed, the chronic sick, unsupported mothers. But many vigorous younger people have become very inventive in eking out an insufficient official income. This is not to concede the argument of those who believe that the world is full of scroungers (that modernized version of a more ancient fear that the poor-house was becoming a castle of indolence). Indeed, without the expedients to which some of the more able and energetic poor have recourse, the social peace would be seriously threatened; the stability of the system of which the rich are such stout defenders depends crucially upon the secret world of unofficial enterprise, which absorbs the energy and abilities of those who might otherwise become severely estranged from it. This is why all the publicity given to efforts to stamp out fraud, to pursue those improperly claiming benefit, is all pure mummery. A few ritual prosecutions signal the disapproval of authority, and above all reassure those who are working, often exploited and ill-paid, that something is being done. In fact this can only skim the surface of all the clandestine and marginal ways in which people survive; and those who are loudest in their denunciations of spongers know quite well that a certain submerged *laissez-faire* economy is the necessary and acceptable price to be paid for maintaining social stability.

It is always interesting to contrast the stories of how people get by today with memories of the thirties and before. Then, people talk of how they went out with a wicker basket to gather mushrooms, or nutting or blackberrying, to increase the supply of food for sale as well as for consumption; gathering sloes and crab-apples; picking herbs for remedies – comfrey leaves and dock leaves; flowers for sale – violets, bluebells, primroses; dandelions – leaves for food, roots for grinding into coffee, flowers for wine-making; scavenging for fuel on the coal tips and in the woods; making a meal out of a ham bone and a few vegetables, keeping hens, poaching rabbits and game, making and mending, patching and darning, repairing shoes on a last in the cellar, making clothes. These appear archaic contrivances now, not at all suitable for dealing with the contemporary experience of being poor. It is not a question of the efforts required in order to subsist, but of getting the money for at least a few of the purchases from which the poor are excluded. And in spite of recession and hardship, it is essentially the availability of money – by hook, and not rarely by crook – that keeps many poor people, if not satisfied at least attached to the society to which little else reconciles them.

One of the reasons why all attempts to measure poverty in terms of money always remain unsatisfactory as soon as they exceed barest subsistence is that poverty in the rich world is an elaborate artefact, created by a dynamic process between money on the one hand and its inextricable and living relationship with social and psychological structures on the other. Money is thus always only one half of an equation that is not static, but is continually evolving; so that even as the income of the poor increases, it can always be recuperated by the rich through an ever more complex process of adding value to the necessities of the poor, or of finding new and more expensive ways of answering basic need that will maintain profit and increase. It is the rich who control both the experience and the measure of poverty. This is why the only way in which the poor can imagine escape from poverty is by a sudden accession of money, by means of which they can, at one leap, move ahead as individuals of a dynamic process that goes on perpetuating poverty and manufacturing new forms of dispossession, even in the presence of the most spectacular creation of wealth. Hence the power of the big win, the lucky number, the windfall, Lady Luck; and it should not surprise us when the poor decide to make this ideology work for themselves. It originates, after all, not with them.

A new culture of surviving has grown up in this shadowy and largely unexplored territory. Just as there existed a secretive world of working-class resistance at the time of the industrial revolution, so there exists today a hidden and closed culture; but with this difference, that it isn't a life apart, but has been shaped in the image of the dominant market culture, of which its values are an exaggeration and reflection. This is why it is in the interests of authority, as well as in the interests of the poor, to keep it out of sight. As a caricature of majority values it does not show them in a flattering light; it is necessarily conservative, parasitic and dependent. It is a parallel rather than a submerged culture. Its detachment from any significant political consciousness makes it profoundly attractive to the rich, a price well worth paying, because it is not they who pay. The sub-culture clings, as it were, to the underside of all the rhetoric about the need for rewards, incentives and enhanced profit.

The way in which sections of the young and vigorous poor live, those whose energies are not required for any positive contribution to society, has certain elements reminiscent of the Victorian underworld, but many other features which have no roots in our past. Perhaps it resembles the experience of poor whites in the United States: a life of recklessness and spontaneity, intense emotion and fast living, allied to a heart-on-the-sleeve sentimentality, a here-today-gone-tomorrow fatalism; a celebration of the arbitrary and aleatory, the image of the wheel of fortune; a saga of feuds and passions, people who take the law into their own hands, fierce loyalties, betrayals and implacable revenge; a hedonism and living in the present of people who prefer to be known by their Citizens' Band names, symbolic of an assumed and elective identity – Sapphire and Lady X, Zombie and Gipsy and Hot Rod and Phantom; a life that is part fantasy and play-acting, part shaped by a media-determined mixture of frontier life, video and trucking society. It is a life of sepulchral fantasies where, after a couple of bottles of vodka, a group of young adults will go off in the night to a country churchyard and dig up the graves of the long dead; a fascination with the occult and the beyond, late nights spent with the Ouija board, contacting the spirit of slaves or Red Indians or pirates; a life of junk-food, adult comics and battered Cortina Mark Twos.

This picaresque fantasy life is the ideological counterpart of a far more modest semi-outlawry: it is the cultural expression of a marginalized or informal economy. What is, in effect, a relatively small area of unofficial enterprise creates a space in which quite disproportionate fantasy luxuriates. The poverty and destitution of an earlier stage of capitalism permitted less extravagance of imagination: literal survival occupied all the space of the informal economy, and its cultural expression was far more prosaic – the penny dreadfuls, the stories of Maria Marten or Sweeney Todd, tales of ghastly murders and crimes, all recounted in realistic detail. The more florid contemporary version exists in the benevolent shadow of welfare capitalism which has assured physical survival.

The ideology, brutal and damaging with its simplistic morality and intense passions, is that of people who say of their lives that they feel 'empty'; who have to make things happen; who fill the long tedious days with phantasmal projections of a reach-me-down culture that belongs mainly to the entertainment industry.

As they talk together in the warmth and indolence of a long summer afternoon, Crystal Gayle on the record-player, talk turns to darker stories: a gang of bikers coming over to get their own back on somebody who grassed one of them up; Michelle, who had petrol poured through her letter-box and the house set on fire, had to jump out of the bedroom window with her little girl in her arms; she broke both ankles; a boy who crashed his bike into a lorry at 90 miles an hour, because he felt he had got as much of this life as he could. He had been given a fabulous funeral, a wreath in the shape of a motorbike, life-size. There is the story of the boy who got so high on pills that he held his hand over the gas flame until it was cooked like steak; the lad who could only gain acceptance by the group by displaying his recklessness and lack of fear; and for a dare had crossed the central reservation of the motorway, and driven a mile on the wrong side. The stories of lawlessness and excitement have a strong competitive edge; many are exaggerated, and for the most part, they all end in minor lawbreaking. It is boredom, Christine says, that makes you want to cause things to happen; and in the vacuum of those empty functionless hours, the fantasy sometimes spills beyond the overworked imagination, and invades the real world in an act of cruelty or violence. This is what made her accept a 'contract' to beat up the wife of a stranger she met in the pub one night, and for which she and her friends were paid £100.

It isn't difficult to see the relationship between this daredevil and freebooting resourcefulness, and the world of more legitimate risk-taking and enterprise, with all its rewards. It is a caricature of a free market economy.

Even so, there is something alien in the menacing fantasy and the deadpan violence; the amoralism; the paramountcy of money, the rootless identity and the unstable relationships. It is like a visit to another culture; a defensive and enclosed world, in which adults seem to be playing at being children, while the children play at being adults, showing off the gold in their ears and their cute hair-dos, their disco-dancing and posters of Boy George; while the babies are almost like dolls, passed around and petted, pacified with sweets and cough-syrup to keep them quiet, and a dose of whisky when it's time for the child-parents to go out; and the toddlers eat lollies and biscuits and crisps, drink Coke and flavoured milk, listen absently to the sexual scandal and horror stories, gaze briefly at the flickering video where a man is inventing some new outrage upon the body of a captive woman; and the grown-ups talk in fatalistic terms about broken hearts and starting over of Country-and-Western philosophy, how you always hurt the one you love, raindrops hiding the tears, the heartaches, the grudges and the retribution – now it's your turn to cry, and watch me walk away like you walked out on me.

But that isn't the whole story. The fantasy only partly conceals a bleaker, almost unbearable reality – Kelly's four children taken into care because they had run beyond her control and wrecked the house (the oldest is six); the boy-friend accused of beating a two-month old baby and fracturing her skull; the father who molested Christine for ten years ('I thought that's what all fathers did'); the brutalities of six months in DC, the dishonourable discharge from the army. The pain of Billy is almost tangible when he talks of what drove him to leave Aberdeen and come South. He was separated from his wife and had three bairns to bring up. He lived in a tenement, in a room with an old-fashioned gas-fire that didn't have a proper extractor.

'It was a freezing day in January, and the lad came home from school and said 'Can we have the fire on Dad?' The snow was on the ground. It was only a small flat, the boy and girl slept in the living-room. And I left the fire on low when they went to bed. But they must've got cold in the night and turned the fire up. When I got up in the morning, this fire was blazing away. I couldn't wake them; they were both unconscious. He was six, and she was five. I rushed out into the street with them, and the neighbours came out, and we rolled them in the snow to bring them round. The girl came to: but by the time the ambulance arrived, the lad was dead. The Gas Board had known that the extractors were dangerous; they should all have been changed long before. We were told by a solicitor that we could claim big compensation from the Gas Board – the room had been full of carbon monoxide. When she knew what had happened, my wife came back to me. After a loss like that, we should try again to make a go of it, the important thing was to be together. So she left the bloke she'd left me for and came back. But little by little, I realized it wasn't me she'd come back for but the claim against the Gas Board. I wasn't interested; it wouldn't bring the lad back. She said we should sue them for every penny we could get. I said I don't want compensation, I want my bairn back, and that I couldna have. So she left me again. She had only come back for the sake of the money she thought she was going to get.'

All these stories are from an inner city area; a few summer days spent with the people who come and go in the terraced houses, with their crumbling plaster, make-shift furniture; and outside, the pot-holed roads and neglected pavements, small factories to let, corner shops and second-hand clothes stores; 'short-life' housing, doors swollen with damp, gardens full of rubbish. it is a formerly respectable street; built on a slope, so that the roofline of each house descends in well-defined steps. There is a view of the whole suburb – the blighted inner area, with the shells of mills, workhouse and chapels still brooding shapes; the central shopping area with a gleaming white tower; the vast spread of new estates on the hills. The houses in these streets have deteriorated; the wreathes of acorn- and oak-leaf-moulding at the corbels have cracked and worn away; doors have been reinforced by pieces of plywood painted black or mauve; brickwork has been painted crimson. The chassis of an abandoned car has not been moved, and has collapsed into the road; there is a scattering of broken glass; dust and waste paper in constant movement.

The economic activities of this group of the poor are rather unspectacular by comparison with the fantasies; they consist, for the most part, in modest undisclosed earnings, casual and unofficial jobs, petty crime, receiving, a parallel system of barter and exchange, the provision of services, and even manufacture out of discarded or obsolete goods: front rooms are full of oily motorbike parts, clapped-out engines, old record players, leather jackets, lengths of material, bits of radio and television sets, sewing machines, broken toys, clothes that have fallen out of fashion, part scavenged, part nicked, sometimes bought or received from charity. The old people look at the newcomers – the boys with their decorated and customized motorbikes, the luminous paint and metallic sheen, death's head transfers and Nazi emblems, their denim, leather and chains; and the girls with their tattoos and short skirts, and they are frightened and repelled. How can they say anything to these young people about labour as the source of their pain and also of their hope, when so many of the young have never worked? At the same time, the young do not know how to express to their elders their own different sense of what it is to be poor. How can a party of Labour touch them, when they have been raised to a vast luxuriance of fantasy that has bred in the margin of the security that Labour struggled for? They have grown up to think of money not allied to work, but as something mysteriously as likely to be found through a big win or a break-in or a talent for disco-dancing or a Bingo jackpot, as it is from selling their labour. The old people, schooled by the oppressive discipline of those factories, see simply that these oppressions have been removed from the lives of the young. They can understand it only as they would have understood their own deliverance from these things, as a setting free. But what they do not see is that so many of the young have been released into absence; no function or purpose gives definition to their lives, no collective experience shapes their development. It is in this vacancy that aching and amorphous needs grow. There is a terrible pity in it, the boys circling through the echoing streets on their bikes, engines tuned to reverberate, in a search for escape from the escape in which they have grown, with their dreams of violence, fantasies of action, longings to do something in the world; while the old are stranded, with a lifetime of memories that are of use neither to themselves nor to their grandchildren. The only shared experience of the young is the collectivism of mass markets, and the cults that grow up around their own alienated substance, locked up and sold back to them in ways that deny them access to it; and they circle round commodities, in the same way that they circle the streets on their bikes, exiles, in a measureless estrangement from their own lives.

They survive, even though the human cost is high. Crises flare up and die; the social workers intervene sometimes, briefly, and then pass on to even more urgent calls. The problems remain inaccessible to politics; and you remain a powerless spectator at a wrecking of lives, a marring of the youth and health of young people.

For what makes the condition of the poor so much worse is that most of us do not want to reach it; we scarcely even know that it exists, for as long as it all shows up only in crime statistics and not in any more radical threat to the majority, it can be contained. Individuals can be persuaded to take personal responsibility for a pain that is socially produced; and society, in consequence, gains absolution from the consequences of its own practices. That is not to say that there are no damaged individuals who would remain so in any imaginable society; only that the socially created element that compounds the pain has been effectively denied. The result is that people carry a burden which is the obverse of all the concern for the individual of which we are so proud: of course we cherish individuals, especially when they will obligingly internalize so much misery – that single largest artefact of a society that offers selling things as its ultimate balm and its deepest truth.

The poor live in a distortion of the society we all inhabit; a more naked version, a cruder exemplification of its values. The reason why the voice of the poor is stifled is that they tell us too much about ourselves; our bartered freedoms and diminishing autonomy and dying control over our lives. In this way, we intensify the injury to them. But we should be under no illusion that there is anything easy or cushioned about poverty in its contemporary form.

There is a vast uncharted realm between subsistence and sufficiency; and another country between sufficiency and the strivings for satisfaction in the rich societies of the West. This terrain has been obscured by our experience of passing between a capitalist version of poverty and its version of plenty; this immediate shift from extremes occludes all the space in between, in which a more human life might be constructed.

All societies involve the interplay of (often scant) material resources and (mostly abundant) human energy, ingenuity and skills. In most societies the latter have been the more significant feature. In recent times, however, the productive power of the Western world has been applied in such a way that the former have been in the ascendant. These have eclipsed the human resources, caused older forms of skill, earlier storehouses of wisdom, to decay and to be replaced by marketed substitutes. This is the key to what Illich has described as 'modernized poverty'.[1] The erasure of the ground between bare survival and sufficiency has created our experience of oscillating between a debilitating poverty and an oppressive plenty which nevertheless always falls short of being enough.

A way of life which depends on quantitative increase for its own sake, the society of the autonomous economy, will never be able to relieve poverty; for all definitions of it are pitted against some inhuman measure that robs them of meaning.

At times, it has been possible to feel the re-making of poverty. It is like an invisible presence in the lives of the poor; a process of creating penury and insufficiency out of plenty.

I have known Valerie for some years. She lives with her three children (aged eight, six and five) in a new house on a new estate. She is separated from her husband, anxious to be a good mother to her children, determined not to let them go into care. But she is afraid. She fears being overwhelmed by them. She pleads, begs, bargains with them; negotiates exhaustingly to gain their compliance, their co-operation. One day when I was there she was asking them to tidy their room; she said, 'Go and have a look at it.' The foam quilts were on the floor; they had been torn, and there was a drift of pieces of greenish sponge all over the room. The single beds were overturned. On the floor were pieces of silver wrapping-paper from sweets, pages torn from books, the limbs of dolls; broken things, pieces of plastic, a china mug. There was scribble on the walls in biro and felt-tip, pervasive smell of urine from the mattresses, which had also been torn – even the open window did not dispel the sharp smell. The light switch had been torn from its socket and hung from the wires; the plaster around it had been poked with a pen, and lay in a small crumbled heap on the wooden floor. The walls were bare of any ornament, though there were sellotape marks where some posters had once been fixed. There was nothing in the room that had not been wrecked; a frightening incontinence. Valerie locks then in the room until they will do as she asks; but the devastation is only made worse. Kieron opens the window and says he will jump if his mother will not open the door.

The rest of the house is little better; the mud has dried on the rubberized floors and comes away in reddish dust; clothes have been dropped, and left as they fell; earrings, shoes, fluffy animals stained and discoloured, patches of spilt drink that have dried sticky and sweet-smelling; the gas-stove is choked with saucepans that have overflowed;

[1] Ivan Illich, *Tools for Conviviality* (Calder & Boyars, London, 1973).

clean clothes have been thrust into blue plastic bags; the chairs have been wrecked by having been jumped on; there are holes in the red plastic of the sofa. The television is the only thing that works: this, says Valerie, is the only way she has of regulating the children's behaviour.

The children are full of energy and life, and Valerie's love for them makes her pour upon them everything she can lay her hands on. She does private cleaning when they are at school (and the irony of the state of her own house is not lost on her); she has done soldering at home when they are in bed; she denies herself, eats nothing but bread, toasted almost black, and margarine, wth cups of sweet tea. She is thin and indifferent to her appearance, though she gets clothes from a friend whose husband works for the local authority. She senses in her children the growth of disordered wants and hungers, unchannelled needs and appetites she cannot satisfy; she is confronted by a voraciousness in those she loves best in the world, an undifferentiated avidity that she cannot still.

She lives on a housing development on the edge of a new town. The estate is constructed like a medieval village, with timbered gables, around a central green. The houses are fawn-coloured brick, roofed in dark red tiles; but although only five years old they show signs of significant wear and tear: some of the timbering has warped and is being replaced; the blue paint on the doors has chipped; the inferior metal letterboxes are tarnished. A lattice of cotoneaster and pyracanthus shrubs forms a spiky web that catches crisp papers and bags and sweet-wrappings.

The estate consists of nothing but houses. Valerie seldom goes into the town centre, which is five miles and a 45p bus ride away. There is a small shopping centre, a doctor's surgery and a chemist's shop on a bigger estate, a mile away; and that is the furthest limit of her excursions for weeks at a time.

During the time I knew her Valerie hired a video to keep the children happy during the holidays; but it was repossessed because she could not keep up the payments. The telephone, which had been installed while her husband was still there, was cut off, even though it was her only way of keeping in touch, not only with her family in Ipswich but also with friends in other parts of the town. She did not see her mother for three years because neither could afford the fare. The gas bill went unpaid; and this, together with arrears that had accumulated during her first marriage, meant that the accumulated debt was several hundreds of pounds. The same thing happened with the electricity. Now she has rent, gas and electricity payments stopped at source, so that she draws £15 from the DHSS for herself and the three children; this is augmented by £19.50 child allowance.

Most of her income goes on food. For two or three months she kept a record of her expenditure. The most obvious feature of the food she bought was that much of it was ready-made and processed. It looked like convenience food; in fact it is the most expensive way to eat, and it depended entirely upon the tastes that her children had grown up with: an addictive *need* had long ago been created for certain products; and they would not eat anything else. This meant that she was buying mechancially reconstituted meat, burgers and steaklets; processed cheese, canned goods – ravioli, spaghetti, tinned peas; soft drinks, sweets, instant puddings, chocolate, reassembled and barely identifiable luncheon meat, tinned steak. The innocence of these sad purchases for a family of four is only too apparent. For instance, the breakfast cereal – plain puffed wheat with sugar and chocolate – meant that she was actually paying for a basic staple that had been processed in ways that made it absurdly expensive. Much of the food the family ate was highly value-added, had been through elaborate and costly industrial processes, ready for consumption in a form that cost Valerie disproportionate amounts of her income. Crisps and oven-ready chips are two of the most expensive ways to eat potatoes, and frozen ravioli the dearest way to eat pasta. The inflation of price through processing, and the moulding of children's taste so that they become addicted to what they know ('They like what they eat rather than eat what they like' in the words of Lappé and Collins[2]), help to keep the poor poor.

More than this: it is difficult to discover the origins of the recon-structed hamburger meat, to know out of whose mouths the grain was taken that fed the beef and made our convenience somebody else's malnutrition. (When we speak of the lightening of the workload of women through convenience foods, it is not possible to suppress our knowledge of the provenance of them, and to know the price that is paid by other women, and children too, in the Third World.) And to complete the circle, as the production of food becomes more and more complicated in the West, it means that nutrition decreases as more chemicals and additives are involved in it. Looking at the items in Valerie's store cupboard – packet soups, jellies, soft drinks, sauces and preserves – it soon becomes clear there is a formidable range of stabilizers, preservatives, emulsifiers, permitted colouring: tartrazine, potassium sorbate, sodium metabisulphate, water-holding phosphates, ammonium alginate, propionic acid, carbon dioxide, hexamine. Valerie, with all the pressures on her life, the clamour of the children for the food they are hooked on, the desperate dispossession of her life, can know nothing of these things; just as she is unaware of the provenance of what they consume, or of what they contain, or of the dubious nutritional value of the things she so lovingly prepares for the family. It does not

---

[2] Frances Lappé and Joseph Collins, *Food First* (Sphere, London, 1982).

even occur to her that the children's behaviour, the hyperactivity she is afraid of, might be influenced by the additives, the colouring, salt, sugar, the unknown effects of the particular mix of chemicals.

The real charge to be brought against the advertising industry is the way in which it recreates a certain kind of ignorance, dissociating the purchase of things from their origins and constituents. It isn't so much that it persuades the poor to buy things they do not want, though that doubtless occurs too; but that it envelops all transactions of buying and selling in a cleansing anonymity which absolves us from any responsibility for the implications or consequences of even the most trivial purchase, the most casual impulse buy. As Marx observed. 'Just as every qualitative difference between commodities is extinguished in money, so money, on its side, like the radical leveller it is, does away with all distinctions.'[3] What advertising does is to present all exchanges in an atmospher in which commodities are offered as objects of pure, transparent honesty; and the processes that are often long anterior to those simple and shining transactions are lost in the promotion of their universal desirability. We can see here the clouding of understanding which prevents Valerie and millions like her from seeing that their poverty is produced by the same processes as those that dispossess the poor of Asia, South America or Africa. But we can glimpse something of the vast work that needs to be done, in order to show the poor of the rich countries that the hungry of the earth are not our enemies, but our allies; that we are all subordinated to the same global mechanisms that damage us and those we love.

Attached to the supermarket where Valerie shops – one of the biggest in Britain – there is a lecture theatre constructed around a mock-up of a kitchen. Here the company organizes classes in home economics for schoolchildren – the elements of cooking – and stages lectures and demonstrations. Negotiations recently took place with the local Social Services department for women on low incomes who found it hard to cope to receive instruction in basic cooking skills. This supermarket chain was one of those that pioneered convenience foods in the 1950s. As a food industry developed in which food processing diverged increasingly from nourishment, many simple skills in the preparation of food decayed. This supermarket has found that competition from newer fast-food chains and take-aways has rendered even the rudimentary work required for the serving of frozen and factory made meals unacceptably laborious. In a way, the company has itself been undermined by the very success of its own promotion, which for years was based on urging people to set aside their knowledge of cooking; a process which paves the way for less wholesome but far more expensive eating. Colin Tudge points out, for

[3] Karl Marx, *Capital* (vol.I, Lawrence & Wishart, London, 1977).

instance, that the traditional potato pie of Lancashire, for all that it was born of austerity, is 'nutritionally unimpeachable', as well as being satisfying to the taste.[4]

The convenience of so-called convenience foods is essentially to the transnationals and agribusiness. Against the argument that they release women from labour, it must be said that there is no reason why the preparation of food should continue to be 'woman's work', and that making meals is not an ignoble undertaking. The price for the convenience is paid elsewhere – not only in higher food bills, the energy squandered in processing, the unforeseeable consequences of adulteration needed to prolong the shelf-life of perishables, the absorption of pesticides, although all that is bad enough. But the companies that sing their purified products every night on television spread their net wider and wider across the world, and increasingly depend upon luxury crops and commodities, ranching and plantations from which the poor have been displaced. In January 1979, Brooke Bond-Liebig Kenya took a seventy-five per cent interest in Sulmac Company Ltd, which grows carnations, ferns, chrysanthemum cuttings, sisal and vegetables on estates. The flowers and vegetables are for export to Europe, express by air freight, to meet the demand for off-season and exotic vegetables and winter flowers. Brooke Bond is here contributing to an established trend in agribusiness investors of using scarce land in African countries to grow food to supply a luxury market overseas. The frivolous nature of such market 'needs' is illustrated by Sulmac's estate at Masongaleni, which has 'the world's biggest production area of asparagus plumosus, a fluffy foliage which is very popular as a green support for bouquets'.[5] Not only is Kenya encouraged to 'develop' its resources to meet the industrial world's demands for tea and coffee, it is now also encouraged to 'develop' to meet the demand for fluffy foliage for bouquets! In 1980, for the first time since Independence, people had to queue to buy maize, and large quantities were imported.[6]

It requires no great imagination to see the parallel between the growing dependency of the rich and poor world alike on the same dispossessing power of forces working through transnational companies that control whole crops, from seeds, fertilizer and pesticides through harvesting, processing with all the additives, to marketing and distribution. The ruin of older strategies for survival in the West has its equivalent in the Third World, as subsistence farming continues to give way to agribusiness; and the lives of the poor are governed increasingly by the same influences,

---

[4] Colin Tudge, *The Famine Business* (Penguin, Harmondsworth, 1979).

[5] Brook Bond-Liebig Kenya Annual Report 1979.

[6] C. Dinham and B. Hines, *Agribusiness in Africa* (Earth Resources Research, London, 1983).

across continents and cultures; influences that are in the business not of feeding people, but of making money out of hunger in all its forms, physical and spiritual.

Not far from Valerie lives Phyllis Gregg. She came to this estate soon after the death of her husband. The interior of her house, in contrast to Valerie's, is neat to the point of obsession. Everything is arranged symmetrically on the mantelpiece: some brass candlesticks, a wedding photo, pictures of the grandchildren. The furniture is threadbare, but there are linen covers pinned to the back of the chairs; a Constable reproduction on the wall, some gold-rimmed teacups in a bow-fronted china cabinet. Mrs Gregg lived in Nottingham; she has come here to be near her sister, but above all to forget.

Her husband was a foundryman, who lost his job early in 1980. He had worked since he was fourteen. 'And he worked there for over forty years. When he started, his job used to be to cook the men's breakfast on a shovel over the furnace. Just after the war, I've known him work from Monday Morning till Tuesday night with only breaks for meals, all day Wednesday, all day Thursday, then Friday morning till Saturday dinner-time. He'd come home, sit in the armchair and doze for an hour, then back on his bike for another 12-hour stint.

'But when he lost his job, it broke him. He just sat still. He'd never had time off. He was a strong, healthy man. But once he stopped going, he sat; and he started thinking about his health. He became obsessed with it. The idea that he was ill seemed to grow; it grew like another person, between him and me. His state of health was like an unfaithfulness to me. That's how I felt it: the presence of another person, the shadow of someone I couldn't compete with. I'd often heard women talking of how they sensed when their husband had another woman, was seeing somebody else. Well, that's what it was like, only it wasn't another woman. We'd been married 35 years; and we loved each other. Not silly, romantic love, you soon grow out of that; but the sort of love where you expect somebody home by the clock, and if they're a couple of minutes late, something catches in your throat, an anxiety, you know. He came home from the foundry, and he'd go into the back garden, do some digging. He had a pigeon loft; he loved the pigeons. I've known him sit out there half the night if one of his favourites was sick. But that was his only relief. Work was his life. He enjoyed work – not the foundry, but the people he worked with, the company. He was born to work. He only went to two places all his life; and he was 54 when they made him redundant. The firm closed. He had some redundancy money; it went on the house, the garden, the pigeons.

'But then he went downhill. He started imagining things wrong with him. There were noises in his ears; then he had heart trouble; and then he had cancer, or so he thought. But the cancer was in his mind. That's what he had – cancer of the mind; this thing growing there, in his imagination. He got so he was forever examining himself, dosing himself with all these medicines he got from the chemist. You wouldn't believe what our bathroom looked like; he must've spent hundreds of pounds. He kept on going to the doctor; but he was retreating all the time from the real world, into the dark, somewhere inside, where I couldn't follow him. He sat in the chair, with his arms folded, not doing anything; waiting for the pain, an attack, death. He wouldn't be able to breathe, and then he'd panic, his face would go blue, he'd get all agitated. He'd wake up in the night and say he was choking. We sent for the ambulance; they'd take him to the hospital, and discharge him the next day – nothing wrong.

'I could feel the distance betwen us. I couldn't make him laugh any more. I couldn't get a reaction from him. The daughter used to come in after work; and there wasn't even a flicker of acknowledgement; and as a little girl, she'd always been the favourite, she could do no wrong. When the son came over it was the same.

'Nothing interested him, except this obsession with his health – or rather, his sickness. He was like a man who'd got a girl he was infatuated with. It was an imaginary illness, a ghost of a disease. He wouldn't even read the paper. He watched TV; whatever came on. And he always hated watching TV mindlessly, you know. He sat so that even when the flies settled on his face, he wouldn't lift a hand to brush them off. It made me want to go out and find somebody else to give me some comfort; but I couldn't have, even if I hadn't been 57, and fat, with varicose veins. It made me so angry with him, with the world. But I didn't dare say anything. He was ill; it was obvious he was ill, although not in the way he thought he was. When I got impatient, he used to accuse me of not caring. But I did care. I did. He kept on saying no one understood how bad he was, nobody could do anything for him, nobody ever felt as ill as he did. It was as if the illness was the only thing that could understand him.

'In the end, he walked into the canal. He went out one night, warm night it was, in summer. He got up and said he was going out for a walk. He hadn't been out for weeks. I said 'I'll come with you.' No, he wanted a bit of fresh air. And I knew what he was going to do. I didn't know, but I had this premonition; and I did nothing to stop him. You must remember, it had been going on for three years. But I felt I could have prevented it, and I didn't.

'I can't tell you the guilt and remorse that I didn't go with him, or at least follow him. He fell in love with his sickness, you see, that's what happened to him. And he proved it, by giving up his life for it in the end. His illness became another person, and then it finally became him, who he was. Where he had been a strong man, a foundryman. He used to get thirsty, we'd go to the club; I never begrudged him his few pints. He used to love the pigeons, but of course, he neglected those as well. One night, he went out and wrung their necks, all of them, and put them in a big black rubbish bag. People don't know the half of it. I watch the politicians when they come on TV. They say 'Yes, we care about the unemployed.' Nobody cares. People can die of it, and they don't even care about that either. That's the real sickness.'

She falls silent; hands arthritic and swollen, in her lap, thumbs tapping gently together give the only sign of her inner agitation; the budgerigar in its cage hanging free on a chromium stand, twitters and scatters seed through the bars. The rain on the shrubs outside trembles in silver beads. Mrs Gregg draws the curtains against the dark afternoon.

Peter and Corinne came to live on the estate after being moved out of the demolition area in the city centre. In the old house, the windows rattled, the paint had peeled from the woodwork, the yard was foul with water from the overflowing drains; the children always had throat infections. Julie is 6, Helen 4, Samantha 2 and Neil 9 months. The new house represented the fresh start they had been looking forward to; what a relief it had seemed, to get away from the aggravation of the neighbours, the fear Corinne felt of going out alone, even in the daytime, let alone after dark, with all the stories of mugging in the underpass and rapes in the park. Peter has been out of work for four years; but in spite of the lack of money, everything suggests things are getting better. They bought a carpet from Corinne's mother's catalogue; the grant from the Social provided beds and curtains and a cooker. There is a TV; and they have the use of a video which a girl they know wanted to be rid of because it was stolen. They have even found some ornaments for the wall. The window looks out on to a green, where banks of daffodils are about to flower.

But since they have moved here, Corinne says, Peter has changed. Peter says 'I think our marriage is on the rocks.' It is a strange alien idiom in his mouth, with his homely North-country accent: even the way in which he talks about the relationship with his wife is the implanted language of the entertainment industry. The two older children look on: Julie is nursing Neil, and rocking to and fro with him, in the attitude of a mother comforting her child. Corinne starts to cry; the tears run down her cheeks. She runs into the bedroom, and throws herself onto the bed. Peter sits in the living room. Helen clings to his legs. He rolls a cigarette. Peter is 23. He says he needs to hang loose for a little while. He wants to find himself. He is too young to have so much responsibility. He hasn't had any life. You should be out enjoying yourself while you're young. 'Corinne thinks I'm out, giving some woman one. I've got a friendship with a woman who's forty. We're friends, that's all.' He follows his wife into the bedroom, and sits on the edge of the bed, with his back to her. The children follow, and range themselves around their parents, watching.

'It's all happened before', says Corinne. 'Whan I was carrying Helen. He never told me, somebody else did, a friend of the woman.' Peter complains 'That's the past. I was immature.' He says that Corinne nags him; she wants him to account for all his movements. She bosses him, she doesn't trust him.

Corinne gets up and stands by the window; the packing-cases which they used to move with are sodden with rain, overflowing with paper and rubbish; some washing has blown off the line and landed on the laurel bush that is the boundary of the back garden. Corinne says Peter won't talk to her. Peter says he can't talk about his feelings; he never has been able to. Corinne's way, when she is hurt, is to talk about everything. His way is to be silent. People are different.

Peter says 'Men need their freedom.'

'What about my freedom,' asks Corinne.

'You can have yours.'

It's no freedom, with four kids, is it?'

The children watch and listen.

The discussion reaches a block; a tense, heavy silence; resentment and incomprehension. Neil has fallen asleep in Julie's arms, and she sets him down on the bed. Peter says that he and Corinne need some time apart from each other.

'I don't', says Corinne. 'Is this your way of telling me you want out?' She lifts her face; the tears have left a tidemark on her cheek; her eyes are swollen. She says: 'We've been here before': the feeling is just like it was when her first marriage ended. 'Is it because I'm too old?' Corinne is 25. She complains that her husband goes out all the time, stays away half the day; the whole day; will never tell her where he has been.

'She knows where I go. I go to see Tessa. She's 41, I'm 23. She's had a bad time.'

'So have I' says Corinne.

'Her two-year-old is in hospital. He got savaged by a dog. Alsatian crossed with a Doberman, when he was only a few months old. It tore his scrotum. He might not be able to have children when he grows up.' Tessa left her husband. He made her do things she hated – made her go to bed with a Lesbian, locked her in a room, and wouldn't let her out until she agreed to do what he wanted; took away her clothes. Then he came back to the house one day while she was out, and smashed everything up.

Corinne has transformed Peter. When she met him, she was married to a postman, and Peter was living in a hostel for single homeless men. Peter had been unloved by his parents, and had found comfort with a gang of boys; they were into drugs and drink; taking and driving cars, petty theft, shoplifting. Peter had had two periods of probation and a community service order. When he met Corinne, he recognized her as the person he needed. At the time, Corinne's marriage was already disintegrating. Peter always said that if it had not been for her, he would now be either in prison or dead. He had once tried to kill himself in the hostel, wounding himself in the stomach with a butcher's knife. When Corinne's husband left her Peter moved in. He found comfort and security with her for the first time. He achieved a stability he had never known. He threw away the leather jacket, cut the hair that hung over his eyes, kept himself clean. He could begin to confront the lack of love of his own childhood and adolescence. Indeed, Corinne mothered him, gave him confidence; permitted him to express all the anger and sadness of the unloved child. She provided him with a haven in which he could grow and develop. It was a role in which she felt happy; indeed, she wanted nothing beyond it. It is the pity of their situation that Peter now feels that with her help, he has grown up and continued to develop. She loves him in the same way that she did at the beginning; and Peter feels that such a love is now stifling.

Their relationship reflects this intensely emotional bond: their sexual relationship has not been easy; occasional violent love-making, helped by fantasy, pictures or films. Peter insists he is no longer the person he was when Corinne 'rescued' him. But it seems to her that his survival has been at her expense; that she has surrendered something vital for his sake; that hers is the experience of loss. Their positions are the reverse of what they were at the beginning. Then, he used to plead with her never to leave him, to stay and look after him. And now Corinne is begging him not to go, because she doesn't want anyone else.

Corinne recognizes that this is a familiar story for women; but that doesn't lessen the pain.

Peter did leave and they were divorced. But he didn't go to live with Tessa. He met Tracy, whose marriage was also shaky. Her family perfectly matched the one Peter had just left. This only made it the more bitter for Corinne: why does he have to leave one family for another that is almost exactly the same? She was angry and bewildered. But she was also aware that Peter was not as whole as he had believed himself to be; you don't recover from the sort of childhood he had in the space of three or four years. She knew it wouldn't last. He was trying to find a way into a family that already existed breaking through the fissures in other people's relationships; he moved in with Tracy after she had thrown out her husband. And that, says Corinne, was exactly what he had done with her. In this way, this was only his repeat of a deeper haunting – that of his own young life, when he had circled around the relationship between his mother and father, and the other children, unable to find a way into the affections of any of them. Corinne draws some faint though unrewarding comfort from her understanding, and from her prediction that it can't last.

There is nothing of even this modest comfort for the children. When Corinne feels despair, or she can't cope with the children, she will go and lie down on the bed. Helen, who is four, says 'My Daddy doesn't love us any more.' She strokes her mother's hip with her hand, and says 'That's why Mummy cries.' The children cling to male visitors, and won't let them go. They have already received ample instruction about life – that you can't really be sure of anyone; and they have learnt to take such consolations as are available, the sweeties and the money; the what-have-you-got-for-me frankness when people come to the house, the calculation – even though the bag of sweets is soon used up, the comic savourless, the novelty fallen apart. But at least you know the limits of these compensations; unlike those mysterious, shifting affections, the volatile feelings, the uprooting of adult feelings, the removals and arbitrary disappearances.

For the adults it is no longer a question of staying with the children when the relationship had broken down – that frail attachment that had once seemed so strong. The official imagery of family life still pours from the media, mothers immaculate and knowing, children smiling with pleasure; and Corinne feels hurt and deficient because she cannot give her children, not only the things other children enjoy, but also a father, a sense of belonging to a 'normal' family, as she says; even though, of the thirty houses in the square, there are no more than half a dozen children who are still with their own natural parents.

Corinne is left stranded. Peter is free to find consolation where he may. Corinne, with her £43 a week, and the £26 child allowance, has to keep five of them. It isn't that you can't afford to live; but all the things you can't have, says Corinne, seem the more desirable precisely because they are just out of reach. The weekly money is accounted for in advance. The burden of empty time is the worst thing; not the work and the drudgery, but the void: this is when people do desperate things, to make something happen, do the meter, invite the workman doing the repairs to the road in; One of her friends asked the telephone engineer to go to bed with her; and then arranged for her husband to burst in at the right moment, so they could blackmail him out of a few quid. Corinne becomes exasperated with her children; she feels she has nothing of herself to offer them when the money runs out.

'It gets unbearable. You threaten them, you hit them, you feel frightened of how destructive and hateful you feel inside yourself, things you didn't know were there.' One night, she hit Samantha too hard; and was afraid to stay in the house alone with her. She wanted the children taken into care, because she was no longer sure she would be able to control herself. The feeling passed; but guilt and a terrible loneliness followed. Corinne says that the feeling of solitude makes her, when she is feeling bad, confess things to them, speak to them about emotions they can't understand, tell them of feelings they shouldn't be burdened with. And then she is ashamed afterwards that she hasn't been able to keep it to herself.

It becomes easier to see how the ideology of increase and growth corrodes the lives of the poor. People's relationships become a caricature of the social mechanism: a market economy of the emotions. What can you get out of people for giving the least you can; what is the psychic balance of gain and loss; how are you to get the fun, the enjoyment, the sex, the entertainment, the money that you need, and at whose expense?

Eddie, disabled by a works accident twenty years ago, lives in a purpose-built bungalow for the sick and elderly. A shabby, neglected interior, with furniture provided by Social Services. They had to burn everything from his old house, because it was so ruined and dirty. Eddie lives alone with his dog. He is in his early sixties. He will not open the door to any offical visitors, because he is afraid they will take the dog away, or remove him from his home because of dirt and neglect. He says he was born unlucky; in fact, being born at all was his first stroke of bad luck. Everything in his house speaks of loneliness and indifference. The half-empty tins of food have become mildewed where they have been left to stand; the bucket of urine, unemptied, is under the kitchen table; the dog-food has clung to the filthy tin plate; crumbs of food lodge in the mesh of the coco-matting. Eddie has a single light-bulb which he takes with him if he wants to go into another room in the dark. The small garden is overgrown with brambles and bindweed. There is a strong smell of dog; shit clings to the porcelain of the lavatory bowl. Eddie shares a tin of food with his dog – whether it's dog food or steak-and-kidney makes no difference. There is grease on the mugs; the single saucepan is stained; and the gas-stove will hardly light from the overflows which have clogged the rings – mostly of packet soup, which, apart from sausages, is the only thing Eddie cooks. There is a packet of sliced bread on the plastic tablecloth, a tub of margarine, open and covered with crumbs and fluff. Teabags have been thrown into a rusty metal waste-bucket, which has seeped in a deep amber stain on the floor. There are dog-hairs everywhere.

Eddie wears a collarless shirt, ribbed with grime; his neck is dirty and his greying hair matted. There are yellow stains at the crotch of his grey flannels. As he walks across the floor, his slippers stick to the grease. There are grey fingerprints around the door-handle, and streaky paw-marks on the door and walls. Eddie is quite indifferent to the world; he doesn't read, and although the TV is permanently turned on, it is not properly adjusted, so that the image flickers and contracts and the sound is blurred. He says not to touch it; he always has it like that.

He was a window-cleaner, but fell from a ladder and injured his shoulder. He lost a finger in a factory accident. His only interest, he says, is in his books: a whole shelf of porn, women with half-closed eyes and half-open mouths, sitting on chairs with legs apart, or lying on satiny beds; most of them are well thumb-marked, and in lurid colours: the ugly, explicit imagery of expropriated imagination. Eddie never married. When he was younger, he relied on prostitutes; but even that finished when he stopped work five years ago. He was made redundant at that time from the nightwatchman job he had done for ten years. 'Redundancy, that's the story of my life', he says. 'That's what they'll put on my grave – He Was Made Redundant.'

Eddie was an only child; and he felt he was an unwelcome interruption in his parents' life together. 'They were wrapped up in each other. They never had time for me. They used to go everywhere together, but they never wanted me stringing along. One night, when I was about twelve, I hid in the wardrobe, because I wanted to see what they did together. I watched them do it, on the bed. That's how I learned the facts of life.

'I never asked to be born. Well, nobody does. But if you have them, it's your job to look after them. All the years I was a kid, I was out in the cold. Outside, that's where I always seemed to be. Waiting for them to come out of the pub; being sent out to play, being given money to go to the pictures, when what I wanted was to be taken by them. They used to go on their own. Waiting in the porch for them to come home, being sent to the shop for chips, instead of having dinner with them. I tried to make them take notice of me, by being good. Then, when I got a bit older, I thought 'Well, if I can't do it that way, I'll do it the other way.' I made them take notice, didn't I? I set the bloody house on fire. They came home from a darts outing, and all the front room was burnt out. They never did find out how it happened; they thought he must've left a fag burning.

'That's what I mean about being born redundant. I was always the one who got left out.'

I was shocked to learn that Eddie is only 61; he looks much older – mid seventies. His dog is his only companion. Sometimes, she sits on his lap, almost smothering him. He then has periods of punishing and rejecting her. He delights in making her suffer – go for a couple of days without food – and then making it up to her by lavishing sweets and affection on her. 'She's all I've got.' The dog sleeps at the bottom of his bed, on a once pink, but now filthy eiderdown.

When we consider the position of the poorest, we do them a grave injury if we take no account of the texture and feeling of individual lives; but we perpetrate an equal wrong if we ignore or elide the social determinants which produce their poverty.

7

The Remaking of Women

Any discussion of the remoulding of human beings so that they will fit an always evolving division of labour must come back to the central position of women. This is particularly important at a time when 'service industries' are invoked as an answer to the problem of future employment. The word 'service' should alert us to the fact that it is women who are going to be most drastically restructured for this new form of capitalist service, just as they have been before, whether as private servants or as unpaid labour in the home. Of course, women have often been swiftly absorbed into paid labour at times of emergency – during the world wars, for instance – and then expelled unceremoniously back into the home when the urgent need for their labour has passed. In some industries the work of women was always indispensable. Marx pointed out the tendency of capitalists to substitute the cheaper labour of women and children for that of men as machinery became more complex: 'The more modern industry becomes developed, the more is the labour of men superseded by that of women.'[1] For the most part that did not happen: the value of the work women could be induced to do for nothing proved an even greater source of value. Only recently has something Marx saw as imminent in the 1860s became more general, coinciding with the mutation in the employment structure that we have seen in our time.

It is a commonplace social observation that many women – often with young families – entered the labour force for the first time in the 1960s and 1970s. But the way in which this neutral social 'fact' is presented (i.e. that women now make up about forty-three per cent of the workforce) diminishes its importance. It has been represented as a benign and even progressive social evolution: many women have had their first experience of release from the constrictions of home and family, have come into contact with a wider world, have learned the lessons of the workplace, have seen the possibilities of sisterhood as they came into often brutal

[1] Karl Marx, *Capital* (vol.I, Lawrence & Wishart, London, 1977).

conflict with male-dominated trade unions as well as management. Many women have felt that were doing two jobs, because they were not, in most cases, relieved of responsibility for the children.

These processes that have caught women up in their toils have not always been perceived for what they are. They too have involved a sort of *migration* from one culture to another. Women have travelled an epic voyage; and a long and often painful road it has been too, from a decayed working-class domestic culture, with its vestiges of extended family (which fell into rapid decay after the Second World War) to a new culture that ought to have been more enriching.[2] This has meant a profound restructuring of the experience of working-class women; but because it has involved so little surface disruption (except in the lives of those affected), it has not been seen for what it is. Where capital has always depended upon the uprooting of people, driving them from the periphery to the metropolis, from one end of the Earth to the other, the same effect can now be achieved by the internal manipulation of human beings; the changes can all be worked within. The upheaval, the driven compulsions all recur, but the old resistances (especially those male-oriented trade unions) are not helpful; and as a result women have had to bear the burden of disruption and reshaping, without acknowledgement of the epic through which they were passing.

The old domestic culture attached women to the home, indeed imprisoned them, although it is worth asserting that the accommodations they made, their secret and often unrecorded adjustments, constituted an underground resistance, an unsung and often heroic response. Richard Hoggart's sketch of working-class women (published in the 1950s but drawing on his childhood experience) was sufficiently general to deserve being cited.

It is evident that a working-class mother will age early, that at thirty, after having two or three children, she will have lost most of her sexual attraction; that between thirty-five and forty she rapidly becomes the shapeless figure the family know as 'Our Mam' . . . By forty-five or fifty, ailments begin: you hear during the poorer periods that she is 'nobbut middling' just now. There may be rheumatism, or a regular backache from a twenty-year-old prolapse. The big fear, the one which recurs constantly in conversation, is of a growth, visualized as some huge and ramping cancerous organism . . . The lines on the face of an older working-class woman are often magnificently expressive – but they are hard earned. We should not try to add a glamour to such a face; it has its fineness without any artificial light. It is often a face with a scaly texture, and the lines, looked at closely, have grime in them; the hands are bony claws covered with densely lined skin, and

---

[2] P. Wilmot and M. Young, *Family and Kinship in East London* (Routledge & Kegan Paul, London, 1957).

again the dirt is well-ingrained there: years of snatched washes, usually in cold water, have caused that. The face has two marked lines of force – from the sides of the nose down to the compressed lips; they tell of years of 'calculating'. They 'belonged' in the house; were always at home when the children arrived from school, the man from work. Shopping, local visiting, an hour up the pub on Saturday night might be her only excursion.[3]

This description now sounds extraordinarily archaic. It is true that her public role did great violence to her own needs and inclinations, and for many women it was an oppressive and joyless experience. But her self-effacement and subservience to men had an inescapable and functional cause. The cherishing of the man's body and the labour-power it possessed was all that stood between survival and the workhouse, an income and starvation. In terms of the available responses of the early industrial era, it was not ignoble. I well remember a conversation with the wife of a former miner in South Wales, who said that she had always got up to see her husband, and later her two grown-up sons, off to the pit; and she was always waiting to welcome them with a meal when they came home, no matter what shift they were working. When their work-times didn't coincide, it meant that there were whole weeks when she never got a night's sleep. But to the suggestion that this represented a terrible denial of herself, she said fiercely. 'You never knew if that was the last time you'd see them alive. I had a brother killed in the pit. And his wife always said she had the consolation of knowing that she had given him breakfast and kissed him goodbye before his last journey. Do you think I should sleep, while those I love go off in the dark without offering them a little comfort?' She said she was well aware of the oppression – it affected them all; and her expression of love was, for her, a humanizing gesture, and therefore an act of resistance. It is easy to be scornful now about the sexual division of labour and the position of those women who were denied in every conceivable way; but that scorn is possible only because of the struggle, the coming of the welfare state, the long fight against degrading living and working conditions. Their sacrifice and drudgery appal us now; but we do their memory a cruel disservice if we disregard those for whom it was an act of love as well as inescapable duty.

But what is at issue now is the nature of the changes that we have lived through; and how working-class women have experienced those changes. The decay of the domestic culture was a result of the decline of the old heavy industries, the achievements of the welfare state, and the growing control of women over their own fertility, the coincidence of which makes it difficult to extricate one single cause. But these things led to a moment of greater fluidity, a point where the position of working-class women

[3] Richard Hoggart, *The Uses of Literacy* (Chatto & Windus, London, 1957).

could have been spectacularly improved, where the rigid ascription of
male and female characteristics could have been broken and redistributed
in ways that were truly liberating. The release from the role of oppressed
mother, worn out with drudgery and childbearing, the round of washing,
scrubbing, whitening the door-steep, cooking, blackleading, occurred at
the time when the role of women in the wider community – the help to the
woman lying-in and to the bereaved neighbour, feeding the children of a
sick relative – also subsided; all the demands of the immediate
neighbourhood were lessened simultaneously. Escape from the traditional
woman's role, with its miseries and its strength, led for a majority of
women not so much to the opportunity for self-realization as to
imprisonment in a different kind of stereotype, though equally in the
service of men: from that of comforter and consoler into that of sexual
object. This new stereotype was a creation of mass markets; and its
furthest effects have been to lead many women from one kind of captivity
into another. The consumer markets suppressed many of the 'traditional'
characteristics previously attributed to working-class women – all those
associated with self-effacement in serving others; while the opposites of all
these things came into prominence – fashion, cosmetics, care of the self.
Fast-food industries, labour-saving domestic appliances offered a
wonderful freedom from that image which many millons of women had
inhabited like a prison. And, in important ways, it was a setting free.

This reconstruction of women coincided also with the mitigation of the
demand for heavy manual labour among large sections of the male
working class. But the hardness and toughness associated with the sheer
endurance required for intense physical work remained; indeed, even
became more entrenched when the workload was alleviated. Those male
characteristics stayed the same, even though they ceased to be
indispensable for the survival of the family unit. In other words, what is
now called 'machismo' only because exacerbated when its reason for
existence had decayed. Men, fearful of the void that might otherwise have
confronted them, only intensified their familiar attributes.

For women it was different. For them a quite different set of
characteristics was heightened; not those associated with self-sacrifice and
'motherliness' (these would actually have defied even the most dedicated
manipulators of women's sensibility, those whose mission was to create
mass markets; and if for no other reason, this is why the role of crushed
working-class women had to go); and in its place images of glamour,
sexiness and self-display were encouraged – the cultivation of all those
features so long neglected. The fact that this change reflected in part a
changing subordination to the needs of men was perhaps not felt by
women as too irksome at the time. For it gave countless women a genuine
feeling of release; even though it was occuring at the same time as women

were entering new and often unfamiliar kinds of employment; new sectors of the economy which recruited them at lower costs than men might have commanded. Indeed, they were pioneering the change to new service industries and the tendency towards assembling rather than manufacturing in factories.

In this way, for men nothing really changed, apart from the lightening of the workload; whereas for women the shift was far more drastic. Eager to embrace what looked like liberating experiences, women were actually being marketed for men. Men did not undergo anything like the same process of having their psyche dismantled, their feelings restructured. Perhaps this is one reason why men have become a greater conservative force than allegedly more 'conservative' women.

What really occurred, of course, was that an only partial account of both women and men – a limited range of the possible characteristics of both – was exaggerated and frozen by the mass consumer markets of the fifties and sixties. What did not change was the subordinate status of women; only it was a different kind of subjection from the earlier form – in much the same way that the re-making of the working class in general during this period results in a different mode of dependency upon capitalism. Everything seemed to be in a state of fluidity and change; but as things settled it became clear that the subaltern position of women within it remains constant, no matter how far-reaching the apparent changes.

At the moment of dissolution of that older working-class culture, these newer stereotypes were captured and then perpetuated in attitudes determined by mass markets – capitalism's version of solidarity. Because these offered such an obvious contrast with an oppressive past, and because real freedoms were involved, it all looked far more benign than it may now appear. (And it is essential to understand the fullest implications of some of these freedoms offered to working-class women by, for example, convenience foods: what appeared as liberating commodities in one part of the world were increasingly experienced in Third World countries as agribusiness dispossessing them of their traditional subsistence. Not only this; but the more basic foods are 'modernized' i.e. processed, the more they cost and the less nutritious they become. For instance, as potatoes becomes dehydrated or powdered, or turned into crinkle-cut chips, potato crips or potato snacks, the more expensive they become per pound, and the greater the added chemicals and fat; by this process the 'caring' for children's nourishment as expressed through the buying of more expensive food becomes the very opposite.)

The new culture that has grown around this mutation in working-class life reflects the changing needs of capital; but because capitalism has proved so adaptable, so wonderfully protean in its metamorphoses, it is far easier to blame men for having retained archaic privileges than to attack the deeper structures and influences, that ideology which makes current dominant images of male and female look to many people like acceptable, even desirable, accounts of human possibilities.

It is in this light that all the rhetoric – especially in the 1960s – about the 'sexual revolution' masked what was simply a movement within a deeper stasis. Male and female responded to the reconstruction implicit in an appearance of 'liberation' in the metropolitan countries, from the production/reproduction model to the fantasy/consumption model; in other words, to capitalism's own mitigating response to its own cruelty, it's own 'reward' to its own inflictions.

In this way the manipulation of appearances – the glamour, the sexuality, the desirability of a working class transformed from its former shapeless, ugly dowdiness – corresponds to that reshaping of the more general external decor of capitalism's landscapes. The experience of violence, the unhappy consciousness, the dissatisfactions are all produced within; out of sight if not out of mind; distant and detached from the system that creates them. Indeed the outer aspects – the stereotypes themselves – do offer consolation and reassurance to those who inhabit them. They provide a reference point, an illusion of security, a created sense of sharing, which is itself like a caricature of other forms of solidarity. The sexual stereotypes provide a haven, a refuge, something to hold on to at times of disturbance and change. Mass markets create a simulation of a shared predicament: solidarity through capitalism's own products, as opposed to the defences of a working class built up in opposition to it. It is this that feeds the immobilism and conservatism of large sections of the people, and that is the despair of socialists and feminists. The restlessness and uncertainty of life within capitalism makes people cling to the easy stereotypes, with their familiarity, their selling back to us an identity that has been stolen away. The reinforcement of a machismo that is functionally obsolete, with all the industries of fantasy that underpin it, together with the version of women that the capitalist market-place projects, appear to offer people a place of safety; even though they mangle and diminish real human beings as they try to wrestle with the inconsistencies and discrepancies. It should not surprise us that so many of the energies of men, lately confiscated for the labour of production, should be partly released into an obsessive preoccupation with marketed sexuality, where women appear in a new guise of service; and it should not surprise us if women often become the victims of those energies – violence and rape and cruelty – that can no more be totally absorbed by fantasy than they can by relentless labour.

It has been the most magnificent achievement of the women's movement that it has managed to create a separate space, another way of being in this shifting entrapment of women as they are tipped – like those pale helpless bodies in a Bosch painting falling into hell – from one oppressive role into another. Nevertheless, the consolations which those sheltering stereotypes offer people should be treated not with scorn but with an imaginative understanding of the fears and vulnerabilities they conceal, the apparently merciful asylum they provide for internal torment. For the images of manhood and womanhood which the culture sells do seem to offer protection, even if they are as constricting as walls of glass.

The congealing of mass-market decisions taken at any given time, and as a reaction to earlier experience from which they appear to offer deliverance, causes the choices and preferences expressed to congeal also; the pent-up feelings harden into the shape they assume, like boiling metal spilled from a container in which it has been seething. These then become a major determinant on the next generation. And the transmission of these immobile stereotypes offers comfort and meaning through change; even though it may actually be a false comfort, for it merely delivers us to a market-place which can only urge us to behave in conformity with the stereotype we occupy; discomposing our sense of self, and reconstructing it in the image of all those dispersed and fragmented components that can be sold to us, a sort of identikit of merchandise. And this vanquishes autonomy, progressively erodes identity, much as work and poverty once did. In this way the result for women is the same as it was for those generations inhibited and crushed by self-immolation in the service of men. As we pass gratefully into the image provided for us, we surrender more and more of ourselves; like Alice passing though the looking-glass, we are bound to accept a preposterous and yet compelling logic which we have no power to influence or control.

The passage from the repressed needs of women in the old working-class culture to the different elided needs in the new, illustrates the range of possibilities within capitalism. All of them suppress, bypass, exclude or deform those characteristics which do not serve it. Woman as domestic service and comforter is metamorphosed into woman as labour and sexual object. Caring was associated with self-denial, whereas sexual and emotional self-expression get caught up in a tangle of marketed sexuality, an imprisoning network of mendacious images and false surfaces. Even women and men have been landscaped in conjunction with the cleansing of capitalism.

The migration of women only ripples the outer calm of social and economic life; and that is why its closeness to earlier experiences is not easily seen. It is experienced by individuals as a personal, private itinerary.

The beginnings of the transformation of the living places of the working class in the 1950s, the slum clearance programmes and rebuilding of the towns and cities, looked like a deliverance. The new estates, even the tower blocks, the city centres with their geometric and unornamented shape, demanded that they be properly decorated and maintained. The very box-like emptiness of the rooms seemed to cry out to be filled with attractive things. They imposed their own imperative of cost; unlike the shabby slum houses with their chipped paint and crooked windows, their dusty chenille and old-fashioned furniture. It began to be necessary to live up to an external standard; one that was obligingly set by the sudden appearance of plate-glass windows in all the shops of the city, which offered an uninterrupted view of the promptings and suggestions of everything that was available. This coincided with a profound change in the purpose of home, which became a place of comfort and retreat and entertainment; in contrast with the shabby overcrowded interiors of tradition. At the same time, in spite of the newness of everything, the fact of being at home came to seem to many women claustrophobic, and increasingly oppressive. With the decline in demands of the neighbourhood, the dispersal and depletion of families, the long mornings at home, the convenience foods, the depersonalized contact of the supermarket, the decay of older kinship and neighbourhood networks, the fleeting and emulous friendships with people who had become more mobile, to whom you confided the dissatisfactions and anxieties of your life, only to quarrel when you discovered what you had confessed was known all over the estate; feeling you had nothing to say to your husband when he came home, and not quite knowing what to offer the children; the rainswept concrete, the radio programmes that failed to capture your interest, Crown Court on television in the empty mid-day hours and the televised images of distant wars; the newspapers and the cups of tea, the desultory shopping, the decreased housework that so easily became an obsession; in the long hours occurred a languor, an ennui that women had never known before. If they complained to their mothers, the older women were not sympathetic: 'You don't know you're born. We could have used all the washing machines and hoovers forty years ago.' And they told how *their* mother had washed for eight and then had to go out to other people's houses to do their washing, and had baked all their own bread; had a routine of work as inescapable as time itself. There seemed a terrible mismatch between the needs of older women and the improvements that had come too late for them. Many women felt that the easing of domestic labour had led them into boredom and lack of purpose. There was a lot of talk in the papers about new town blues. They went to the doctor with depression. Many were given 'tablets'; tranquillizers, even though a surfeit of tranquillity was what they were suffering from. The possibility of work was grasped eagerly – the independent income, the friendships, the chance to do something.

It is important to understand that the changes we have lived through represent neither pure gain nor all loss. This is a false antithesis, and it severs the discussion in the wrong place, so that endless sterile discussions occur around progress versus nostalgia. Any argument that focuses on either/or is false; the truth is that the same structures remain in place, that the purposes of capitalism have not altered, and that gains in one area are likely to be neutralized by loss in another. The release from the old domestic culture has been ambiguous in its effects. For one thing, work – almost any paid work – was welcome to women; and the possibility of earning money that they could control, that they could use to buy things to enhance the lives of their children, looked irresistible. The longer-term consequences take some time to appear.

So women went into the service jobs; shops and selling, public services, health care, school dinners, factory and assembly work, offices. The work offered the chance to provide the children with things that had always been out of reach. It seemed to offer the individual woman a mixture of traditional selflessness – the giving role – combined with the opportunity to meet people, and to widen that diminished circle of family and neighbourhood. Throughout the 1960s and 1970s hundreds of thousands of women entered work. Flexible hours were arranged, twilight shifts organized, apparently to accommodate them; but at the same time this casualized work, took many workers out of protective legislation, continued a process of deskilling. What women felt was above all a sense of relief; having control over money beyond the man's wage (the true amount of which he frequently failed to disclose to her). And in addition there was the sweetness of companionship at work. What a release it was! To be able to joke about men and sex, share experiences, compare notes, pool ideas. Even the tensions at work – disagreements with management, wage-claims – gave many women a chance to experience trade union activity. And then there was the flirtation, the repartee, the common bond of working together; it all made women feel so much more alive, even though they knew they were underpaid, were being used as a source of cheap labour.

Of course there was the other side of it. To get home at five o'clock and find the crumpled newspaper from the previous night, the washing up left in the sink to soak, the cornflakes sticking to the side of the dish, the milk turned sour and clinging to the bottle; and in winter the cold house, which meant the gas fires had to be turned on and your coat kept on till it had warmed up a bit; the cloud of breath, the windows streaked with condensation; the smell of frying, chips, egg and bacon; the children's clothes, left where they had stepped out of them, toys scattered on the floor. It required fresh reservoirs of patience and energy to get everything ready for the evening meal. And then it was time to turn on the television. And somehow, when the others got home, they were all too tired to say very much; the stories and experiences that might have been exchanged remained untold; the things stored up to amuse and interest were submerged. Everybody's face turned towards the television; the pressure was removed.

Yet that was not all. The changes were accompanied by another kind of ache. The children, for one thing. They seemed to grow up so fast; between the sink and the stove, when you turned round they looked older. Or was it that there was never the time to pause, to enjoy their curiosity, their wonder, their questions. It seemed as if something was missing. Shouldn't it have been possible to talk more with the children, to tell them things; weren't you supposed to instruct them, to amuse them, occupy them – to bring them up, in short. And yet, what could you say? Nothing seemed certain; you couldn't teach them anything, they knew so much already. Even right and wrong, those things your own mother had been so particular about, didn't seem so easy, apart from the obvious things about stealing and not bringing trouble home. There was having money and there was having no money, that's what it seemed to amount to these days. And then, the children seemed so able to fend for themselves. They began to stay out later; and they didn't always appear at mealtimes. As they got older, they wanted money to buy food out – Wimpy, Kentucky Fried, later Macdonald's and take-aways. Well, it made life easier, as long as the money kept coming in; but you sometimes met your children with their mates, walking in a group down the main shopping street, carrying striped cardboard containers, dipping their fingers in and eating, as though they hadn't time for a proper meal; and yet, they weren't in a hurry to go anywhere, they weren't doing anything in particular. In fact, they were always moaning about how boring it was round here. The time you might have given your children dissolved somehow into money.

But on the other hand, going out to work made possible things that you had never before dreamed of. You could buy fashionable clothes for the children; educational toys; furniture for their room. Even so, things did seem to wear out so quickly; fashion changed before you'd had time to draw breath at the previous extravagance that you'd tried to resist. But in spite of the money you were able to spend on them, the children were not conspicuously more grateful. They simply absorbed it all, almost as a matter of course, and them seemed eager for more. Women found themselves saying: This isn't a house, it's a hotel . . . The kids only sleep here . . . I'm just the ever-open purse . . . I see so little of him I've forgotten what he looks like . . . Parents felt themsleves obscurely shy of their children; not in the way that you had been with your own Mam as you reached adolescence and she had tried to tell you clumsily about menstruation, but shy of them as social beings. Where did they go? What did they do with their time? Why did they seem indifferent to cold, hanging round the chip-shop in the middle of winter without a coat? What did they do in those unused garages underneath the flats? And whoever was writing all those terrible things on the concrete of the walkways? An anxiety tugged, beneath the surface; something unspoken. You couldn't quite put your finger on it. They were so easily led; it must be the company they kept – whoever it was. Nor was this the end of it. The self-containment of the children meant that in the evenings, when you stopped worrying, what was there? There seemed so little to share, beyond the family income. And in the absence of a shared project, things seemed to unravel so easily. There wasn't the same zest in the relationship with your husband.

Life became a different kind of treadmill from that of the old domestic slavery. Life was undeniably easier, and yet at the same time full of tensions and anxieties. Worries that had scarcely been noticed suddenly became overwhelming. Would everything be all right, would the kids grow up normal, were they safe? Then, more urgently, could you fit the supermarket in before going to work; what if there's a long queue. It became important to be efficient: defrost the chicken in good time, not forget to replenish the toilet paper. And at the same time, the dependency on the week's shopping went hand in hand with a declining faith in your own powers. What could you say to the woman whose little boy had been run over? You gave a pound to the collection, but you dreaded meeting her face to face; what would her grief do to you, how would you feel? Could you cope? Why did you go out of your way to avoid that older woman, who seemed able to speak of nothing but her dead husband? What would happen if mine . . . Heart. Cancer. Is that a growth I've got? It became easier to go and buy a symbol to show how much you cared for the children and your husband. And you did care for them, in spite of the impatience, the weariness; if only there was some way of showing it a bit more satisfactorily. That time when he had the accident at work, and they said he was going to be all right, you cried and cried. And when you went into the children's rooms, with the bunk beds and the transfers of prehistoric monsters and the posters of stars you didn't even recognize, you could feel your love for them, intense, but circling round inside you somehow, failing to find expression except in what you could buy for them.

Women were led into an employment structure that was evolving from heavy male-dominated industry into services; many of them more casual, less skilled. They have in some ways prepared the way for cheaper labour: is this the inheritance they will leave their children, those they care for most in all the world? Have they been unwitting accessaries of events and changes that appeared benign, the furthest consequences of which they could not have foreseen?

In some ways, their desire to do the best for those they love has led them to be instruments of discontinuity with the older labourist tradition: lower wages, unorganized labour, jobs rather than work. In turn, their children have been led into deeper dependency on market relationships that have grown, even as family relationships have become more de-roled and unstructured. And the children, raised in another culture, migrate back to a casualized, deskilled labour market, subordinated by money to goods, tastes, needs that in their turn depend on a global patterns of exploitation – fast foods, cheap fabrics, confectionery, the divorce of taste from nutrition, of choice from its consequences.

It is these terrible contradictions – the improvements and the pain, the sense of release from old ways of servitude into new and unfamiliar ones, freedom and renewed subordination, that make it difficult to evaluate the changes. You can feel the ways in which the human material is manipulated, pulled into new shapes required by capitalist renewal. Occasionally, individuals embody these processes in a dramatic way: Yasmin Kemal, as migrant, woman and young person, has a deeper understanding than most. Yasmin is now twenty-eight. She was married at sixteen, divorced at twenty; she has two children, both boys. A small Turkish woman, with dark eyes and great energy and intelligence, she lives on a big estate in North London; has opted to bring up her children alone. 'People say it isn't natural, it isn't fair on the children. Any man who comes in, they're all over him.' She married, as she says ironically, for love; went against the tradition of an arranged marriage because she was sure she knew better. She says she woke up four years later, with two kids, her husband out every night with the boys.

'Turkish women are very unaware of their bodies. I hardly knew what had happened to me. My mother came here from Cyprus; she worked as nanny with British army familes. She still doesn't speak English. She went through two arranged marriages; neither of them worked out. She was left with two children the first time, then with five of us. But she still believes in arranged marriages.

'I don't have any contact with my brothers and sisters, but she and I have become quite close. When I was divorced I went to live with her, and she tried to fix me up with an arranged marriage. I just stayed there long enough to get rehoused.

'I knew nothing. I was very inexperienced. I'd never done anything on my own initiative until I got married. I left school at fifteen, was married less than a year later. My mother saw the chance of a British passport as a meal-ticket. She came to this country convinced that we'd get educated. But of course the schools are much less disciplined than schools in Turkey, with the result that you don't learn anything. You just waste your time. That's how immigrants' hopes get deceived.

'When I was alone with the children I tried doing work at home. I was sewing kilts, 50p each; the most you could do was one or two a day; and then the children got no attention, and were bored and unhappy. I made dresses. The company brought you a bundle of work to do, and then collected it a few days later. You didn't know who you were working for. The kilts were sold for £15 each. There are women who earn £70 or £80 a week, but they're up at six working, they eat their meals at the machine, they can't leave it.

'I did some work making Christmas crackers. Working with glue. You can feel yourself inhaling it, it can get you addicted. So I gave that up. I went into a factory. Where's your insurance card? Haven't got one. Right, start immediately. Wage was £18 a week; and you had to take it, because you'd worked unofficially. Then, when they chose to sack you, they had no obligation to pay what they owed you; and you couldn't do anything about it, because it was illegal. There is a kind of contract between worker and employer that's based on blackmail. It suits both sides, and it escapes regulation. At the moment, my mother and I earn a bit by doing cooking for Turkish weddings and celebrations; not officially of course.

'It isn't easy being on my own. But I wouldn't accept a man just for the sake of saying I've got a man. A lot of women do that, because if you haven't got one you're vulnerable. I've had insults, ever since I've been here; dog shit through the letter-box, and as I walk by people make remarks about all this filth that's living in these flats. If there was a man here they wouldn't do it. It's hard to bring children up alone. Part of it has to be done by bargaining and bribery – if you do this you can see what you want to on TV; if you tidy up your room or whatever, you can have that. You worry about them. If they get into bad company, make one mistake, it can follow them for ever. It's all right while they're young, but as they get a bit older you start to think, when they're fourteen or fifteen, you can't control kids of that age. They're a law to themselves.

'I hate being on benefit. Somebody wrote to the Social, saying I had a man here. There's a lot of that – people telling on their neighbours. Half past eight one Saturday morning, two men came. I didn't believe they were from the Social at first. I said you can look round if you like; which they did. It was humiliating. They said you can have a man stay two nights a week; if he stays more than that you're cohabiting. Anyway, if a man is living with a woman, that doesn't mean he's keeping you. It's more likely to be the other way round. They look through the clothes basket to see if you're washing for a man, look in your cupboards, see if you've got any luxuries like food.

'I can see both sides. My brothers say to me "We told you so" because I wouldn't accept an arranged marriage. I think if I had the chance again, I'd live with a man rather than marry him. I can see the strengths of the old ways – family loyalty, people stick by each other. But then, once you break the rules, that's it. You're out, and out for good. But then with the freedom of English girls, you see so many people ruined by it – drugs, drink, debt. This flat costs £34 a week rent. Everybody's in arrears.

'I lived with my husband in a street in North London; they were all white families, all working. It was a cul-de-sac, and you coudn't avoid them. They'd all be out on Sundays cleaning their car, you didn't dare go out. We couldn't live there. You felt you were on show. We felt conspicuous. You're glad to get back into a place where there's all sorts of people, people have got too many problems to worry about yours. When I got this place I thought there'd no hassle. But the kids get called Pakis, these flats are full of racists. I've started a Turkish women's group. That isn't easy to organize; the men are suspicious of what you might be teaching the women. They like women to remain ignorant, naive, unaware; like I was.

'I had a bad time at first. I went to the doctor and I was given tranquillizers. I got to the state where I'd get up, give the kids their breakfast, then I wanted them out of the way; I wanted to avoid them so that I could sleep the time away. I was so slowed down like, that I never got round to doing anything. The flat got into a mess, I just wanted to escape into sleep. I had a social worker, who came and took them to the nursery – that was supposed to help me go out. But I didn't. I would only go out once a week, to do the shopping. If anything ran out during the week, that was just too bad. The rest of the time, sitting in a stupor, dreaming, sleeping. Eventually I realized that was no way out; and there never would be unless I found the strength to do it for myself. So I got up one day and said right, that's it. You mustn't let it crush you; there's enough people who are destroyed by it, women especially. I have strong opinions. I think people respect that. If you show you're strong, it draws people to you. They ask you for advice, they tell you how they feel; and you know, because you've been there yourself. A lot of people don't realize what they have inside them until they're up against it. I could've gone under. I have a lot of friends who are feminists; middle class. I think relationships between women are more close. If you want to express your feelings with women, you can. If you want to hug each other, you do; nothing sexual of course. Men don't like it. Men like to keep control; being the provider – even when all they're providing is social security money. That makes them worse in a way, because you know it's not on account of their big macho act about going out and doing a job and being the breadwinner. But that makes them very touchy about their pride.

'A lot of Turkish women are trapped in the home. They never go out, literally. They do some of the worst jobs, homeworking. I used to make soft toys; glue and nylon everywhere. Poverty here is different from poverty in Turkey. It's easy to say there's no real poverty here; but it's a different sort of poverty. There's hunger in Turkey; here, there's despair, there's loneliness, there are all sorts of reasons why people can't cope.

'The things people do for their kids here is tragic. They do it from love, but it's mistaken. Women go to jumble sales for their own clothes, but they buy expensive things for their children – Doriada plimsolls, T-shirts that cost a fortune because they have a trendy motif on them, track-suits – there's a children's boutique on the main road honestly, twelve-year-olds go round looking like fashion-plates. It's ridiculous. They've no food at home, their houses are poor, but the kids go out dressed up like advertisements. That's poverty in its way.

'I'd like to be a community worker. Maybe I'll have a relationship when I'm thirty-five, the kids are grown up. It's better they should have one good parent than two bad ones. You feel guilty towards them when your marriage breaks up. You think it's your fault. And then I feel guilty to my background as well, going against the custom and refusing an arranged marriage. It means you carry a double burden of guilt which it's hard to explain to someone who isn't a migrant. I must admit I don't have much to do with the neigbours; I'm afraid of being rejected. I was very lonely, but I'm not now. I do too much; and the secret is not what you can get out of life, but what you can do. I don't go out at night; if you haven't got a boyfriend or a man, people don't ask you out. You can walk round this estate in the middle of the day and see nobody. The corridors are silent and empty; it's scary even in the daytime. At night there have been a number of attacks on women. You see men standing in the garages, exposing themselves. I just don't look or speak. Nobody sees anything round here. Women get attacked, people must hear things but nobody wants to get involved.'

Interlude

That our Western version of poverty is a cruel and elaborately wrought construct designed to keep alive a redundant need for growth and expansion can be demonstrated by the merest glimpse of the kind of poverty which is the fate of the majority of humankind. Without dwelling on the horrors of famine in Central Africa and the Sahel – that most excruciating and self-conscious form of death that is starvation – the less extreme but more generalized daily poverty of the South does its work more slowly, less spectacularly on the emaciated bodies and exhausted spirits of those who are drawn to the ever-extending and formless cities. I have chosen the cities, because by the year 2000 most of the people in the world will be urban; and secondly, because the growth of those cities illustrates that the pattern of development willed upon the whole globe by the developed North is nothing other than a repeat of the experiences through which we ourselves have passed. Indeed, those carefully dismantled landscapes of poverty which have haunted our culture since the beginnings of industrial society have been reconstructed in the cities of the South. The enhanced technological achievements of our century only taunt the poor more effectively than the palaces of production, the lights and luxury of the nineteenth century metropolis: the pavement dwellers live in the shadow of the skyscraper, the fantasy architecture of the tourist hotel, the marble and concrete slabs of bank and finance house.

Pranab Bardhan, development economist, says in *The Political Economy of Development in India*:

I am told that mothers in the affluent western countries often urge their children to finish their plates by reminding them of the hungry people in India. It may or may not be an effective strategy to make the rich eat more in the name of the poor, but it is interesting to recall that only a few centuries back the children in some of those same countries grew up with stories of the fabulous riches of India; some of them as adults ventured out to find the quickest routes to India, even stumbling on new continents on the way. But over the last century or two India has been more often associated with endemic hunger or poverty, and the stories of the extravagant wealth and splendour of the Maharajas have not succeeded in dispelling that association.

It is precisely the perpetuation of this relationship of plunder that is the object of all the pious rhetoric about 'mutual interdependence' of North and South. For our wealth is dependent upon the continued poverty of the majority of the world's people, just as definitions of poverty in the rich world depends upon ever-more convoluted and bizarre reformulations of what constitutes wealth. For instance, in 1979, almost a million people on the south west cost of India who depended on fishing were thrown into poverty and underemployment when some Japanese and Indian firms put fifty-two trawlers to fish off the coast. The fish was for export: that year India earned from the state of Kerala 97 million dollars exporting fish, but while this transaction was going on, 60 per cent of the population of the state suffered from protein deficiency. The fish went to Japan, the USA, France and Britian, much of it in the form of frozen prawns. And there, people who could not afford prawn cocktail or scampi *à la* king in the smart restaurants were made to feel their poverty the more keenly.

What we must understand is the way in which the disabling wealth of the rich world, which deforms and undermines human energies in the ways we have seen, is indissolubly tethered to the wear and tear of the human flesh and spirit that we see in the worn-out bodies and spent energies of those who live on the edge of survival in the South: and that their liberation can be achieved only in harmony with ours.

> *The Arithmetic of Poverty*
>
> *Decide, mother,*
> *who goes without.*
> *Is it Rama, the strongest?*
> *who may not need it that day*
>
> *Or Baba, the weakest?*
> *Who may not need it*
> *much longer.*
>
> *Or perhaps, Sita?*
> *who may be expendable.*
>
> *Decide, mother.*
> *Kill a part of yourself*
> *as you resolve*
> *the dilemma*
>
> *Decide, mother*
> *decide . . .*
> *and Hate.*[1]

[1] D.Appadurai, 'The Arithmetic of Poetry' in *Other Voices, Other Places* (Christian Aid, London, 1983).

8

The City: Bombay 1983

There are subtle gradations of poverty, even in the hutments on the
sidewalk. The shelters that people have built vary. For one thing, if the
slum is officially acknowledged to exist it may well have certain amenities
like piped water or electricity: but even in the unofficial slums there is a
wide variety of dwellings, from the relatively stable structures which will
withstand the rains, made of corrugated iron with sloping roof and tiles,
an imitation of a house, and furnished with a metal table and metal folding
chairs, bamboo beds with a base of string. This kind of shelter merges into
more insecure places, made of packing cases and tarpaulin; while these, in
turn, yield to something more like a tent, with strips of polythene or
hessian, with a heap of stones on the roof to prevent it blowing away; while
others are dry bamboo leaves and rattan, pieces of rag bleached of colour
by dust and sun. Some of the slums line the main roads, with one wall
formed by the outer part of some monumental colonial building – a post
office or government department. In many of them it is impossible to
stand upright; the fire for cooking fills the space with the smoke of banyan
wood or cow-dung.

Living in the city has advantages – you can get a *khoondi* (a thin metal,
gourd-shaped container) filled with water from the hosepipe that plays on
the gardens of the agricultural college, and there is always something
edible to be scavenged from the heaps of vegetable matter around the
street markets. However ugly urban poverty, the proximity to food
supplies means that people do not die of hunger in the way that can occur
in remote country places. The lowest level of shelter are those fragile
structures of cardboard, little more than places to lie in, the most
temporary of all living places. Below this level, there are families and
individuals who live on the street itself. In the more prosperous parts of
the city many of them live by begging, or by staying close to the market for
some product or service they have to offer – the women braiding tresses of
marigolds or jasmine, not as temple offerings but to decorate the hair of
tourists; an hour's work may be rewarded by a five-rupee note. The

families on the pavements of Colaba who live by begging consist only of women and children; they are seldom seen with their men – just as the beggarwomen of Victorian London kept their men out of sight, but might whistle for them if there was an opportunity to rob someone in a dark corner.

The sons of some of the street familes sell hashish, postcards, nuts roasted on a little brazier and carried round the neck on a tray, decorated with strips of coloured paper, and sold in little newspaper cones at 50 paise a time; the boys walk up and down from early morning till late at night, making perhaps ten or fifteen rupees a day, and sinking exhausted by the sea wall for a few hours' sleep. One boy said he was working for the sake of an education; and from beneath his *lunghi* he drew out a battered 1920s commercial English textbook.

An old woman – that is, in her fifties – sits with her two naked grandchildren stretched out on a piece of hessian, as though offering them for sale; one, a child of about two, has a bandage on his arm, which had been broken and set at an angle that made it impossible to move. The grandmother says the parents are dead. She is an old woman. She cannot look after them. She has heard that there are rich foreigners who are looking for children in Bombay for adoption. Do I know anyone who could help?

The young women squat or stand outside the hotels, or at a discreet distance from them, with a baby on their hip; and the tiny ragged children run alongside the rich, the tourists who arrive in Bombay but seldom stay for more than one or two days at the most. The children are tireless, running beside the foreigners saying, 'Babu', 'Sir', 'khana', apprentices in fawning; and they act out more and more dramatic afflictions in order to move the hardened hearts of the well-to-do. A woman with two babies on her hip which is deformed by where she has always carried her children, says that her husband has killed himself. He was on strike from the mill; and he could find no work but stealing. He was arrested, but jumped into the sea to escape beating and prison. It becomes a little easier to understand the naked, almost reductive quality of the reporting of the nineteenth-century observers in Britain: the biography of the destitute has the universal skeletal quality of bones showing through the skin.

The Tulsi Pipe Road leads to Worli and Parel to the north, the mill districts. The distress of prolonged strike was acute by the spring of 1983. Some of the workers have left Bombay; others have sold everything that had; some are working – under a different identity – at other mills, in defiance of the union; others have found casual and poorly paid work. From Dadar station you walk under the railway bridge, where the market straggles in the shade of the overhead lines; cows, goats and hens pick among the rotting produce; people poke among the blackened cauliflower leaves, peel, offal, picking anything that might be saleable and placing it in a basket. The road is green with trodden vegetable leaves. Thomas Archer, writing of Bethnal Green in the 1860s, might have anticipated this scene:

Most of the women and children perhaps at one time or another carried on some miserable domestic craft involving little outlay and earning infinitesimal returns. Some took in stitchwork for the Whitechapel sweaters; others wove cages and baskets from cane and withies, or made bandboxes, matchboxes, clothes-pegs, flypapers and the like . . . Cows fed on the vegetable refuse that cluttered parts of the streets and alleys . . . The skins of strayed and stolen cats, cage-birds, pigeons, rats, guinea-pigs, ferrets and other small creatures were offered for sale . . . In such districts, most children either went out to scavenge and pilfer what they could about the streets or were put to some miserable, often vitiating employment.[1]

In many of the bustees – the huts that lean against the high walls that enclose the mills – people are working in such desultory demeaning employments as Archer indicated. A boy is mending some badly frayed hessian sacks with a big darning needle and string; but the fabric is so worn that as soon as he pierces the material it tears. He is paid three rupees to repair fifty sacks, most of them beyond repair. He is close to tears of vexation. That work will take him all day at least. He is eleven. Two young women are weaving a bamboo basket, which has the same design as the shallows of Mayhew's coster girls. Outside one hut a woman sits at a battered Singer sewing machine, working away at the metal treadle, and stitching plastic comb-cases – fingers of cheap red material, some of which split and spoil, and which pile up in the dust at her feet. She is paid five rupees for a basketful. The work requires great speed and accuracy.

The huts along the road are provisional and insubstantial, weighted with stones on the dun-coloured roof of rags; sere, dusty palm-leaves discoloured by the sun. A length of faded cloth hands over some of the doorways; in the midday glare these are thrown back to reveal a makeshift structure of bamboo sticks, knotted together with string, some of them so low that they can be entered only by crouching, or even on all fours. The huts are built against the peeling wall which goes on for perhaps three-quarters of a mile. There is space on the dusty sidewalk between the bustees and the road; and then the gutters, which are choked with stagnant waste. Greyish water mixes with the dust into a dark paste; the sun beats down, shadowless and enervating, and the road shimmers with the fumes of the traffic. In front of some of the meanest hutments there is a patch of poor earth; and here and there a twig of bougainvillea, a tiny growth of ashoka tree, even a plastic flower, lovingly protected by a few

[1] Thomas Archer, *The Pauper, The Thief and The Convict* (1965).

stones; it recalled those images of Victorian London, where a scarlet geranium bloomed on the windowsill of grim tenements.

Many of the people on the street in the middle of the day are children and old people. A boy of twelve with a hessian sack over his shoulder is looking for waste paper. There is virtually nothing for him to pick up here; and although he has been working since daybreak, he has only a few crumpled pieces in his sack. His father left the family, and his grandfather threw them out; his arms are thin, his feet hardened, the skin cracked. In front of one hut, a mother is searching her child's hair for lice; an old woman with straggly grey hair, her face contracted with pain, lies on some rags. Her back is being massaged by a younger woman; the wasted flesh shows the rib cage through skin that looks as fragile as paper. A boy of about 8 is washing himself with water from a yellow plastic jug from a rusty corrugated barrel. An elderly man lies in the gutter with his mouth open, his face covered with silver stubble; as the traffic passes, it sets in movement clouds of dust which settles on his skin. A younger man moves him so that he is an a more protected position, and places an empty tin under his neck as a pillow; it is labelled Dried Milk.

Inside, even the poorest huts are clean. A girl sweeps with a tired mechanical gesture the area in front of her shelter. She uses a bundle of twigs to beat the dusty earth; an older woman makes a similar gesture with a piece of rag, so the particles of dust are kept in perpetual motion. Inside, most families have the same battered utensils: a blackened cooking-pot, a pan in which the *bakri* a flat unleavened bread, is cooked. Three bricks enclose the fire, the ash of yesterday's fire joins the waste in the gutter, and the choking curl of fresh woodsmoke rises. The smell clings to the dry leaves and tarpaulin. There is no chimney. Even the poorest offer something to a visitor – a tiny piece of precious *bakri*, a fragment of areca nut. Where the sidewalk opens out there are huts on both sides, so that there is a narrow path between them, a sort of 'street', but so narrow that it is only just possible for two people to pass. One of the public standpipes has been twisted and broken, so the women have to walk several hundred yards to fill the battered aluminium vessel with water. They manage to wash themselves and their clothes in minute quantities of water; and all in public. The only privacy lies in the self-absorption of others. The rags of washing are spread on the roofs of the huts to dry in the sun. There are few men around. They will have gone looking for work or money, labouring, carrving, working in the rich parts of the city, setting up a stall to sell some small commodity or to offer some trifling service. One woman's husband walks each day to the beach at Chowpatti, selling green coconuts to the tourists. He carries a tray on his shoulder and a knife with which he slices the tops from the nuts, and offers the juice to drink. Each morning he has to buy the produce from the market, and then walks the five miles or so into the city. He walks around Marine Drive; and takes *bakri* and chutney to eat. He will earn 10 or 12 rupees a day.

This is the mill district; many of those who live in the shadow of the walls would ask nothing more than to get work there. The workers live, for the most part, in the chawls – tenements. Many of these are built of brick or stone. Three or four storeys high, they are constructed round a central courtyard; some form enclosed squares while others have one or two sides open. They are far more substantial buildings than the self-constructed shelters on the highway, built for rent, and therefore occupied only by those in regular work. Some have worn and weatherbeaten shutters, crude shades of rust metal or wood bleached white as bone. Some of the windows are covered with wire netting, others protected by bars, prison-like; but never glass. Some have balconies around the upper storeys, metal grilles in a zigzag motif, or patterns wrought in imitation of Gujarati wood-carving. The yards are mostly of beaten earth; but here and there are flowers or a plantain, a cluster of green bananas from which hangs a bright crimson flower. Elsewhere, pools of stagnant water collect in the courtyards, dark grey and fetid in the uneven ground. The rubbish accumulates where the animals scavenge – hens, dogs, thin cats and goats, and at night the rats. There are heaps of cinders and ash from the cooking fires. Although the chawls have communal wash-houses and lavatories, the smell of the wind from the sewage and the polluted sea makes the atmosphere sulphurous and oppressive; occasionally the city is choked by smog, a chemical and greasy mist; a contemporary re-creation of the sooty fogs of nineteenth century London.

Many of the chawls are bisected by corridors, which are like wide stone thoroughfares within the buildings through which the air can circulate. The one or two-room dwellings open off these. The doors are simply wooden planks nailed together, with a diagonal bar; most are closed with a bolt or padlock. In the corridors there is a perpetual overspill from the crowded interiors: a string bed in a wooden frame, a padlocked chest of belongings – dowry jewellery, perhaps, or a few family treasures. Children squat on the cool stone, old women sit on mats of rattan, stitching or weaving garlands of flowers. There is a broad flight of stone stairs leading to the next floor. These are crumbling and concave with wear; some have been repaired by rough applications of concrete and metal strips to prevent erosion of the edges. There is considerable variety in the style and standards of the chawls, very much as there were subtle variations in the streets of the Lancashire mill-towns: some of the yards are filled with the bright green blades of plantain, which prevent the area from being filled with detritus, and canna lilies grow under the windows; others are so neglected that they are awash with stagnant water, a sump of garbage.

Each door opens onto a high-ceilinged, single room, with a small kitchen annexe created by a concrete dividing-wall which reaches three-quarters of the way across the room, without a door. In the kitchen there is a brass faucet, and an opening in the stone floor for the water to run off. On a shelf in the kitchen are the cooking utensils – a pot, some aluminium trays; and in a wooden cupboard, green-painted, foodstuff in tin containers and metal jars: rice, flour, spices. The living area is dominated by a large wooden bedstead; what looks like a gunmetal filing cabinet is a wardrobe. There is a fixed wooden cupboard, painted grey, closed by a metal strut that spins on a nail at the centre. High up on the wall are some shelves with a row of polished aluminium vessels, and some brass pots and jugs. These are the best things, used only on special occasions – a display that is perhaps the equivalent of the glass-fronted china cabinets in British working-class homes, with their best china that was rarely used. The wooden base of the bed is the only place to sit, apart from a folding metal chair that is the father's place. In the daytime, the bedcovers are rolled back into a neat bundle at the head of the bed. The cover is a patchwork, pieces of cotton material – like those quilts and rag rugs that used to add a touch of colour and comfort to otherwise cheerless homes in Lancashire. A shirt, a pair of trousers and some shawls hang from a nail in the wall over the bed. The wooden shutters at the window – which has the protection only of wire netting – are closed against the heat of the day. The walls are bare breeze-block bricks, and have been painted dark green. There are pictures on the wall – Krishna, Lakshmi, goddess of wealth, one calender advertising Dunlop and another Air India, with a picture of blossom reflected in the mirror-like calm of the lakes of Kashmir. There is a twig of faded flowers on the shelf in front of the little Krishna shrine; and some family photographs in tarnished brass frames: a brother in America, a cousin in England. In this apartment twelve people sleep: father and four boys in the bed, two grown-up sons on the floor; mother and three daughters sleep in a cot in the corridor, with the two small children at the foot of the bed.

The lavatories that serve the whole block are at the end of the corridor: dingy tiling, a pervasive smell of urine, a constant nuisance of flies and mosquitoes. The rooms are airless, even though the day is relatively cool.

A millworker in his late thirties, Ashok has been on strike for over twelve months. He would willingly go back to work. Four members of the family, including his mother, work at the mills. His wage is normally 700 rupees a month, about £50; though exchange rates are not particularly useful because the structures of prices, expectations, etc. are not at all comparable. He would be quite happy with another 100 rupees a month, but the union leader, the charismatic Datta Samant, has insisted that they hold out for an extra 300 rupees a month. Ashok says they will never get the increase they have asked for. In the meantime, the family has no income; they are helped by Ashok's brother who works on the railway. Ashok works at the Tata mills, which are completely closed; some of the other mills are kept open with blackleg labour. He is bitter, because some of the strikers from his mill are working in the other mills as blacklegs. His boys, aged fifteen and sixteen, do casual work. They had to give up any hope of continuing their education. One of them had a job with Cadbury Schweppes, but lost it through sickness.

There is something familiar in these dark, unornamented interiors: the painted brickwork recalls Victorian kitchens; the family pictures, the best metalware, the overcrowding, the help of the extended family during the long strike, the reaching out to the neighbours. Those families who have one or two members working will help those who have none – not occasionally, but as a regular commitment. One man who works as a bus driver has been feeding his neigbour's children, or rather, his wife has. Ashok is a skilled fitter; he maintains the machinery in the spinning-sheds. It pains him to see machinery stand idle and deteriorating, just as he cannot bear to be not working. I asked him why the employers don't take on others who are out of work. They fear violence. Ashok's daughter is in the eighth grade at school. He would like her to get on, but he cannot afford to buy the books she needs for her studies; he knows someone who may get her a job in a plastics factory. That too brings a pang of recognition: my mother, who ran home from school on her thirteenth birthday to tell her parents she was going to the Grammar School, was taken out the next morning and found a job in a factory.

Next door to Ashok an elderly woman lives with her husband and son; the old man has had a stroke. He can do very little, and is unable to speak. But at least there are only three people living in the room – a rare luxury of space. The son is to be married and the bride will join him here later in the year. To make some money the woman feeds six men, morning and night, men who are working in Bombay separated from their families. Many such men sleep in the open air to save money, which they send to their families. One comes from Aurangabad, perhaps two hundred miles away. Not all the people who sleep on the sidewalk are destitute: indeed, they may be among the most resourceful, cherishing their ambition of the return home with some money, or even of migration, with their little roll of money tucked into a leather bag tied round the waist. You can tell them from the defensive postures in which they sleep, unlike those who have nothing, who lie out in attitudes of more complete repose.

In front of the tenement, on a piece of waste ground in the shade of the building, an old man sits with his iron last, a tin of nails and a few pieces of leather, some stick-on soles. A woman is mixing cow-dung with coal-dust, and rolling them into flat fuel-cakes which she spreads on the earth to dry.

An old woman is selling bananas, just a few withered fruits in a bowl; she appears to be asleep, but she sits bolt upright, alert to any potential customer or thief. A paan-seller mixes the saffron and spices with crushed betel and areca; an old frail man, wearing a sports coat over *khadi*, watches over half a dozen red apples spread in the dust.

The next chawl has a balcony, with an elaborately patterned grille, that girds the block at first-floor level. A woman of about fifty is seated on the threshold of her apartment, from which she can look down onto the little square below. Six people live here. The woman has an extensive display of brass pots, bowls and containers, tumblers and jugs, which fill shelves on an entire wall. In her single-room apartment she has constructed an upper deck, which stretches from the back wall halfway across the room, suspended like a balcony and reached by a rough wooden ladder. The room is sufficiently high for this to be possible without making it too cramped. The upper deck has a wooden balustrade, made by her son, to prevent the children falling. She is very proud of her home, which is one of the most comfortable in the block.

Her daughter is eighteen. She has worked since she was thirteen in a factory that makes plastic and polythene bags. She travels an hour to get to her work each day; and earns 250 rupees a month (about £4 a week). She works fifty-four hours a week. The chemicals in the factory are a constant irritant. The skin has peeled from her hands, making them blotched and raw; and she tries to conceal them when she talks to strangers. She is to marry next year, and will go to live with her husband's family. Her mother works in the mills, but in recent months has worked as a domestic servant with a Parsee family. There are four girls and one boy: he is the youngest, a beautiful and much-indulged child. They had despaired of having a boy to look after them when there are old. Girls get married and leave, but boys bring their family to the parents' house. Children says the mother, are the wealth of poor people. She sends out for some Coca-Cola for their visitors. The gesture of hospitality is translated into buying something which they think is worthy of their guests. They have learnt the economic message well. The purchased drink is invested with greater value than their own everday tea-kettle; and a simple act of warmth and goodwill is annexed by forces which benefit neither the giver nor the receiver. The fluted bottle of Coke stands on the best brass tray, an ugly symbol of the magic of the markets, and its hold over the poor, disgracing their homely offerings. It costs four rupees.

Next door seven people occupy the single room; next to them, eight; then six. The last one is the most wretchedly furnished of all. There is no bed. A women who has recently given birth lies on a pile of rags in the corner. Her husband is a millworker, but has been on strike for a year. There are five children under ten. The baby was stillborn. The woman grieves silently, does not speak. This family is bitter against the strike leader, saying that he is seeking his own glory and does not care how the people suffer. They have seen their standard of living decline, from a time when the man was earning 600 rupees a month. They are now reduced to eating just rice and *bakri*; sometimes even to begging. The oldest boy is ten. He goes scavenging for rags. As he goes past the market stalls he swings his sack to knock things to the ground. He apologises and offers to pick up things he has scattered – potatoes, carrots, plastic hair brushes, pocket-mirrors. Once he stole a watch. They are sometimes fed by the brother's family, who live in a neighbouring block. The brother works in 'service', which means a government office. Once a day the children are fed by a government scheme, which is administered through a medical charity for women in the neighbourhood. This charity operates from one of the tenements: wooden benches along a peeling saffron-coloured wall, where a pitiful procession of women with young children, many of them emaciated and malnourished with eye infections or diarrhoea, queue with inexhaustible patience to see one of the doctors. When it is time for the daily feeding of the children, two women from the centre arrive in the public square between the chawls with a nylon shopping bag full of a mixture of wheat flour and dahl; 400 calories of food for each child. They dip into the bag with an enamel scoop, and the children hold out plastic cups, beakers, bowls, to receive their share. Some of the children are so small they can scarcely hold their dish straight; but they walk off with it, treading carefully so as not to spill one grain of the precious stuff. Some of them share even this modest portion with other members of the family. One small girl collided with some bigger boys running out of the chawl, and she spilt her portion in the dust; tears streaming down her face, she tried to scoop it back into the bowl, mixing it with dust and small stones as she did so.

Behind the chawls there is a piece of waste ground, with animals tethered to a wooden post. Cow dung, straw, decaying matter. On the other side of this open space the hutments begin again. For the most part these are of asbestos or corrugated iron. Some have roofs of Bangalore tiles; others have strips of wood weighted by rocks. Some of these huts have floors of cement; one even has floor tiles. These somewhat more elaborate structures indicate the existence of an established slum. People here see no reason to move on, even if there were anywhere else to go to. Though the buildings appear impermanent, networks of neighbourhood support are well rooted. Once again, the echoes are heard from Victorian England: the mother who had to go out at dawn to break stones for the road, leaving her seven-year-old to bring the baby to be breast-fed, was like those tales of children being brought to the mill to be suckled during work-breaks.

The interiors of the established slum contain the same kinds of utensils as the chawls. But the rent of the chawls is 40 or 50 rupees a month; whereas here only a modest ground-rent is due to the owner of the land. There have been many attempts to get him to improve the public facilities, but he has no interest in anything but his rent, which from three or four hundred dwellings is a considerable sum. The huts are built adjacent to each other, so that most of them have at least one shared wall; these internal walls are really partitions of brushwood or plywood, and as they do not always reach the roof there is an aperture between each house. Everything the neighbours say and do can be heard. This creates a sort of functional privacy, which overcrowded living always imposes: people simply contrive not to hear things that are not intended for them; and at the same time it imposes a discipline which ensures that no one does or says anything to cause surprise or scandal in the neighbourhood.

The huts have sloping roofs, so the rain will run off, and although the front door may be quite low the internal space opens up. But they are dark and airless, and there is no ventilation; in the humidity they can be stifling. Some have electricity, with a bare bulb on a flex swinging from the roof. Others have kerosene lamps, which shed a thin yellow light over the cooking-bricks, the bedstead, the kettling boiling on the fire, with its tea, sugar and milk all boiled up together, and a pinch of cinnamon or ginger to give it greater pungency. There is no running water, only public taps at rare intervals. Open drains have formed their own channels following the terrain of the street (really just an earthen and stony gap between the houses, seldom more than two feet wide.) The drains empty into pits, covered with slatted concrete tops. Irregular outcrops of stone provide the only 'pavement', and these are really stepping-stones, little dry promontories sticking up out of the flow of mud. Some of the buildings have been here for thirty-five or forty years. In spite of the different physical setting, it suggests evocations like that of St Giles Rookery in the 1860s:

Whoever ventures here finds the streets, by courtesy so called, thronged with loiterers, and sees, through half-glazed windows, rooms crowded to suffocation. The stagnant gutters in the middle of the lanes, the filth choking up the dark passages which open upon the highways, all these scarce leave so dispiriting an impression upon the passenger as the condition of the houses. Walls the colour of bleached soot, doors falling from their hinges, doorposts wormeaten, windows where shivered panes of glass alternate with wisps of straw, old hats and lumps of bed-ticken or brown paper, bespeak the last and frailest shelter that can be interposed between man and the elements.[2].

---

[2] Charles Knight, *Passages of a Working Life* 1864–65 (Irish University Press, 1977).

And yet, there is little of the menace of nineteenth-century London; or even of its twentieth-century version. Indeed, the poor parts of Bombay feel safer than those of New York or London. Subsistence poverty lacks the high tension and anxiety of the survival poverty of rich societies.

A woman of twenty-five with three children has lived all her life in the hut she now occupies. Her younger child, six weeks old, is lying in a cot – an open-weave basket – suspended from the ceiling by four pieces of frayed rope; she gently moves the container to and fro, and talks to him as she does so. On shelves high around the edge of the hut are the family's belongings – clothing, bedding, beakers, cooking-vessels. There is a cylindrical metal stove, about a foot high, with an aperture for the fuel; and there is a small opening in the roof, though the smoke stagnates in the room, and the wooden frame of the hut is charred black. Dust clings to all the uneven surfaces. The man is a conductor on Bombay's buses, and earns about 500R a month. The woman has now been sterilized. What she wants, she says, for the child sleeping in the cot that oscillates gently in the afternoon heat, is education: that is the most certain path out of the slums. This family has divided its hut into two rooms; and has created a platform, three or four feet above the cow dung floor. Every monsoon these streets are flooded. Furniture, clothing, beds, are carried away by the water that gets trapped between the densely built huts. It will flood the whole area to a depth of two or three feet; and those who have not secured their belongings out of reach risk having them ruined. During this rainy period – two or three months – the whole family will live and sleep on the ledge they have built, marooned in a space four foot by six. After the rain come the outbreaks – typhoid, dysentery, cholera, when the sewage is lifted out of its more or less regular channels and contaminates the whole district.

The landlord will not clear the detritus from the public square; and the badly nourished children are prone to constant infections of the eyes, throat, ears and chest. Over five million children under one year old die each year in India; sixty per cent of them within a month of birth. Tuberculosis is common, and I was taken to see some people wasting away, bodies so thin it seemed impossible they could still house a living soul, tormented by coughing. One man in particular had read a great deal in his long illness; he was always advising his neighbours, writing letters for them, as though in facing certain death he had become wise in a way that other people had not. He reminded me of Jack London's docker in *People of the Abyss*, who died of TB.

As in all slum areas, people over a wide neighbourhood know each other. Many are related by marriage, and a dense mesh of kinship overlays that of sheer physical propinquity. The supports and networks are like those we knew in the established working-class areas of Britain: an unexpected feast shared with neigbours when a boy 'found' a chicken; a neighbour returning from a visit home to the country; the young men coming back from the Gulf with a huge stereo and a washing machine, which people are invited to admire, as objects of beauty and prestige rather than function. At times of sickness and death, people know what to do, at least in human terms, though adequate medical care is often unavailable or too expensive. There is nothing romantic about the way people live – their social conditions only add to existential burdens of sickness and insufficiency. But the ways in which they respond to each other do not want dignity or mutual regard. Our inability to transfer proper human responses to our improved circumstances in the West remains a reproach and a great mystery to us: they have been subtly worked out of our daily lives, have become part of that preparation we have to undergo to be ready for intensive selling; this is why all the purchased consolations are necessary, even indispensable. This is perhaps the source of the longing, the perpetual dissatisfaction that eats at the lives of those who have everything.

In one hut, a woman whose husband has died has invited a cousin to live with her and her family. Everybody knows he is not her cousin, and that they share a bed. But with the help of his income she cares for his children. He works as a water-carrier, taking the train into Bombay each morning – trains so overflowing with bodies that almost every week there is a fatal accident to someone travelling into the central area.

When you go back on to the main road, where the really squalid shelters are, you realize that if the established slums had proper sanitation, if there was enough work to provide an income sufficient for familes to feed themselves, so that people were not left at the end of each day to a sleep of such exhaustion it is like death, they would not necessarily be undignified places to live. Indeed, they would probably represent something a little below what the living standards of the whole world would be, if its total product were evenly spread (an estimated $2222 per head in 1983). The threat from the very poor is not that they want to imitate the extravagances of the rich; it is simply the need for enough food, freedom from preventable disease, secure shelter and a social function. These demands are of course dangerous: it is their very modesty that is such an affront to the dilating wants of the rich and of the global system which they embody. The poor ask only what could be so easily granted. This is what makes us uncomfortable and ashamed, and therefore angry, so that we are forced into postures of self-justification, and search for alibis for their poverty – in climate, or population, or ignorance. And the rich of the poor world, those treacherous elites whose lives are the models of an alien colonizing culture, have learned all the phrases and received wisdom of their Victorian antecedents: The poor like it, that's all they know, it's what they deserve; the Indian is basically lazy, the Nigerian is very unsophisticated, the Brazilian is stupid; it's the caste-system; the poor are fatalistic, say those insulated by luxury hotels and secluded villas. (J.K. Galbraith has observed that the conserving of energy, which the rich mistake for apathy, the reluctance to change, is actually the only sensible response to an ageless unchanging poverty.[3]) I was solemnly assured that when communal latrines had been built in one slum, people had filled the bowls with flowers and contined to defecate in the gutters; but my informant was perhaps forgetting that those who are used to squat lavatories are unlikely to change habits for the sake of a piece of Burslem porcelain. But all the dehumanizing clichés echo down the years; and it creates an eerie impression to hear in the Taj Mahal hotel the certainties of the rich of early industrial Britain: Joseph Townsend's *Dissertation on the Poor Law* in 1786, for instance, in which he said that it is a law of nature that there must be poor, 'so that there may always be some to fulfil the most servile, the most sordid and the most ignoble offices in the community . . . Some check, some balance, is absolutely needful, and hunger is the proper balance.[4] Or Malthus: 'The power of population is infinitely greater than the power of the earth to produce subsistence for men' and 'at nature's mighty feast there is no cover for him' (the pauper).[5] or Ricardo: 'By engaging to feed all who may require food, you in some measure create an unlimited demand for human beings'.[6]

From time to time, the public authorities clear the slums. People are rounded up and herded into lorries, and many of them taken 'back' to places they never came from; some notional law of settlement governing the locus of their disposal. But it doesn't last long. There have been efforts to clear all the main thoroughfares; but after each clearance all the easily demolished shelters will have been rebuilt within a few weeks.

As evening falls, two boys are still foraging in the heaps of waste by the roadside. They are collecting paper; but because it has to be dry, they have spread it out on the earth near their hut. They will receive 70 paise a kilo. To earn four or five rupees, they must work all the hours of daylight. One of them, the eldest of five children, has no father; the other boy's father is crippled by polio. The children's income is the only regular money the family has; and they feel it as a heavy responsibility, these grave, thoughtful 11-year-olds. One of them says he would like to go to school; and he does sometimes attend one of the charitable night-schools in the slum, only he is always so tired he cannot concentrate, and has sometmes

[3] J.K. Galbraith, *On the Nature of Mass Poverty* (Penguin, Harmondsworth 1966).
[4] Joseph Townsend, *Dissertation on the Poor Law* 1786 (University of California Press, 1971).
[5] Thomas Malthus, *An Essay on the Principle of Population* (Everyman edn, London, 1973).
[6] D. Ricardo, *Works* (Royal Economic Society, London, 1951–55).

fallen asleep in the hut that a Protestant minister uses for his school. The boy's father sits at the edge of the road. His legs are withered, and crossed like sticks. He moves by shuffling along on a piece of thick rubber, a length of car tyre wrapped in hessian, which is tied to his abdomen with string. He doesn't speak, but maintains a dignified watchfulness while his son speaks. He does not approve, but is powerless to exercise his authority over the boy he depends on. Sensing this, the boy goes back to his work. In the meantime, a girl of about ten has arrived with some water, and the youngest boy brings firewood. There is a cooking pot in the lean-to but no utensils. The family eat from the pot. There is a seven-year-old, a girl who has a speech defect and can make only whimpering noises. She goes to the stalls at Dadar market. Most of the stallkeepers know her, and will give her some oddments of produce – an unripe aubergine, some purple onions.

The most obvious feature of any poor city in the world is the vast expenditure of energy required for survival. The intense activity of these places reflects the desperation of getting through the day. These are not places of inaction and apathy. They are full of movement; occupations of sometimes incredible humiliation for those who practice them: the myriad forms of servitude in the marketing of the most trivial commodity, or offering the most degrading of services – from shoe-shining to child prostitution, from the immaculate waiters in the rich hotels to the swarms of dusty children collecting rags, papers, glass, rusty metal, plastic, whose work places are heaps of ordure and rotting material that form man-made mountains overlooking the slums and shanties.

That nothing should be thrown away strikes the visitor at first like a collective exercise in conservation. How careful it all seems, the children prudently turning over every scrap of chemical-impregnated rag, picking out the filthiest bits of paper, jagged shards of glass. But when you consider the wear and tear upon bodies that will still probably be unable to make good the energy used up in the day, unable to buy enough food for themselves, let alone those who depend on them, it begins to appear somewhat different; particularly when you return to consider the poor of the West. The age-mates of these children in the inner cities, in the ghettos of North America, the HLM blocks on the edge of French cities, are in the very opposite condition to that of the youngsters crawling on the rubbish heaps: they are fallen into idleness, futility, unemployment, inertia. Many of them become de-energized and without purpose. Their creativity and energies have failed to be roused by all the riches of the West. Their society has nothing for them to do. Many of our young of the rich world are a mirror image of the young poor in the Third World: their energies are wasted, because they have not been called forth. Nobody has asked anything of them, so they remain undeveloped, without any realization of the resources, the powers and strengths that lie locked up, wasting, within.

So what look like two contrasting societies in the capitalist world are actually linked, symbiotically and to each other's mutual damage. Both involve the most prodigal waste of human resources – one in the struggle to maintain life in ways that are degrading and destructive to body and mind, the other in the inactivity and inertia of having nothing to contribute to the world. The deepest irony is that the captive state of our young people is a direct result of the 'liberating' wealth of capitalism. They have grown up to seek meaning and purpose in purchased consolations, market distributed rewards; money has extinguished their energies, just as money exhausts the poor wasted bodies of those desperate enough to do anything to survive in Bombay or Bangkok or Mexico City.

Under the Gateway of India, or the Apollo Bunder, a great triumphal arch commemorating the visit of George V and Queen Mary in 1915, there is an expanse of cool marble, in the shadow of the pink stone monument. Here lives Salim, with his wooden shoe-cleaning box, its four tins of Cherry Blossom Boot Polish, four shoebrushes, four toothbrushes for getting into the crevices, and rags for shining the shoes after they have been polished. When a customer approaches, Salim removes the laces from the shoes first, then places two pieces of cardboard inside them, to protect the socks. He works thoroughly and is proud of his skill. Salim is eighteen. His family came from New Delhi, but now they are scattered. His father has a petrol pump in Madras.

As a child, Salim worked on the railway station at Madras, selling tea to passengers, hopping across the lines as the trains came in and out. One day, a train started unexpectedly as he was leaning against it, and he fell under it. His legs were severed just above the knee. He was then twelve. He was ill for eighteen months after that; but the stumps eventually healed. He wears blue denim shorts, from which the remains of his legs protrude. He came to Bombay four years ago to earn a living, and to save up some money for two artificial legs. These will cost 5000 rupees. He has a battered skateboard, which he uses to propel himself across the stone floor of the arch, a gift from an American businessman whose shoes he once cleaned. He is a warm and intelligent boy, with a dazzling smile. He is fed by friends who work in the kitchens of nearby hotels – leftovers, which are lavish. He sleeps on the stone under the arch, where the rats run freely at night, and the smell of urine and polluted harbour water comes in strong whiffs.

Salim has vowed to save enough money to have the legs fitted before he will return to New Delhi. He knows that the fare is 140 rupees. He left his mother there because he did not want to burden her; and he will not go back until he can do so independently. He wears a white shirt, and at night wraps himself in a single grey cloth; his shoe-box is his pillow. He says he has many friends; those who eke out a living around the Bunder form a fellowship of mutual help and support.

One of Salim's friends keeps one of the motor launches that take tourists out to the Elephanta Caves – a decrepit vessel that chugs desperately out of the harbour every couple of hours, threadbare motor tyres as lifebelts. Malik is from Madras; he has a superior boat, competing for the trade to the caves; he brought his with the money he made selling hashish. He started this as a child, when his father died of TB and his sister came to Bombay, where she lives as a prostitute. Mike is a sixteen-year-old. He wears a woollen knitted hat, a dingy, torn shirt and black trousers. He lives rough too. He says that he came home to India when he was eleven; and his English is perfect, as indeed it should be, for he was born in Bristol. He wanted to see India, so his parents left him in the care of a friend who was returning to Kerala. This woman brought him as far as Bombay and then abandoned him. Whether she did this because she ran out of money or because it had been pre-arranged with his parents, he doesn't know. Indeed, he says he prefers not to know, because if it is confirmed that he has been rejected it will make him too sad.

His is a curious story, a boy lost, alone in India. He has no money. He sold his passport to somebody who wanted to go to England. He says vaguely that his guardian took his money from him. His father is a bus conductor in Bristol; he offers this information as though to reassure me that his story is not invented. He says you can live on very little money in Bombay, if you know how to go about it: hustling, stealing, charity. There is a group of youngsters who work together: a boy with a monkey on a chain, an older man with a cobra in a basket and a flute to which it will dance. A young man with a dog says that it can read his thoughts; and this dog will go up to any member of a crowd who the man designates while the dog is blindfolded; he actually whistles to it at a level that the human ear cannot detect.

Mike says he misses his family; he has written to them, but they do not reply. He says he wouldn't want to go back to England. 'We don't want to leave here. We have a beatiful palace built for us by His Majesty King George the Fifth,' and he indicates the arch, the stone smooth and pink in the afternoon sun, framing the grey flank of Elephanta Island, the polluted sea sparkling in the sunlight. He says that he has no one. He now speaks fluent Marathi as well as English; he doesn't care what work he does, only he won't touch hash or any other drugs. If you want to deal in hash, you have to pay the police. 'Fuck them.' (It was odd to hear the word 'fuck' in India; his use of it seemed the best authentication that he had indeed grown up in England.) He doesn't want to risk prison, like his friend who spent two years in a Maharashtra gaol for robbery. It had been a degrading experience: chained on the way to court, beaten by a length of rubber, a diet of chappatis without ghee, food sometimes withheld by the dadas who controlled it, and for whom favours had to be done, bidis or use as a sexual object. He too had been turned out by his father, after his mother had gone back in shame to her parental home.

There was a curious sense of Dickensian orphanings in these stories, children wandering in the city and being self-sufficient. Salim gave his address as the Shri Krishna Motor Launch, Apollo Bunder; a world of great voyages and coincidences, governed by hopes of a charitable deliverer, a *Deus ex machina*. It suggests that even some of the more baroque plots of Victorian novelists were less absurd and gratuitous that we have come to see them. They were, after all, writing at a time of great migrations and wanderings of people, when children were abandoned, sold or abused, and familes dispersed. I offered to go and see Mike's parents in Bristol. But no; he liked his orphaned status, and he was adept at using it to attach people to him, tourists in particular, for they are the kind of people who find him a romantic figure, and are more likely to part with a five-rupee note than to offer to something practical.

The ways in which people make a living here show the ingenuity that only abjection and despair can inspire. Neither great poverty nor great wealth can emancipate people: they form a symbiotic symmetry, and the oscillation between them is a repetitive and endless depletion of caged energy and trapped human powers.

The boy who said he had been mutilated by his father to give him a genuine cause for beggary reminded me of the nineteenth-century faking of sores and wounds, 'covering a patch of skin with a layer of soap and applying strong vinegar so that what appeared to be matter-filled blisters formed'; [9] touching up the stumps of healed amputations so that they should appear fresh – these things we have known before.

In the richer districts of the city, in Colaba, people have developed skills that are of use to the rich: you can see, in embryo, the distortions of the free market that drive people to fulfil all kinds of demeaning services for the very rich, to the neglect of their real skills and needs. There are people who have learned to cut slices of pineapple as delicate as lace; or to construct displays of fruit salad on a base of melon-rind. I saw a fire-eater, with blackened mouth and rotting teeth, who filled his mouth with petrol before blowing a flame four feet into the air; and people threw coins onto a piece of rag in the road. There were carvers of bone and ivory itinerant performers with cobra and mongoose; a family conducting a team of black bears. People stand for hours with their single commodity; the booth with the machine for crushing sugar-cane, with its dense serrated wheels that

[7] Cited in Kellow Chesney, *The Victorian Underworld* (Penguin, Harmondsworth, 1970).

eat up the fibre and produce a glass of sweet liquid; the paan and bidi sellers; vendors of bright green cockatoos in bamboo cages; the sellers of green coconuts. All the vendors who have no licence have to keep watch for the police, and whenever the police arrive they hide their wares – either giving them to legitimate stall-holders or perhaps lodging their bananas or coconuts in the rocks below the sea-wall, and sticking their knives in the foliage of the pipal-tree. One boy – about 14 – wasn't quite quick enough as the police-car drew up beside him. The policeman seized his tray of fruit, and one by one threw them out to sea as far as he could, confiscating the knife with which the boy chopped the rind. This boy is from Kerala. He has come to Bombay to earn money to help out his father who has lost his fishing-boat. It costs 15R to get a licence. The boy is angry and humiliated. He unwinds his *lunghi* and climbs down onto the boulders to retrieve his coconuts from the water; but they have been carried out too far by the tide. A friend of his had been drowned, swimming after produce that had been dumped by the police. He'll start again tomorrow.

On the sidewalks people offer for sale all kinds of goods, many of them imported consumer objects, in addition to the clothing and food. There are hair-dryers, cassette and video recorders, umbrellas, toys, balloons, books, novelties. The kind of things that look superfluous in the rich world have an even more glaring incongruity in the presence of this poverty. Some men are twisting coloured wire into shapes representing men on bicycles; you can feel the warping of human ingenuity that goes into the creation of trivial diversions for the rich, whose money purchases them, not only the object in question but also ignorance of and absolution from the violence that is done to the poor in the process. While I was there the city was full of vendors of magnetic fish – little coloured darts that propel themselves across the surface of a plastic bowl full of water. There are rows of shacks, with battered typing chairs and typewriters, with typists copying out certificates and testimonials; a man is selling application forms for jobs in government service; writers of letters wait outside the post office. I met a teacher of English who could scarcely speak the language, and none of whose students could speak an intelligible word of it. He goes from place to place, moving on before those he teaches have a chance to discover how little they have learned. The ear-cleaners wait with their small sticks and pieces of cotton-wool; the shoe-shiners, some of whom have only one brush and a tin of polish; the hash and ganja-sellers. Much of this is distributed through a complicated network of sub-contractors, with the result that much of the substance is seriously adulterated. The stone-breakers and the dung-collectors; young men offering massages on Chowpatti beach, looking for the rich foreigner who will rescue them from the indignity òf that particular service; the makers of nameplates, with their rows of brass, plastic and bone rectangles; the

carvers of wooden galleons and animals; the man who stuffs and sells
cobras; the shavers and barbers by the roadside, with only a chair, a brush
and some soap; the photographic booths, the vendors of pekoras and
sweets, belphuri, herbs and tomatoes; the offerings of Ayurvedic
medicine, bizarre decoctions in plain bottles against fever and the evil eye;
the rickshawmen, sellers of rattan, bamboo, wood, plywood, plastic,
polythene; the sweepers and beggars; people corroded by leprosy. Others
have deformities of all kinds; they line the causeway to the Hadj Ali tomb,
remaining in their places until the water laps over the smooth stones and
threatens to wash them away; women who guard the shoes outside the
temples, the man who sat beside his empty plastic bowl in the street for six
days, never moving, until he died, silently; the astrologers and casters of
horoscopes, the sign painters and makers of rat poison, the sellers of potions
that do everything from curing snakebites to the creation of eternal youth.
There are those who sell ancient text books; the tiny wood and metal shack
has a sign saying School of Commerce; a lean-to calls itself The Bluebell
School of English; while a middling bungalow advertises itself as a Clinic of
Neurosurgery. One of the most touching sights was a street-family, where
the grandfather was teaching a child of about six to read by the lighted
window of a restaurant; it was ten o'clock at night, and the little boy could
hardly stay awake, but he was repeating the words as his grandfather said
them.

On Grant Road station the beggars sit at intervals on the steps over the
street; children with deformed arms wrapped in bandages; old women
with babies in their arms. They sit impassive, detached from their own
afflictions, for they are in the business of selling pity. At various times of
the day, they are brought *bakri* and water by an elderly man; then, late in
the afternoon, the children are relieved by others, who take up the same
position. It is clearly organized, but they would not say how it is done or
by whom concerted. In 1865 Thomas Archer observed:

Standing by the terminus of the North London Railway you may witness the
periodical visits of slinking and bedraggled women – weedy as to their apparel and
with the attenuation and pallid hue of much gin on their faces – who come to take
off one or more of these poor little wretches the money they have 'picked up'
during the day. Any one of these women may be the mother of one or more of the
children, or may merely employ them to do her cadging. Sometimes she brings
them slices of coarse bread and butter wrapped in a dingy handkerchief.[8]

One young man who was begging lived with the beach-dwellers and petty
thieves along Chowpatti beach. His father had mortgaged his small piece
of land in Gujarat for a loan which he had not been able to repay. Instead,

[8] Archer, *Pauper, Thief and Convict.*

he had offered the rich landowner his son's labour. But that was like slavery. The boy and his brother had run away, jumping on and off trains. He doesn't know what has happened to his brother; but he knows he cannot go home again.

The central area of the metropolis is of course scarcely typical. There is nearly always enough money for people to get by, scavenging, hustling, begging, even if there is no legitimate work. More typical is the crowded slum on the northern edge of Bombay, a settlement on the very limit of the city.

Ghatkopar is a shanty village on the slope of some barren sage-grey hills, where the sun glares through a dusty blue-grey haze. The terrain flattens out at the bottom of the slope, where some new apartments are being built, there is a concentration of factories in an industrial zone, and the road leads to Ghatkopar station. One part is an official slum; but that finishes abruptly, and becomes the sprawling unofficial place whose existence is not recognized. But although deprived of services, there are many who know how to tap the supply illegally and sell it to others, and there are people who have built up a thriving enterprise selling water to those who are too old or infirm to climb up and down the hill.

The foul water pours down the hillside, and collects in the hollow at the bottom, where the garbage and detritus accumulate, where pigs and goats wander, and there is a constant stench from the stagnant, semi-solid lake which it forms. A road is being driven through the area to serve the new apartments. Some women sit in the sun, sari over their heads, skin blanched by dust, with a hammer breaking boulders into small stones for the road.

The hierarchy of poverty on the arid hillside ensures that the better dwellings are at the bottom of the hill. The higher you go up the steep scarp, the meaner the huts become, just as the vegetation, sparse enough even at the base, grows more thinly as you climb. The space for the huts has been carved out of the hill itself, in a series of rough, narrow terraces. The lower ones are several yards wide, but towards the top they are only ledges in the natural slope of the hill, so it looks as if people could lose their foothold at any moment and fall into the ravine. From a distance it looks at bit like a medieval European hill-town; but when you approach you can see the heterogeneous materials that have gone into its construction, the jumble of palm-leaves and pieces of old packing-cases, some of them still stamped with their contents or place of origin, like Assam Tea and Karachi and Liverpool,or This side Up, With Care. The people at the top of this natural pyramid are poorer than those lower down even though the bottom of the slope is more pestilential, have fewer possessions, and the labour of carrying water or firewood becomes more arduous. Around the pool of rubbish grow lilac flowers on thin grey bushes, in some places called 'shameless', because they will grow anywhere, in others 'hardworking', because they grow all the year round. On the other side of the unfinished road are the factories, many of them belonging to multinational companies. The more solid homes of factory workers contrast strongly with the improvised slum-dwellings; just as their lives are altogether more regular and disciplined – the strongest discipline of all being the vast reservoir of labour living on the side of the hill, the thousands of people waiting to take any job that should fall vacant.

Because the slum does not officially exist, the people have to fend for themselves. Water has been brought here illegally, but is available only a few hours a day. At noon the tap is surrounded by people carrying kundhas, barrels, pots; one woman carries a tin labelled Acrylic Emulsion on her head.

Although the slum is on government land, the huts and shanties are often sold in private deals between individuals. If people become unemployed or sick they may sell a more substantial hut and move up the hill, to hack out a piece of flat earth near the peak, which remains as yet uncluttered and bare. The better huts may be sold for R7000–8000. Many of those at the bottom are used as small enterprises. Some are the result of charitable income-generation schemes, designed to extend family earning power – batik or sewing; others are doing outwork for the multinational companies, like the sweated trades in the old East End: people are making sportswear, tennis and running shorts, stitching T-shirts with familiar logos and emblems. Others are sub-contracting, and have sometimes been set up with a bank loan to help with raw materials, a sewing machine, a stock of goods. One woman was making pot-scourers. Inside a dark, narrow hut, a machine was knitting what looked like a continuous cylindrical stocking of red twine. This is cut into equal lengths, sewn by hand at top and bottom, and then sold as those pot-cleaners that can be bought in hardware shops for a few pence. The woman whose business it is buys great hanks of red, orange and blue twine; and now employs two young men who work the machine, sew the scourers and deliver the product to the company. In another hut a whole family works, plaiting gilded fibre into belts and threading them with mother-of-pearl shells, so they can be cut up into lengths to make girdles for evening dresses and saris, or used as hair ornaments. The man who runs this enterprise employs family and neigbours; he produces immense quantities of the distinctive braiding, which is looped in long, gold-coloured chains around the hut, stored on shelves, thrust into polythene bags.

Elsewhere, two boys are making earrings: simple studs, which they fire with a crude and smoky blow-torch to melt the alloy and make it more malleable. There is no ventilation in the hut. They are seated on high stools at a bench, bent almost double over their work, and inhaling fumes and smoke. One of them coughs from time to time, a dry, tubercular rasp. They work up to twelve hours a day, and sell the earings to shopkeepers in Colaba. They make about 30 rupees a day, but they have to buy the metal; they are members of the same family, and between them have sixteen dependants. Next door a woman is weaving thin strips of raffia across the wooden seat of a cane chair. She can make one of these a day for one and a half rupees. If she worked all day, she could conceivably make two; but she has five children, two of them under three. The pattern is intricate, and the raffia has to be carefully woven. It is a strain on the eyes and the back.

These are the best dwellings, and there is some activity in almost every one. They are unevenly built, close together. Most have sloping roofs, many with red tiles. The rough boulders of the natural landscape protrude here and there, incongruously forming a piece of furniture in somebody's home, and sometimes draped with a piece of cloth to form a chair or table; the boulders are black and highly polished, scoured by dust so they gleam in the sun. The passages between the huts have been smoothed with cow dung, which hardens like concrete; though by February it is cracked and fissured after several months of dry weather and the desiccating wind that blows round the hillside. Some of the passages run with rivulets of dirty water and excrement; the smell is overpowering. Hogs, goats and dogs roam the area of waste. Suddenly, the narrow gorge opens out. By the water tap some women are cleaning aluminium utensils, applying a paste of abrasive mud to make them shine. Then the road turns upwards and the huts deteriorate. One has been built as a go-down, and is stacked from floor to roof with plastic – sheets, bags, lengths of polythene. Another is full of rags, which children collect and bring here to be stored before they are sold back to the factories. Many of the rags are impregnated with chemicals, which cause eye and skin infections. One woman makes two rupees a kilo by selling the plastic bags in which milk is sold. She opens up each bag with a knife, washes it thoroughly, dries it and returns it to the factory. Her hut is full of the evil-smelling squares of plastic.

People sit at sewing machines in the open fronts of the buildings, making shirts, shoes, skirts, all paid by the piece at some insignificant sum. Here, as Paul Harrison suggests,[9] we can see the sameness of the capitalist enterprise in its global reach: Ghatkopar would recognize the conditions of Brick Lane. Even the folklore of the sweated trades is the same: the story of a week's labour expended on sewing or knitting a garment for luxury wear, for which the worker receives a derisory sum,

---

[9] Paul Harrison, *Inside the Inner City* (Penguin, Harmondsworth, 1983).

and then sees it offered for sale at ten or twenty times the price she was paid.

It is easy to be nauseated by the chaotic development, and not to see the gradations of poverty, just as visitors to the working-class streets of Victorian England were so disgusted that they failed to see the subtle distinction conferred on people by their possession of a brass door-knocker, a passage through the house, or a piece of foliate moulding above the front door. In some of the better parts of Amruth Nagar, channels have been dug to drain away the foul water: the channels are then covered with smooth slabs of stone, which mitigates the nuisance. Many of the people in this part of Bombay are from Uttar Pradesh, and are said to be natural entrepreneurs. Indeed, many of the people professed to despise factory work, though they could earn more money there. Perhaps they – like the handloom weavers in Britain – prefer not to surrender the last vestiges of control over their work, even though it means living in greater poverty.

As you go deeper into the slum area there is a clearing where a small market has been set up: tomatoes, aubergines, a few oranges, grapes are for sale. A boy is selling pieces of blackened banana, fruit that has spoiled. He cuts the bad parts away; beside him is a pile of fruit he hasn't yet started on. He cuts away with surgeon-like skill, removing only the parts of the fruit that are rotten, wasting nothing that could be eaten. But even these unsaleable bits are snatched up by some small children. As he discards the sticky black stuff, they fall on it and eat it; a swarm of flies hovers over the sweet fruit and the faces of the children smeared with it.

The Samaj Seva Niketan (House of Service for the People) wanted to start a school in the area. They had to buy a piece of ground – very small and narrow – big enough to accommodate twenty or thirty children at a time. It cost 3,500 rupees, even though the land was neither theirs to buy nor the vendor's to sell.

In the *balwadi* (nursery) there are forty five-year-olds. The teacher is a young woman of twenty, from an untouchable family, a passionate and devoted woman who will do anything to help lift up those of her caste. She is a little like those pupil teachers in late Victorian elementary schools, close in sympathy and experience to those they taught, but unqualified and frustrated. She feels inferior because she cannot speak English. Many people stive to send their children to schools where the medium of instruction is English. There is one just outside the slum, called the Little Flower School of English. It is in a shed.

The teacher lives with her brother-in-law. Her father died, and the family gave the piece of land they owned to someone else to cultivate for a few years, while the rest of the family came to the city. Under a law designed to stop exploitation by big farmers, the land reverts to those who cultivate it after a certain period; and under this law, the family lost their land. They are too poor to pursue it in court. The teacher says that the people of Amruth Nagar are exploited whatever they do. The medical facilities are sketchy – just a clinic run by charity. The public authorities treat people without respect; facilities are inadequate and stretched. If you save up and go to a private doctor, he will send you from specialist to specialist, until the bills mount up and you pay out all the money you have. Many people stick to traditional medicines, herbal and ayurvedic remedies.

Like all migrants, those who have come from Uttar Pradesh have a sense of dual lives: here, life is only provisional. One man has a picture of his wife from the village on the wall. He lives with his wife from the slum. He says there is no conflict. He cannot be with his real wife, so he takes one for the life his is leading; but since this life is not real, nor is his present wife.

We go back through the slum. A boy of twelve is sitting on a stone near the well. He works in the plastics factory, but hasn't gone to work today because there was a quarrel between his mother and father. His father was drunk and beat her. Children are not supposed to be employed in factories under the age of sixteen. I ask him how he manages to get round the regulations. He shrugs. All the children who can get jobs take them. You think you're lucky, even though the work is hard. You can be fined if you do anything wrong. You lose pay if they decide you are not working hard enough. If the foreman doesn't like you, he finds you the worst work – carrying heavy loads or working with the chemicals. He says that when he returns to work tomorrow there may be no job for him, because he has taken the day off. He is an intelligent boy, who wants to study. He has an uncle in England. He takes out a well-thumbed letter. The post-mark is Wolverhampton; it is dated two years ago.

The water is now running freely at the tap, on the edge of the square that serves as both playing space for the children and communal latrine. Women are washing clothes, pounding them with stones. It is a marvel how little water they require to keep clean. A small plastic jug, containing not a pint of water, serves to wash a five-year-old thoroughly: just a little water in the palm of the mother's hand, a thorough rubbing of the scalp; and then the remains of the water poured over her. The energy and effort required, not just for survival, but to maintain dignity and self-respect, are awesome; and give the lie to the prejudices of the rich.

The most coveted jobs in Ghatkopar are in the grandly named 'industrial estate'; not because they are particularly well paid, but because they are unmistakeably part of the modern sector. The conditions in which people work there have not been seen in Britain since the time of Engels.

The factories are a series of stone sheds, often ramshackle and crumbling, merging one into another on two sides of a rough road encumbered with waste, industrial debris, dented oil-drums. The workplaces are sheltered from the sun by rough strips of sacking sewn together. Some of them are sub-contractors to multinationals: Colgate Palmolive has a toothbrush factory, Johnson & Johnson make soap; there is a subsidiary of Philips. The soap factory has uneven heaps of greasy discoloured tallow piled against the wall. Although the official Maharashtra State miniumum wage is 18 rupees a day (about £1.50), some of the women in the soap factory earn only half as much; and although the lowest legal age for factory work is 16, there were many children as young as ten on the estate. Nowhere is the discrepancy between the finished product – especially toiletries and cosmetics – and the conditions in which it is produced more clear. When the soap reaches the market, it is bathed in a pure promotional light of desirability and hygiene, which effectively insulates the consumers from the producers – that most significant of divisions in the contemporary capitalist project, which keeps its subject and exploited peoples well separated; a process made far easier by an increasingly global division of labour.

Most of the enterprises are small, and for a good reason: when a company employs more than 22 people, the workers are entitled to form a union. There is a forge with an open furnace: the temperature outside is about 35°C; as you enter, the heat takes your breath away. The men are almost naked, and the flame burnishes their emaciated and sweating bodies; the scene is reminiscent of those testimonies from the Black Country of the early industrial era in Britain.

In the next factory, dark and dusty, where the noise is deafening, aluminium cooking-oil containers are made. Each worker has a single semi-skilled function. Marvari, a woman in her twenties, has worked here for eight years. She works eight hours a day plus three hours overtime; and receives 15 rupees for her 11-hour day. She operates a press, cutting the metal sheets into strips. These she passes manually to a woman who sits over an open flame, and whose job is to make the metal pliable. It is then bent in the required shape for the oil-can, and this is rivetted by a man operating a machine; thence they go to a woman who punches a hole for the opening at the top; and finally the base of the can is fitted. After they have been inspected, they pass to an area in front of the factory. There, two boys, about 12 and 14, sit with blow-torches and soldering irons, attaching the thin strips of metal for the handles. They do not work inside the factory, because their work is sub-contracted. A rough screen of palm-leaves leaves a lattice of sunlight across their back; their eyes stream from the fierce torch flames.

But these are not the worst work-places. Bhavani Plastics makes sandals. The workers are mainly women and children. The factory has a lower storey, with a kind of overhanging balcony reached by a wooden staircase. The soles of the sandals arrive downstairs from the moulds. A boy of about 15 sits over a metal spike which pierces the sole, so that the straps that will form the toe-thongs can be inserted. This is done by a group of women, who thread and glue the plastic. One woman of about 30 describes how she got her 11-year old son a job here. He was a good (i.e. fast) worker, and when the company opened its new factory in Gujarat, they took him with them. The family had no choice, because his father has TB, and the boy was being offered 30 rupees a day (£2). They have promised to send him home once a year.

In the upper part of the factory children spray the sandals with an automatic paint-gun, orange and blue. They are unprotected from the overpowering fumes of the paint – you can feel its effect after just a few minutes. Their hands, faces and clothes are stained with the lurid colours; the oldest is 16, the youngest 10. Bhavani Plastics have donated a sapling in a painted oil-drum to improve the environment; it stands on a heap of rubble and stones against a background of barbed wire.

Sundip, a child of ten, goes from factory to factory, delivering tea. He carries a blue plastic crate containing glasses, and a battered tea-kettle. He wears a torn white shirt, khaki shorts and white plastic sandals, and lives in the 'hotel' which employs him – little more than a glorified tea-stall. He has to work as and when he is needed; his hours of work are not calculable. His mother abandoned the family. His father and stepmother collect his wages from the employer. He doesn't know how much he earns.

In a large four-storey building – significantly the most imposing structure in Ghatkopar – a number of industrial units are collected under one roof. Companies vary in their employment practices: reasonable training and conditions next door to unbreathable air and derisory pay. Here is the Colgate toothbrush factory. Wages vary between 8 and 20 rupees a day, according to age and skill. A boy sits cross-legged at a low metal table, softening the bristles; he passes them to an older man operating a machine which punches the bristles into the head of the strips of blue and yellow plastic that form the handle. The next machinist trims them to an even length. They pass to a table where women inspect each one and ensure that the bristles are fast – this is one of the lowest-paid jobs. A man operates a machine that seals each one in polythene, and they are packed for distribution by a boy of about 15. More than 40,000 toothbrushes are produced each day.

The Palmolive packets are printed in a neighbouring unit. The same company also prints other familiar packets – Surf, Director's Whisky, and cartons of Best Prawns, for export with the labels printed in English, French and Japanese. One former mill-worker pointed out that protein-rich food was being exported to the overfed from a country half of the population of which suffers from protein deficiency.

The Palmolive packets leave the printing unit a smudgy dull red colour. The colour is made fast by yet another sub-contractor. The varnishing room contains a single machine; on the wall there is a picture of Ganesh, with four Colgate cartons as a frame.

In a small electrical company I met some of the lowest paid of all. One woman was getting 8 rupees a day, and travelling for 2 rupees from Thane, one of Bombay's expanding satellite towns. Thus her net income is 40p a day. Labour legislation is easily avoided through sub-contracting, which effectively conceals chains of exploitation. In this factory I saw women using a press which I had seen in operation in South London, punching holes in strips of metal for electrical fittings. Their wages were about 15 rupees a day, compared with the £15 or so per day which their equivalents – ironically, also Indian women – were receiving in Croydon. Here is what 'becoming competitive in the world' actually means. The sub-text of the Thatcherite rhetoric suddenly springs to life; but at the same time, so does its opposite – the need for an effective global solidarity, a sense of kinship between our own lives and the plight of these exploited women and children, the urgency of creating, not a diluted or weakened labour movement, but one that is far more dynamic and internationally aware.

One of the biggest factories belongs to the Bombay Oil Company, screen-printing on plastic containers – Parachute coconut oil, brake fluid, dishwashing liquid. As the coloured plastic cylinders arrive from the mould, two boys of about 14 hold them over fierce torches, to burn off imperfections, which fly off in a blaze of sparks. They are then smooth enough for the printing – the directions for use, the product logo. This is done by women. Then a boy with a razor blade sits and scapes off every fleck and smudge of paint that has overspilt in the process.

Many women in Ghatkopar who can't get a job in the factories do domestic work. A cleaning woman will earn about 50 rupees a month for doing two hours a day in a private flat. Most will have three jobs each day, which often involves walking long distances. I spoke to Multi, a thin but cheerful girl of 13. Her mother has polio and her father is mentally ill. She is employed by a rich family in Amruthnagar. She gets the left-overs of food, so her family at least eats better than most. She is treated kindly, plays with the child of her employers, and is paid 80 rupees a month. She talks about all the money she has saved, and says that one day she will have a house with a fan – the highest luxury she can conceive. Her greatest ambition is to get a job on the industrial estate.

Nothing, it seems, is forgotten so readily as poverty; or perhaps it would be more accurate to say that nothing is so swiftly lost as sympathy with the poor. So many after-images of our own experience are here, where human labour is cheap and ill-organized, where people emerging slowly from ancient rural cultures are ill-equipped to understand and resist the processes through which they must pass in that man-made determinism we call 'development': that artifical fate that accords so well with traditional cultures where passivity and endurance have been the only rational human response in the face of a dispossession that seems without remedy.

The process of awakening from a traditional rural poverty is not so easily seen in a city of eight million like Bombay. It can be measured more clearly in a community closer to its rural hinterland.

9

The Hinterland: Nagpur

Nagpur is in the very centre of India, 500 miles east of Bombay, and less than forty miles from Gandhi's ashram at Sevagram. It is the second city and former capital of Maharashtra. Nagpur is marked by traditional subsistence farming, by patterns of colonial domination, when it became an important cotton-growing centre, and by the subsequent modifications demanded by the influence of the world market. It is a centre of orange-growing and teak production. It was the site of the foundation of an important part of the great Tata industrial empire, which opened its cotton mills on January 1877, the day Queen Victoria became Empress of India, and still calls them Empress Mills.

In spite of a few grandiose buildings among their lawns and flower-filled gardens – the High Court with its white rotunda that seems to float over the dusty city, the GPO with its immaculate beds of asters, salvias and roses, the rose-coloured granite of the railway station designed for ceremonial departures and arrivals – there is little to suggest any Western idea of a city of a million and a half people. It remains diffuse and haphazard in its spread, with only limited built-up areas, where there is a dense confusion of small workshops, booths, shops, cafés and open markets. Roads are thick with dust and overhung by a maze of electricity cables, thronged with bicycles, flanked by roughly finished concrete buildings, shanties and hand-painted hoardings which advertise television sets, cigarettes and the lurid passions of the movies. Every day, it seems, the city is overwhelmed by its rural origins. It seems an improvised and crowded place, filled with small vendors from the land with a headload of cauliflowers or aubergines, grapes, millet, oranges; with pieces of waste ground where cows and goats pick over the vegetable matter decaying in the sweetish languor of the hot air; with cycle and radio-repair shops, stalls and booths of wood and corrugated iron which all encroach onto the roads that are always jammed with cycle rickshaws, carts pulled by humped oxen, brightly painted Public Carriers, cycles and a few cars – Ambassador (the old Morris Oxford) and Padmini (Fiat), a few of them with lace curtains at the back window to shield their occupants from the sun, and creating in their wake a fog of dust that blanches the leaves of the trees and the faces of passers-by.

On the Western side of the city – the Old Civil Lines – there are colleges and schools, grand facades painted in terracotta and cream, colleges of social work, law, commerce and agriculture, the university; most of them in their own compound, shaded by pipal and bougainvillea. Here too is the Ambesari tank – the city reservoir; in January, the adjacent gardens are full of the flowers of an English autumn: dahlias and asters, as well as oleanders, hibiscus and the soaring trunks of teak. It is not like a city at all. But what is immediately striking is the extraordinary animation of people, the high cost in human labour simply to survive; in dramatic contrast to the passivity of people in Western cities being carried in tense silence to their places of work. Throughout the day there is an unabating movement and sense of purpose. Bicycles with their sheaf of purple sugar cane, the ramshackle booths selling tea spiced with ginger, the handcarts piled with bundles of washing or timber or oranges or cooking vessels. The livelihood of whole sections of the city depends upon a single commodity, and sometimes on minute quantities of it. There is a vast network of sub-contracting. For instance, there must be hundreds, if not thousands, of people involved in the selling of bananas. Men stand beside covered carts by the railway station, with piles of several varieties of banana – red, yellow, green plantain. Then there are the women who buy from them a headload which they carry in shallow reed-baskets; loads so heavy that they cannot pick them up or set them down without help. These are then sold at the roadside, or perhaps taken door to door in the richer parts of the city. Other people – mainly women – will be selling just a few handfuls of bananas from an upturned wooden box at the roadside in a poorer district, sitting there for hours, patiently, but without apparently selling any. Even lower in the scale, a boy has bought some blackened and half-rotten bananas and is offering them from his place under a half-collapsed black umbrella near the railway bridge; while in the slum areas, halves or simply pieces of bruised and overripe fruit will be offered by a youth or old woman sitting by the side of the open drain that is also the main thoroughfare.

The arrivals from the countryside begin every morning before daybreak. Some people come by train, others by ox-cart or bicycle. Many walk with a headload of whatever they had to sell: a bundle of chick-peas still on their feathery stalks, tomatoes, jowari (millet), some herbs, eggs or milk. The hinterland of farms and fields, the network of villages far beyond the city, are nevertheless a constant presence within it.

Although it has been one of the greatest achievements of post-Independence India to become almost self-sufficient in food, some of the

problems associated with improved agriculture – the cost of expensive
fertilizer and pesticides – means that some small farmers can no longer
afford to maintain their family plots. Borgaon is a village some twelve miles
outside Nagpur, a mile and a half from the main road, reached by a dusty
track through orange plantations and jowari fields. Villagers here had
gradually forfeited their land, after the introduction of high-yield varieties
of millet and wheat. After the initial year or two of advantage, the prices of
the inputs had risen to such an extent that they could not afford to maintain
their land. Accordingly, one by one, they had sold their land or raised loans
they could not pay back, in order to keep on cultivating it. All the families
eventually sold to two big landlords, mostly for 2,000 or 3,000 rupees. This
answered the short-term needs, but it meant that there would never be
enough money to buy land again. They were then at the mercy of day-
labouring, intermittent and irregular work at harvest or planting. They had
to forfeit their living places, which were demolished to make way for
increased acreage of crops, and were reduced to living in cattle-sheds. This
story also has its antecedents – in the improvements of agriculture in
eighteenth-century Britain, which drove people from the land; only here
there is no vast industrial expansion to absorb them. Some of these landless
labourers will have walked with their families to Nagpur, and are doubtless
to be found on the pavements of the city, cooking their handful of rice and
vegetable in the few tongues of flame that can be coaxed from a little
scavenged firewood, and screened from the sun and the dust by a few sere
palm-leaves. A group of the villagers squatted on some unused government
land in March 1979; and eighteen families were provided with a small hut,
ten feet square. The cost of this, 750 rupees each, was met by the
government. But the cheap structure did not stand for even one monsoon.
They were virtually swept away. Each hut had one door and one window,
with no cross-ventilation. A family of six or seven were sleeping, eating
and cooking in this space. Those who had squatted felt the government help
had scarcely improved their position. The village people organized to
plan houses as they wanted them; and they were helped by the Industrial
Services Institute in Nagpur, which is partly funded by Oxfam. The people
described the sort of houses they wanted, and an architect designed low-cost
structures as they had suggested; with living-room, kitchen, and toilet
connected to a semi-septic tank. When I visited in 1983, the building work
was almost complete: a wide street of beaten earth in a field of whispering
millet. Each house was set well apart from its neighbour, colour washed in
white or pale blue; each one with mud flooring and a veranda, Bangalore
roof-tiles, and walls of brick and mortar. Most of the materials had been
found locally, including mud and river-sand. The people are still poor; they
depend on labouring for the big farmers at the time of the harvest of millet,
wheat, oranges or cotton. Many of the wells in the neighbourhood have

been closed by the landlords, or they are forbidden to the low-caste people of the village, which means that the walk to fetch water is long and arduous for the women whose work it remains. The total dependency on the landlords has been somewhat reduced.

The government land has been partly distributed to those who squatted on it. An experimental scheme was set up to help twenty-seven families cultivate small plots (less than five acres), such a way as to relieve them of the need to borrow money at extortionate interest, which would ensure that their land would not revert to the moneylenders or big landlords again. Under an Oxfam scheme, HYV seeds, fertilizer and insecticide were made available for each family to cultivate half an acre of wheat. In return, each beneficiary was to give back one and a half times the wheat he had started with to the village panchayat committee. This was preserved for the next season to extend the scheme to other farmers. In addition, the families were to be helped with millet to cover one acre, which was to be sown at the time of the monsoon. Each farmer was to return to the seed-bank half the cost of the materials that supported the first year's crop – seed, fertilizer, insecticide and BCH powder. The seed-bank uses the fund to extend the scheme to more families for the next season. In this way, there is no need for outside assistance, no dependency on growing debt. Each small farmer helped by the scheme produced twelve quintals of millet. For the first year, eighty-five acres were under cultivation; by the next three times as many. Self-reliance is the objective – the extrication from dependency in which all the promises of 'improvements' had further enriched the well-to-do, and made the poor poorer. What has occurred here is a microcosm of what has to occur on a vast scale and in even more difficult circumstances, if the majority of the people on the earth are to disengage ourselves from the manipulations of ever greater concentrations of wealth.

Most people in the district of Nagpur are not so fortunate; and it is they who swell the population each day, in a vast migration of those desperate to extend the family income. The most spectacular moment of the day is the return home at dusk, when the dust, beaten back from the centres of the busy streets by women of the scheduled castes, rises in a choking fog and collects in drifts on the ill-defined margin of the streets; with the result that the sunset is always seen through a haze of the most vivid colour: a bright orange that turns to crimson and violet before dying in a dull, misty blue. In the markets, evening is the busiest time, when people have securely in their hand the price of the night's meal, which for many is a measure of the success of the day's work.

Late in the day the youngsters bring their scavenged cargo, and converge on the booths of merchants near the station. In the light of kerosene lamps their pickings are weighed on the balance-scales: piles of newspaper, leather, fragments of plastic, heaps of rags. The buyer unwraps the bundles carefully, to make sure thay are indeed all rags and all paper; finds a stone in one of them, and hurls its contents across the road at the child who had tried to cheat him. The boy runs after them, his small bundle blown about and disintegrating in the wind. The children watch the balance, to make sure that they are not cheated. The price is 70 paise for a kilo of paper (about 5p), one rupee for metal, more for rubber. A boy of eighteen who looks younger, with hair just appearing on his lip, and an uncorrected turn in his eye, says that of his family of eight he was the only boy. Only he and his mother work. He hires his cart for two rupees a day, and is lucky if he gets six or seven rupees' worth of saleable material each day. Today he has some empty bottles, a rusty tin, an old car number plate, two broken shoes, some splinters of glass. He looks undernourished and exhausted. His life, he said, is just work and sleep. He falls into the hut where he lives with his family and gives his money to his mother for the evening meal. He took me to see where he lived: palm-leaves and polythene, a temporary place, on a long piece of ground in Babulkheda, between an open drain and the sparse white monuments of the Muslim cemetery. He no sooner arrived home than he fell asleep. His mother covered him with a blanket; his frail body is all that stands between the younger children and destitution.

The waste material in these places is the bodies of the people, that prodigal wear and tear of the human fabric. Here is the answer to anyone who feels that there is anything ennobling or spiritual about poverty: it is a boy of about eighteen, lying drunk by the roadside while his mother wails and beats his inert body, because he has been unable to bear it and has spent the money he has earned on cheap spirits.

I followed an old woman, perhaps as old as sixty, well beyond the expected lifespan of about fifty in India; tiny, shrivelled, with thin cheeks, iron-grey hair. She was walking patiently behind an ox-cart, waiting for the beast to shit in the road. She then scooped it up and carried it in her head-basket. She then began to follow another cart, tirelessly following until those animals had shit in the road. Slowly, the dung accumulates in her basket. At the end of the afternoon she will have walked several miles, criss-crossing the city. She takes the dung home to her hut in Babulkheda, and makes it into fuel: flat, round cakes drying in the sun. Her family will use some for their cooking requirements; the rest she will sell in the neighbourhood.

The tips of used coal beside the railway lines swarm with women and children, who are collecting dust and cinders, which they make into rough cobbles with a little water; some of the children use their saliva. This too is used for cooking-fires. The coal-tips, perhaps fifty feet high, are piles of dust and spent fuel, on which it is almost impossible to gain a foothold.

The children are always collapsing and rolling down the side of the hill; they get up laughing, black with the dust. They bring to mind those pictures of Britain's coal mining areas in the 1930s, when the pit-brew women worked on the coal-tips, and the unemployed went searching for fuel. In fact there are so many impressions that speak to us of our past that a journey to the poor is more like a displacement in time than one in space. What is at issue is that elision, the leap from the extremes of poverty to extremes of another sort of impoverishment in the West, from the severe undernourishment and depletion of strength of bodies that pay the price in disease, premature ageing and death, to the inanition of the West, where appetites grow and skills decay.

In Nagpur I was able to look at one group of workers who had recently become organised and had freed themselves from ancient traditions of subordination. But at the very moment of victory, they are threatened by technological change associated with the determinism of 'development'.

The cycle rickshaw is a frail carriage of thin metal, with a canvas hood that is raised or lowered like that of a landau. It surmounts what is essentially an elongated tricycle: the passenger carriage occupies the space behind the saddle over the back axle. Some of the rickshaws are decorated with garlands of plastic flowers: others have been painted by their owners; some have the swastika cross on the back; others are stamped 'Hypothecated to the Bank of India'. It is only in recent years that large numbers of the rickshawmen in Nagpur have become owners of their vehicles.

Traditionally, the rickshaw drivers hired the cycles from big garage-owners, some of whom had as many as a hundred vehicles. They were hired out at the rate of about five rupees each a day, which sometimes amounted to half the daily earnings of the drivers. The work is extremely arduous. Nagpur in summer is one of the hottest cities on Earth – the daytime temperature in May is 42°C, and although the temperature after the monsoon drops a little the humidity rises. At that time the countryside grows green, but the dust of the city is churned to mud, making the roads sticky and hard to drive on. The labour required by pedalling is relentless. Most of the rickshawman are thin, emaciated even. Life expectancy is lower than the Indian average of fifty or so. In the middle of the day the rickshaws are drawn up in clusters at the side of the road, and the driver sits in the passenger seat, with his feet up over the metal frame, sprawled in what looks like extreme discomfort, but sleeping the sleep of utter exhaustion. It is impossible to sustain the work for the whole day: a journey of just a few miles makes the veins throb and the sweat pour down the neck and back. Although Nagpur is a flat city, there are long, shallow gradients; and it is often easier for the driver to get out and push the vehicle rather than pedal it. It is not only the well-to-do who use rickshaws, for it is the only way for many infirm or old people to get round the city, as well as the children, going to and from their private schools in bright blue blazers and caps and new satchels on their backs, five or six of them crammed into the rickshaw at a time.

I spent the day with the President of the Collected Trade Unions, which formed the United Front of Rickshaw drivers. Ramsingh Takur hired a driver to take us round the city. It was a disagreeable sensation to be propelled by the driver's enormous effort, to see his body strain as he stood on the pedals. His movements had the desperate slowness of someone drowning. The loss of liquid from his body was so great that it seemed he was melting. The perspiration was only partly absorbed by the cloth he wore round his head. One of the pedals was broken, so that only the metal part remained, and he had to clench his bare foot, prehensile, round the metal bar in order not to slip.

In spite of this, the story I heard is about the vast improvements that the rickshawmen have won in their conditions. In 1973 there was the first meeting of rickshaw drivers that was to lead eventually to the formation of the United Front – an amalgamation of fifteen separate unions. The Front was formed to demand that the Maharashtra Government abolish the system whereby the monopolists could hire out up to a hundred rickshaws a day, and take as rent half the earnings of the drivers, who would be left without enough money to feed themselves and their families. There was a demonstration when the Chief Minister visited Nagpur in 1977: the Minister's office was blocked, and the drivers would not let him leave until he had spoken to them. He promised help. A year later nothing had happened, so they confronted the State Government when it was in session in Nagpur in November 1978. It took until 1980 for their demands to be accepted. The nationalized banks were ordered to grant loans at four per cent interest to help drivers buy their own vehicles, and the monopoly system was in theory abolished. A further law was also passed, stating that the work of the cycle rickshawmen was degrading and inhuman: but since there is no alternative employment, and no other means of cheap transport, this declaration has been permitted to lapse.

Nor did the owners of the big fleets of rickshaws accept this encroachment on their power. The idea was that the drivers, with the bank loan topped up with a small loan from the union, would buy their own rickshaws. The price was about 1,200 rupees. At this time there were attempts to design alternative vehicles that would require less effort for their propulsion: the Oxtrike, designed in Oxford with the help of the Centre for Intermediate Technology, looked as if it might provide the answer, but the manufacture would have been too costly, and the maintenance impossible, so the traditional conveyance remained unchanged. There were two manufacturers in the city. Because of the likely demand for rickshaws by potential owners, the price doubled to 2,500 rupees. To break down this monopoly the United Front, with the help of the Industrial Services Institute, set up an Assembling Centre, and made and supplied rickshaws at the old price of 1,200 rupees.

There had also been a loophole in the law that forbade the ownership of large numbers of rickshaws and their hire for rent. If a woman was a widow, and had no other form of income, she was permitted to own up to five rickshaws, which she could continue to hire out for the day; and there would always be a proportion of drivers who would not be able to maintain payments on a bank loan, through sickness or infirmity. And even five rickshaws would bring the widow 25 rupees a day. It was not difficult for the monopolists to protect their interests through this escape clause. Large numbers of widows came forward to attest that their only source of income was from the rickshaws bequeathed by their late husbands. The big owners were able to buy for a `small sum the oaths of a considerable number of women, and through members of their family or friends thus maintain control over large numbers of rickshaws.

In spite of this, some drivers did become owner-drivers – *chalak-malak*, and by 1983 almost a quarter of the estimated 20,000 in the city were buying their own vehicles.

The coming together of the different unions, which had been fragmented geographically and ideologically across the Nagpur city area, was what made the transformation possible. It resulted in the new owner-drivers increasing their income by far more than could have been expected merely by being relieved of the five-rupees rent they had paid to the garage-owners. The pride of ownership, the sense of independence, have created a quite different feeling. The work is still as exacting, but it seems less harsh when you are doing it for yourself rather than being compelled to pay half your earnings to someone else. The average income has turned out to be closer to three times the amount gained under the former system. You can tell which rickshaws are owned by the drivers – they are better maintained, brightly painted; some have flowers twined around the metal struts that support the hood, others carry balloons, and have an air of permanent celebration.

The cycles are not difficult to maintain. Many of the drivers carry a tin of nails and a rudimentary puncture repair outfit attached to the back axle, and every few hundred yards there is a boy seated under a tree with a pump and repair kit, and a blackened kettle steaming on a trivet over a fire.

Even so, the work remains as it always was, debilitating and injurious. And other threats remain, which are at the same time improvements – and this is how 'development', something advancing, ineluctable, also involves new forms of dispossession. For one thing, the autorickshaws are

beginning to threaten the employment of the cycles. These are based upon
the scooter rather than the bicycle, with a more solid carriage, and room
for two or three people. These have the obvious advantage of being faster,
and, especially, of requiring less effort. They are also less stable. I saw two
or three accidents: one was knocked over as it was struck a glancing blow
by a lorry turning a corner. The occupants, badly hurt, spilled onto the
road. An angry crowd followed the lorry, but it would not stop. The
autorickshaws are also more expensive. The loans on them are unlikely to
be paid back in the three years or so it takes for the cycles. They require
more specialized knowledge for their maintenance: and to support them,
there are a number of workshops which deal with spares and repairs for
autos. They require a higher deposit payment; and although they are far
less demanding, they intensify the hours of work, and the charge to
passengers is higher.

In this way the livelihood of the cycle rickshawmen is already
undermined by the obsolescence of their vehicle, which has, indeed,
become archaic in some of the big cities. I did not see any in Bombay.
Because of the increased cost of the autorickshaws the likelihood of default
in such a competitive undertaking becomes greater. Each individual driver
has to do more journeys, make more money. Unfortunately, the threat
doesn't stop there. There are already a few motor taxis in Nagpur: the
Padminis waiting at the airport and outside the bigger hotels. In the large
cities the taxis tend to displace the autorickshaw, and these then move out
to poorer and peripheral areas. In Bombay there are not even many autos
in the commercial and rich parts; but in the poor suburbs there are
literally hundreds of autorickshaws, all queuing for what seems never
quite enough work.

The process of modernization is thus ambiguous in its gains. Even the
driver who has paid off the bank loan enjoys an only fragile independence.
Gains are always temporary and mitigated, and can always be forfeited by
the intense competition from all those waiting to enter the market, those
waiting for someone to slip out through sickness, accident or default, or
simply because he is no longer physically able to stand up to the work. The
drivers pass from a disorganized subjection to predatory individuals into
the impersonal thraldom of banks. I met one victim of this change. She
had come to the union office, and later we visited her in her hut in
Mominpura. She is a widow of twenty-eight. Her husband had died of TB
ten days earlier. There are still 240 rupees owing on the rickshaw. Her
brother is driving it at the moment and giving her half the money he earns,
but this is not enough to feed either her family or his, let alone to pay back
the money to the bank. All she eats is *bakri* with chutney. She sits on the
hard dry earth outside her hut, rocking to and fro and nibbling a chilli,
with her youngest child of about eighteen months in her arms. She hadn't

even known that her husband was ill until a few days before his death. He had kept it from her, hoping to pay off the bank loan before he died. Her eyes fill with tears at the thought of what he must have endured, to have kept going with terminal consumption. She feels guilty and reproaches herself for not having realized. She had noticed that he had been falling asleep at lot, had been coughing blood; but he had reassured her that he was all right. She had thought he was becoming lazy, because he had not been able to maintain his income in recent months. She describes the last days she spent with him; the sweat on his face, the dryness of his skin, the fits of coughing. This woman has a daughter of fifteen, who is already married and has gone to live with her husband's family. The other children are with her, aged ten and eight, and the baby. She looks much older than her age; and she holds the ten-year-old to her and tells him that he will have to earn some money for them to live; he looks grave and bewildered and accepting, and he tries to reassure her: the gesture of a man, as he strokes her hair.

Although Nagpur does not look like a big city, it has all the casualties of city life. Beggars are fewer than in a place like Bombay, but there is a minority for whom begging is the only life they know; and there are many families and individuals for whom the street is the only living-place. These are quite distinct from the itinerant workers on roads and public works, who squat in temporary camps of bamboo and rattan, and are much reminiscent of the mobile navigators of early Victorian England. Some of the street families have arrived from the countryside, landless labourers, those turned out of their homes by debt or dispute. While I was in Nagpur, a group of tribals (the early Gond inhabitants of central India) had taken up a position outside the palatial building of the Taxation Employees Union, settled with their faded bundles in the lee of the wall that enclosed the compound. The nights can be cold in Nagpur in winter: the embers of their fire glowed in the darkness in the makeshift fireplace of half a dozen bricks, their pieces of vegetable were being cut up on the stone wall; the only container for their cooked rice was a fragment of newspaper. The dispossessed tribals are among the poorest of all, as the lands where they lived have passed into the ownership of big absentee landlords.

Hundreds of people sleep each night under the railway bridges and around the station, lodged on concrete ledges, some lying on narrow metal girders not more than a foot wide. They sleep wrapped from head to foot in dingy, coarse blankets, in full receipt of the blast and fumes from lorries and cars, and the night-long jangle of cycles and the horns of autorickshaws; they lie still as mummies. Among these are some of the most wretched people – those destroyed by alcohol, the mentally sick, those who have been separated from others by sickness or bereavement. A few of these people find their way into the charitable institutions, many of them run by Christian groups. The rest – the beggars, the mutilated, people with bodies used up by leprosy, accident, deformity, syphilis or TB, comprise an underworld which at first encounter is frightening. There was a boy on a trolley who was covered from his shoulders down, his head appearing just above the rough vehicle, with dark curly hair and beautiful teeth, but a completely withered body, so that he was just a head and thorax on wheels; the woman with tangled hair lying on a piece of matting had been a prostitute in Bombay since she was fourteen; she had come back to look for her family when she fell ill, but could no longer find them. She sat under a flimsy shelter of leaves, possessing nothing, not even a cooking pot, completely destitute.

The Missionaries of Charity – a branch of Mother Teresa's foundation in Calcutta – have a refuge to which some of the worst afflicted people find their way. Shanti Bhavan is on the edge of the city: a large bungalow with a stone floor, surrounded by a thatched veranda from which a corridor leads into dim, cool dormitories. Among the forty or so people here are some who have been abandoned by their families, some who are subnormal, others mentally ill or corroded by alcohol. A man sits on the earth of the plot of garden that adjoins the bungalow. He is tending a row of meagre aubergines, just forming, pale on their spindly plants. Although he wears two sweaters he is shivering in the hot sunshine and is perspiring heavily at the same time. It requires almost all the strength he can find to shuffle forward inch by inch on his thin buttocks to lift each vegetable in turn to make sure that are not being eaten by insects. He is torn by a deep, torturing cough, and is in the last stages of TB. He says he is twenty-three, An older man sits on the veranda, scratching pictures in the dust with a twig. He is strapped to a rubber pad, which forms a sort of concave tray around his lower abdomen, and he moves by means of two wooden hand-clogs, capped with rubber, propelling himself along on the rubber platform. His right leg is severed just below the knee, and his left foot is just a stump at the ankle. He worked on the railways; and was in the shunting yards in Nagpur for eighteen years. One day in 1963 a train had been wrongly signalled, and he was run over by a shunting-engine: one leg went in one direction and his foot in the other. He relives the moment as he tells it; the shock and the pain fill his eyes with tears. But the most bitter thing of all was that his wife and brother-in-law ran away together with the money that was paid in compensation by the railway. When he had recovered, he went off on his crutches in search of his wife. One day he saw her across the road, but as he went to cross he was dragged between two cycle rickshaws; and after that he was paralysed below the waist. He never saw his wife again. He lost interest in living, stayed on the streets begging. He was taken in by the Missionaries of Charity two years ago.

His three sons had died; his daughters live with the families of their husbands; he no longer sees them.

On the veranda are the cots of the TB patients, who sleep in the open under the thatch. Inside, the dormitories contain about a dozen beds: metal frames on two metal stands, with thin foam mattresses; men on one side of the corridor, women on the other. Some of the older people are mentally ill. A woman leans against the dark red iron pillar supporting the roof and sings to herself, plucking away at her woollen jumper; another moves about jerkily and laughs wildly from time to time, a desolating, joyless sound. A young man, unbelievably thin, crouches on the veranda and coughs, a dry, fathomless rasp. The woman with the clumsy movement brings him some water in a metal tumbler. She cannot control her hand, and the water splashes on the floor. He looks up at her and smiles, and for a brief moment of rough tenderness she puts an arm round him.

The rooms inside smell of urine and disinfectant. In one of the smaller rooms on the far side of the building two women are preparing the midday meal: a great vat of rice and vegetables on a structure of bricks where a fire of dry wood is blazing. In a second side-room a man sits on a wooden-frame bed, reading a newspaper. He is from Poona, unmarried, and his only living relative is a sister in Bombay. He was educated by missionaries, and speaks perfect English. He used to work in the Philips electrical factory in Poona, but had a stroke and is partly paralysed. He has learnt to sew with one hand, but apart from that, he is without occupation. All he does is read newspapers, for which he relies on visitors. The one he was reading was dated a month earlier. He misses conversation, people to talk with, some kind of stimulus. He says he is grateful for the attention he receives; but once basic needs are taken care of, loneliness and boredom are his enemies. He has to call on all the strength God gives him not to be defeated by them.

On a cot in an adjacent room lies a girl of about sixteen. She shrieks with pain as the nuns dress her wounds. She is a frail, shrunken child, whose hair has been close cropped, and her body is covered with sores. She recoils from men, because she fears they are doctors – those she associated with the pain of having her sores treated. She was picked up from the railway station in Nagpur a few months earlier, half dead; her body was covered with deep lesions which were infested with maggots. For two months she has been at Shanti Bhavan; she can now begin to sit up for the first time, in her special chair; but for most of the time she lies on her cot, whimpering in fear and pain. She was abandoned by her family, perhaps because she is subnormal; although it is impossible to say whether her incoherence is a result of what she has suffered or an inherent disability. Another girl, who was picked up in similar circumstances, has improved to such an extent that she is now employed to prepare the food and help care for the other patients. Solemn and dark-eyed, she carries buckets of water, gives food and comfort to the others. She is not, of course, paid for her labour.

Sister Shamin is from Ghana. She shows me round the shelter, and we go into the chapel, which is also used as a room for visitors. A swarm of ants on the threshold invade the shady interior, which is painted cool blue and cream. There is a notice which says: 'There is no Hindu, no Muslim – Only Man – Guru Nanak'. A table is covered with a green silk cloth. Another hand-painted text on the wall says: 'In His Will is Our Peace'. There is a crucifix above the small altar, and pictures of the Stations of the Cross round the walls. On the altar a light burns behind red glass; there is a single white chrysanthemum in a small pot; a Bible is open on its plain wooden lectern. Sister Shamin says she has no feelings about Nagpur. It is a matter of indifference to her whether she is in India or Africa. She doesn't miss Ghana. She is here to do God's work, and God's work may be done as well here as anywhere.

Mominpura is the muslim weavers' district. It is an established slum, with water and electricity. It lies between two arms of the railway track, narrow where the line forks and widening out, a vast wedge of wretchedness. The railway embankments are about twenty feet high, and enclose the low-lying area with grey ramparts of dusty barren earth and stone chippings. It is a claustrophobic place, hot, fetid and stagnant. All the huts were built by those who live in them. Some are high enough for adults to stand in them; some are made of rough bricks, but most are of corrugated metal, bamboo, plywood and cardboard. Most of the roofs are of polythene or gunny bags, with stones to prevent them blowing away in the hot, searing wind. Some of the most recently built are only a frame of bamboo, covered with discoloured rags and tattered plastic sheeting. When the rains comes in June these will all be swept away. It looks as though it is impossible to cram any more living space into the area; and yet, perched on the embankments in a tiny gap between two huts, people contrive to cling on, precarious but tenacious.

The dark interiors contrast with the blinding sunlight outside. Living places and work places are not always distinct. Many women work at home, in front of the hut, or in small workshops open to the street, some of them using the traditional charkha for spinning, others at handlooms. The weavers specialize in silk-bordered saris, but all kinds of cloth are produced. There are small factories, with a mixture of handlooms, pit-looms and power-looms, sometimes all in the same work-place. Most of these employ only a handful of people, with few having more than twenty employees. Although many are organized into co-operatives for distributing the finished products, the work is insecure and poorly paid.

In the middle of the day, a group of boys were sitting outside one of these small enterprises, eating rice from a newspaper. They don't speak Marathi; through an interpreter I ask: 'How many hours do you work?' The question has no meaning. One boy says he goes to work in the morning and comes home when it's dark. Even so, his earnings are unreliable. His sister works too, and they live with their mother who is blind. A second boy has been living with his brother in Bombay, but has come home because of the prolonged strike. He likes Bombay, and has learned to think of his home town as small and unexciting. He describes to his friends the fabulous wealth of the city, the cars, the skyscrapers; but he himself lives in workmen's barracks.

The conditions inside the small workshops are cramped and oppressive, even though they are partly open to the air. A shop with ten power-looms leaves barely enough space for the workers to pass between them. In the pit-looms young men sit, half buried, wearing nothing but a dhoti, their arms and legs working away continuously as though at some instrument of punishment; the sweat stands out and runs down their arms, as the cloth grows slowly on the frame before them.

Much of the cotton that comes to Mominpura in great bales wrapped in hessian and drawn on handcarts is waste cotton from the Empress Mills. This is sold to middlemen, who then sell it again and distribute it to the small enterprises in the weavers' district.

The Empress Mills cover several acres of ground behind the railway station. The approach to them is down hot, barren roads, flanked by bleached, crumbling walls, a sparse growth of grass and drifts of dust. Inside the main gate – guarded by a kind of white sentry-box, as though it were military installation – there is a statue of Jamsetji Tata, the Parsee founder of the mills and the Tata industrial corporation. There is a courtyard, some ashoka trees and a flower bed with red canna lilies; and then a series of more irregular concrete yards, dominated by the cliff-like whitewashed walls of the spinning and weaving sheds.

Inside these the atmosphere, already stiflingly hot, is made almost unbearable by the humidifiers. Most of the workers are dressed in singlet and shorts. Many look older than they are, are small and poorly nourished, with emaciated arms and legs. Some are clearly unfit for such arduous work, but the prize of a regular job drives individuals on to heroic efforts. As often as they can, the workers go to the door that opens out into the yard for a breath of fresh air.

There is a sense of revisiting our own past, which is heightened by the machinery in the blow-room, the carding-engines and drawing-machines and ring frames. They are all from Lancashire, these heavy iron machines that create a deafening clatter which makes it impossible for people to speak to each other. The archaic ironwork has the faded gilt inscriptions

'Platt Brothers, Oldham, 'Lord Bros., Todmorden', 'Philipson and Co., Bolton'. This machinery was exported to India during an earlier phase of the deindustrialization of Britain, when the cotton industry was already in decline there – some of it in the 1930s, some in the 1950s. The cheapness of Indian labour still promised profit from these lumbering antiquities. But no longer: there are new machines from West Germany and Belgium, which are enclosed in metallic blue casing, and which work at great speed, lessening the need for labour.

The floors are of rough concrete, pitted with holes that are covered by irregular planks and pieces of hardboard. There is a vast movement everywhere of racing bobbins and spools, as the fibres are drawn into great even skeins on metal cylinders. The work requires constant vigilance, and the danger makes a mockery of the notice that reads 'You Have Arrived Safely, Now Work Safely'. There is harsh blue strip lighting that creates a theatrical bluish tinge. Cotton is everywhere: cotton dust in the air like a perpetual snowfall of dangerous fibre. As the managers pass through the sheds they hold a handkerchief to their faces; few of the workers even wear masks. The portrait of Tata, faded and smiling, is garlanded with marigolds and jasmine. Apart from that, there is no ornament in these bleak places – just a vast expanse of black machinery, pulleys and belts, and a visibility impaired by the flecks of cotton, so that you look from one end of the shed to the other (a distance of perhaps a hundred yards) through a sort of flocculent mist. There are accretions of cotton waste on every slightly uneven surface – the extractor fans, the slight bulge in the wall, the oblong blue metal lightshade, all are bearded with a floss like thistledown. After only half an hour the discomfort to the throat becomes acute. People have rasping coughs; there is a constant need to spit and clear the throat and mouth. The workers do an eight-hour day, six days a week. The mill runs round the clock. The most common ailments are TB, asthma, bronchial and lung complaints.

Two women and a man have been waiting all day on a bench outside the personnel office. The women are the stepdaughters of a mill worker who has died of TB. They have come to claim the wages owed to their stepfather before he ceased work. There is a dispute about whether they are the legal heirs, being only step-children; the man's daughter from a previous marriage is also present. They stand, vigilant, eyeing one another suspiciously. The matter becomes very involved. Nothing can be done at present. The stepdaughters say they have children who must be fed; they make a gesture of fingers forming a pyramid taken to the mouth in a gesture of eating. The sum outstanding is only 30 rupees. Both sides are reluctant to depart first, for fear that the other will gain an advantage.

As the afternoon shift comes out, a vast phalanx of bicycles seems locked together as though it is a single, many-wheeled machine. The shadows of men and cycles are profiled by the sun on the white walls. A group of older workers ride along, holding on to each other's shoulders: one in the middle is garlanded and smiling. He is retiring after forty-eight years' work in the mill. One man says that is a real cause for celebration, because not many people survive that long in the factories of India: he must be specially tough.

The average wage is between 300 and 400 ruppes a month, with an extra 200 'dearness allownace', or cost-of-living bonus. Thus the majority of men in the carding-room and on the ring-frames receive about 600 rupees a month – about £40. Of the men I spoke to in the blow-room, one had to keep eight people on his wage, two had seven, four and six, and seven had five. Some of them had other earners in the family: a son who was a hair cutter, a wife who did sewing. One man said proudly that his son was studying at the College of Commerce and Agriculture. Some of them travelled up to ten miles to work by bicycle. A few lived outside the city area, and had a small piece of ground where they could grow vegetables. One man, in his fifties perhaps, said that before he came to the mill his family had only their piece of land some twenty miles away, and they were always hungry. Now at least they eat every day.

The workers patrol the rows of machines, watching that the threads don't break, and when they do, deftly reconnecting them. Each man has six or eight machines to mind, walking up and down, a caged Sisyphean task, while the tiny cotton spores attach themselves to the growth of beard on the chin, making them appear to age even as you watch them. The men are frail against the pounding and clatter of the machines, feeding in the raw cotton from the great bales held together by clasps of metal. As the cotton goes through the cleaning process it is thinned and homogenized, shedding its almost invisible snow; and the sweepers come along with wide brushes, and collect it in a great cumulus of dingy floss that is crammed into the hessian sacks that will be sold to the dealers. They will eventually pass it on to Mominpura, where the handloom weavers and small enterprises cheapen labour even further, the hours worked become longer and the struggle to make a living gets even more acute and competitive.

The mills are just breaking even in spite of the world recession and the need to compete in a global market; but this has been achieved by investing in more machinery and fewer workers neglecting the one resource that Nagpur has in such profusion – people. Forty per cent of output goes for export, especially to South America, Africa and the USSR. They specialize in poplins and in polyester for dhotis. There is a dispensary, with a cool wooden interior smelling of disinfectant, where an inducement of 155R is offered to the men for sterilization. The windows are shuttered and the walls filled with huge, incongruous paintings of generations of Tatas. In theory, the income provided by the mill should be sufficient to give people the security they need in order to feel they can have smaller families. I asked one man if many people took advantage of the 155-rupee inducement. He said he didn't know. He wouldn't do so. His six children are his life, he says; a man without children is like a body without hands.

A man comes to the dispensary after one of the most common of all accidents – a bobbin has flown off and hit him just below the eye: a half-moon cut, bruise and swelling. The wound is washed with disinfectant and plastered. He goes straight back to work; he cannot have been absent from his looms for more than five minutes at the most.

In a corner of the yard is the canteen; a large open space, a sort of hangar with iron pillars, concrete floor, corrugated iron roof and rows of benches. The canteen offers cheap and nutritious food to supplement the often inadequate diet of the workers. Meals were formerly provided, but have recently been discontinued, in favour of high-protein snacks – samosas and pekoras – because most workers prefer to bring their own food in the characteristic metal cans.

Nearby is the personnel office: a dingy, high-ceilinged room with whitewashed brick walls. A big metal desk is cluttered with yellowing papers and invoices and cardboard boxes full of the workers records. The personnel officer keeps a record of all the warnings issued to workers, suspensions and dismissals, fines and sackings for those who are absent too often. While I was there a man came in to beg for his job back. He has been sick. The personnel officer says he knows he has been doing another job, helping his brother to build. The man appears desperate. His wife is ill. He has medical bills. The personnel officer is unrelenting.

The current absentee rate is 20 per cent on any one day; this compares with a rate of about 10 per cent twenty years ago. Like the lament of all employers, the cause of all the troubles of the country is said to be due to 'the relaxation of discipline and the unreliability of young people'; just as it always has been, in all countries and at all times. There are always workers who are taken on by the day, to fill in on any shift that falls below a minium complement of workers. There is a queue of these casual workers waiting at the beginning of each shift. They stand, as the four o'clock shift is departing, anxious and beseeching, looking though the metal bars of the main gate: a symbol of that pool of labour all over the world, waiting for the privilege of admission to the industrial process. Industry seems such a relief from the uncertainty of casualized and occasional labour, even though its rhythmic regularity dulls and deadens the sensibility, wastes the body in the same way; only launches people on the paths of development that we have known, with their forms of dispossession, their unfamiliar mutations of poverty and loss.

I was told a story in Nagpur of a man who sees a millworker come out of the mill and get run over by a public carrier. Instead of helping him, he rushes over to him and says: 'What's your name?' He then rushes to the mill and says: 'I've come for the job that's vacant.' 'There's no job vacant.' 'Yes there is, Rajan's.' 'Well, he's just gone home.' 'No he's not, he's been run over.' I had heard a similar story before, and it was a long time before I could remember where. It had been in Blackburn in Lancashire; and the story was at least as old as the century.

Much has been written about the growing subordination of the economies of the poor countries to the global capitalist markets. We know how traditional crops that were the staple nourishment of whole peoples have been uprooted for the sake of soybeans for cattle-food, or beef-ranching for hamburgers, or the production of luxury fruits and out-of-season vegetables for the West. But all the analysis and research falter when they confront the sources of those global markets: for we are they. Our whole way of life, our freedoms, have been bought in this way. We have indentified our appetites and needs with those of this vast voracious global system that must go on growing. And because it always does so at the expense of others, it means that it devours the poor. And by our identification with it, we become cannibals.[1] This is the relationship that gets lost in all the pietistic expressions of concern; the charitable impulses, the sense of guilt and fellow-feeling – it is all absorbed in generalities about 'interdependence'. Thus, in the Brandt programme for survival: 'The North–South debate is often described as if the rich were being asked to make sacrifices in response to the demands of the poor. We reject this view . . . The countries of the North, given their increasing interdependence with the South, themselves need international economic reform to ensure their own future prosperity.[2] 'Interdependence' is the cloud that obscures the real relationship; and we rest in the primitive magic of the system which comforts us with the myth that we can all get richer painlessly if we will only trust its beneficent workings.

And 'development' comes to resembles that long torturing of humanity that we set in train at the time of the earliest landscapes of industrial society. This is how the Brandt report justifies the urban squalor of the Third World: 'The mass urban poverty of Kinshasa, Mexico City or Carior is a relatively modern phenomenon. For all its squalor it is one step up from rural deprivation. This means that our guidance to the poor has been 'Follow us, imitate and obey'. They have done so, with the result that we see on a world scale what Thomas Carlyle saw a century and a half

---

[1] This idea was developed as early as 1966 in René Dumont's *False Start in Africa* (Sphere, London, 1966).
[2] *North-South: A Program for Survival* (Pan, London).

ago in Britain: 'In poor and rich, instead of noble thrift and plenty, there is idle luxury alternating with mean scarcity and inability.'[3] Capitalist versions of development (and indeed, their East European caricature) and their universal imagery dominate the poor with the power of predestination; offering only progression in the direction of those riches we have seen, with all their disablings and distortions. The emissaries of Western plethoric plenty are ubiquitous in poor countries, those elites whose function it is to cajole or coerce their fellow citizens into imitative postures. The lives of the rich are intrusive in Nagpur, in the fleshy faces of film-stars on the painted hoardings; in the luxury of the closed and silent ministers' cottages – bungalows embowered in bougainvillea, colour-washed in cool lemon and blue, and unoccupied apart from the few weeks when the State legislature is in session in Nagpur; in the young men drinking themselves into insensibility in the bars and cafes; in the wives of the well-to-do who patronize the Slimwell Beauty Clinic in a city of such emaciation and insufficiency; in the schools of social work, where young women achieve a diploma that has more to do with their marriageability than with concern for the poor; in the restaurants where the rich watch Hindi films on the video and consume at one meal more than most people in the city will eat in a week.

The space between a brutalizing poverty and degrading riches has been closed and declared a forbidden zone in this process. For it speaks of a quite different landscape from any we have yet seen; one where economic necessity does not pass abruptly into the necessity for economic growth, which then takes on an autonomous life of its own. In industrial society – capitalist and existing socialist alike – as soon as sufficiency becomes remotely possible, out of the very abundance that promises enough, dissatisfaction becomes a raw material for the manufacture of strange new products; with the result that in the modern world, poverty in all its guises is an over-wrought artefact, conjured out of the very treasures and fullness of the earth.

This is why it is in the rich countries that emancipation must happen first, by our liberation from that underdevelopment of what is a kind of enriched privation. The territory to be liberated is some little way above that of *aparigraha* (non-possession), perhaps something more than the chosen frugality of religious institutions; it is the ecologists' search for sufficiency, the socialism of enough for all those who share the planet so briefly and whose tenure becomes more fragile with each generation. It is the rich who threaten the stability of the world, not the poor. We should be under no illusion. What we are confronting is the last and greatest liberation movement of all, which is that of the vast majority of

[3] Thomas Carlyle, *Past and Present* (Everyman edn, London, 1962).

humankind, including so many of those of us who have been persuaded to ally our fate with those whose wealth and power controls us all. What lies concealed beneath all the vague and charitable rhetoric of concern in the West is the dynamic relationship between the way we live and those spectres at our feast, out of whose very substance our debilitating and unfree dependency is created. The only consolation in this arduous undertaking is that one of hte oldest dreams of humanity remains to be realized; not as an insubstantial dream, but as precondition of our survival, and perhaps best expressed in the Book of Proverbs: 'Give me neither riches nor poverty, but enough for my sustenance.'

Travelling back from Nagpur, I stayed in Bombay again. One day, outside a smart hotel, I saw a beggar family and a blind man led by a child standing beneath an open window. Some tourists were looking down. One of them – a middle-aged European woman – threw a shirt and some baby clothes out of the window. Hands reached out. The child of the beggarwoman and the child of the blind man fought for them. Screaming and kicking each other, they tore at the clothes and ripped them. The woman at the window was amused. She took up a camera and photographed the scene.

10

Afterword

In *The Three Worlds*, Peter Worsley argues that

measures of absolute poverty, such as the WHO's standards of 3000 calories per day as the minimum required by a moderately active man, and 2200 for a moderately active woman, are thoroughly non-sociological, since they not only omit differences in work-intensity or environmental conditions, but crucially fail to take into account the *social* environment. For notions of what constitutes an adequate diet, let alone adequate pay or an adequate standard of living in general, are culture-specific norms, defined by people in specific societies, according to *their* criteria of what constitutes want or plenty, not standards deemed appropriate for them – often arbitrarily – by social workers, statisticians or nutritionists, and measured against some universal biological yardstick. Social want, not asocial biological needs, define health and wealth.[1]

The truth of this argument has itself been exploited by a capitalism that has learnt far more from its critics and opponents than these generally allow. The very plasticity of human needs has become the source of its enormous regenerative power, once the energies of these can be confiscated to provide its driving force. The possibility of capitalist growth and expansion becomes infinite, once it has gained acceptance for the proposition that 'the central problem of modern society is poverty, and the solution to poverty is production and more production'.[2] Human beings are always being made, broken and remade in ways that perpetuate subjective feelings of expropriation and loss, the healing answer to which is offered only by a closer and closer identification of human needs with capitalist necessity. In other words, the malleability of human needs means that they can be tormented into any shape that may be required for the perpetuation of an economic system which was supposed to have satisfied them.

[1] Peter Worsley, *The Three Worlds* (Wiedenfeld & Nicolson, London, 1984).
[2] Raymond Williams, *Socialism and Ecology* (Socialist Economic Resources Association, London, 1981).

And for these waylaid and travestied needs to be answered, it requires not only the deformities that we have seen in the West but also the distortions imposed on the poor of the Earth by the continued withholding from them of the necessaries of life. The symbiosis in which global rich and poor are held cannot easily be broken: it projects itself over the whole plant as a 'natural' evolution, a universal model of development, and a determining influence which all lead, not from poverty to riches, but from one form of impoverishment into another, in which the possibility of sufficiency is elided. These processes can be resisted only by a joint project of rich and poor together; a liberation movement that dares to recognize common ground between them; perhaps a version of liberation theology in the West that will unite and inform those generous but still discrete impulses that underlie the feminist, Peace and Green movements. We should perhaps start by asking the question, not How do the poor survive? (the answer is quite often, not at all), but rather, 'How can it be that poverty has survived at all, passing as it has with charmed existence to emerge, unconquered, in the richest and most 'developed' societies the world has ever known?

Most of this book was written before the news of the African famine became 'known' late in 1984 – that is, before it was made available to the public in the rich world. The famine has given rise to countless acts of spontaneous generosity by individuals, and even by some governments. The pained conscience of the people of the West suggests that there is a real – one is tempted to use the word *hunger* – to understand, a readiness to question the connections that exist between what we are serenely invited to regard as 'our way of life', with its greedy appropriation of a disproportionate share of the world's riches, and those who are brought, by elaborate and expensive technology, to die at our feet in our own living rooms. It seems however to be the object of offical political discourse to suppress any such connections. The easiest alibi, as always, is to blame 'nature', drought, over-population, the spread of the desert; when it is our own nature that is most deeply implicated, above all the nature of our society and its development, which has succeeded in re-creating a lasting sense of impoverishment out of the very riches it has accumulated, and has made us believe that the simple goal of sufficiency for all represents for us, the rich, not emancipation, but a terrifying loss not be be contemplated.